AF683797

PARTNERSHIP TAXATION

RYAN H. PACE
Weber State University

Kendall Hunt
publishing company

Cover image © Shutterstock.com

Kendall Hunt
publishing company

www.kendallhunt.com
Send all inquiries to:
4050 Westmark Drive
Dubuque, IA 52004-1840

Copyright © 2017 by Kendall Hunt Publishing Company

ISBN 978-1-5249-3428-6

All rights reserved. No part of this publication may be reproduced, stored in a retrieval system, or transmitted, in any form or by any means, electronic, mechanical, photocopying, recording, or otherwise, without the prior written permission of the copyright owner.

Published in the United States of America

Contents

About the Author

Ryan H. Pace, M.Tax, J.D., LL.M., is a professor of taxation at Weber State University. He teaches graduate and undergraduate courses in taxation and business law. Mr. Pace also serves as the director of the Master of Accounting program, the Master of Taxation program, and the Center for Tax Education & Research at Weber State. Prior to his teaching career, Mr. Pace was a full-time tax attorney in Arizona and Utah. Mr. Pace graduated from New York University with a Master of Laws degree in taxation after receiving his Juris Doctor with honors from Washburn University School of Law. He also received a Master of Taxation degree from Arizona State University and his Bachelor of Science degree from the University of Utah. Mr. Pace has written several articles in the area of taxation and has participated in many continuing education programs and academic conferences. He has written three other textbooks published by Kendall Hunt Publishing. Those titles are *Business Entity Taxation*, *Individual Taxation*, and *The Legal Environment of Business*.

Part I

Partnership Formation

Chapter 1

Selecting a Business Entity

A. Sole Proprietorship
B. General Partnership
C. Limited Partnership
D. Limited Liability Partnership
E. Limited Liability Limited Partnership
F. Limited Liability Company
G. Corporation
H. Tax Treatment of Business Entities under the Check-the Box Regulations
I. Qualified Joint Ventures between Married Persons
J. Obtaining an Employer Identification Number (EIN)

One of the most common questions a tax practitioner receives relates to which business entity is best to form for a client. Of course, these decisions are not always easy, and often include an analysis of both non-tax and tax issues. While the book focuses on the federal income tax treatment of entities classified as *partnerships*, Chapter 1 provides a general review of the various characteristics of the most common forms of doing business.

A. Sole Proprietorship

An individual who conducts a trade or business as the sole owner and does not house the business in a separate entity formed under state law is a **sole proprietor**. Sole proprietorships are simple to form because no formal documentation needs filing with a state agency to form an entity. Some paperwork is likely necessary, however, to obtain a business license from the local city or county government. Other licenses issued by government authorities may be necessary depending upon the nature of the business (e.g., a liquor license for a restaurant, law license for a lawyer, etc.). Also, a sole proprietor may wish to register the business name (often referred to as a "dba" or "doing business as") with the state, however, so as to prevent others from using the same business name.

A significant disadvantage of a sole proprietorship, of course, is that the individual owner is not protected from the liabilities of the business. For federal income tax purposes, a sole proprietorship is not separately taxed from its owner;

rather, the income of the business is reported directly on the owner's Form 1040 Schedule C and included with the other taxable income of the owner. The sole proprietor typically must make quarterly estimated tax payments throughout the year to avoid potential interest and tax underpayment penalties.

B. General Partnership

A partnership consists of two or more persons joining together in an activity with the intent to make a profit. A partnership is a **general partnership** if the partners do not file documents with the state necessary to be recognized as any other type of partnership (e.g., limited partnership, limited liability partnership, or limited liability limited partnership). Thus, general partnerships are simple to form. Like sole proprietorships, however, a business license and other licenses may need to be obtained. The partnership may also wish to register the business name with the state to prevent others from using the same name. Under state law, each partner in a general partnership is allowed to participate in management of the partnership unless an agreement among the partners limits those management rights.

Delaware Code
Title 6. Commerce and Trade
Subtitle II. Other Laws Relating to Commerce and Trade
Chapter 15. Delaware Revised Uniform Partnership Act

§ 15-401. Partner's rights and duties

. . .

(f) Each partner has equal rights in the management and conduct of the partnership business and affairs.

. . .

A major disadvantage of the general partnership form of business is that the partners are personally liable for the debts of the partnership.

Delaware Code
Title 6. Commerce and Trade
Subtitle II. Other Laws Relating to Commerce and Trade
Chapter 15. Delaware Revised Uniform Partnership Act

§ 15-306. Partner's liability

(a) Except as otherwise provided in subsections (b) and (c) of this section, all partners are liable jointly and severally for all obligations of the partnership unless otherwise agreed by the claimant or provided by law.

(b) A person admitted as a partner into an existing partnership is not personally liable for any obligation of the partnership incurred before the person's admission as a partner.

(c) An obligation of a partnership arising out of or related to circumstances or events occurring while the partnership is a limited liability partnership or incurred while the partnership is a limited liability partnership, whether arising in contract, tort or otherwise, is solely the obligation of the partnership. A partner is not personally liable, directly or indirectly, by way of indemnification, contribution, assessment or otherwise, for such an obligation solely by reason of being or so acting as a partner.

. . .

For this reason, few businesses now operate as general partnerships given that limited liability partnerships (LLPs) and limited liability companies (LLCs) are viable alternatives that provide liability protection to their owners.[1] Partners in a partnership should adopt a **partnership agreement** to govern their business relationship. If they fail to do so, the default statutory rules under state law will control.

For federal income tax purposes, general partnerships are "pass-through" entities (often called "flow-through" entities) and not subject to income tax at the entity level. Rather, the partnership's income/loss is allocated to the partners in accordance with the partnership agreement. A general partnership files a Form 1065 return each year with the IRS and provides each partner a Schedule K-1 informing the partner of the partner's share of the partnership's income/loss. The partner then transfers the information from the Schedule K-1 to the partner's Form 1040 (if the partner is an individual) on the appropriate line.

---

[1] Notice that the Delaware statute provides that if the partnership registers as a limited liability partnership, the partners are not liable for the debts of the partnership.

C. Limited Partnership

A **limited partnership** (LP) is a partnership wherein at least one partner is a general partner and at least one partner is a limited partner. The general partner is not protected from the liabilities of the partnership. Unlike a general partner, however, a limited partner is not personally liable for the debts of the partnership.

> **Delaware Code**
> **Title 6. Commerce and Trade**
> **Subtitle II. Other Laws Relating to Commerce and Trade**
> **Chapter 17. Limited Partnerships**
>
> **§ 17-303. Liability to third parties**
>
> (a) A limited partner is not liable for the obligations of a limited partnership unless he or she is also a general partner or, in addition to the exercise of the rights and powers of a limited partner, he or she participates in the control of the business. However, if the limited partner does participate in the control of the business, he or she is liable only to persons who transact business with the limited partnership reasonably believing, based upon the limited partner's conduct, that the limited partner is a general partner.
>
> . . .

A limited partner, however, must usually give up management rights in the partnership to the general partner and is typically involved in the partnership only in a passive manner.

To be recognized as a limited partnership, the partnership must file a document (e.g., "Certificate of Limited Partnership") with the appropriate state agency. Otherwise, the partnership is treated as a general partnership. As with other entities, the limited partnership should obtain a business license and other licenses as necessary.

For federal income tax purposes, limited partnerships are not subject to income tax at the entity level. Rather, the partnership's income/loss is allocated to the partners in accordance with the partnership agreement. A limited partnership files a Form 1065 return each year with the IRS and provides each partner a Schedule K-1 informing the partner of the partner's share of the partnership's income/loss. The partner then transfers the information from the Schedule K-1 to the partner's Form 1040 (if the partner is an individual) on the appropriate line.

D. Limited Liability Partnership

A **limited liability partnership** (LLP) is basically an underlying *general partnership* except that state law provides the partners liability protection from the debts of the partnership[2] and, importantly, potential professional malpractice by a fellow partner. Typically, however, a partner in an LLP is liable for his or her *own* professional malpractice (since many LLPs are professional service businesses). State laws vary on what types of businesses may register as LLPs. Some states, such as California, only allow LLPs to be used as an entity by professional service businesses such as accounting and law firms.

> **California Corporations Code**
> **Title 2. Partnerships**
> **Chapter 5. Uniform Partnership Act of 1994**
> **Article 1. General Provisions**
>
> **§ 16101. Definitions**
>
> As used in this chapter, the following terms and phrases have the following meanings:
>
> . . .
>
> (8)(A) "Registered limited liability partnership" means a partnership, other than a limited partnership, formed pursuant to an agreement governed by Article 10 (commencing with Section 16951), that is registered under Section 16953 and (i) each of the partners of which is a licensed person or a person licensed or authorized to provide professional limited liability partnership services in a jurisdiction or jurisdictions other than this state, (ii) is licensed under the laws of the state to engage in the practice of architecture, practice of public accountancy, or the practice of law ...

Notice California limits the availability of LLPs to licensed professionals in the fields of architecture, accounting, and law.[3]

For federal income tax purposes, LLPs are not subject to income tax at the entity level. Rather, the partnership's income/loss is allocated to the partners in accordance with the partnership agreement. A limited liability partnership files a

---

[2] See the quotation of Delaware Code §15-306 earlier in the chapter referencing the liability protection for partners in a limited liability partnership.

[3] California appears to be in a minority of states that imposes such restrictions on who can conduct business in the form of an LLP. Nevertheless, before recommending an LLP as a form of doing business, a consultant should be very familiar with state law on this issue.

Form 1065 return each year and provides each partner a Schedule K-1 informing the partner of the partner's share of the partnership's income/loss. The partner then transfers the information from the Schedule K-1 to the partner's Form 1040 (if the partner is an individual) on the appropriate line.

E. Limited Liability Limited Partnership

A limited liability limited partnership (LLLP) is basically an underlying *limited partnership* except that state law also provides the general partner liability protection from the debts of the partnership.

Delaware Code
Title 6. Commerce and Trade
Subtitle II. Other Laws Relating to Commerce and Trade
Chapter 17. Limited Partnerships

§ 17-214. Limited partnerships as limited liability limited partnerships

...

(d) If a limited partnership is a limited liability limited partnership, (i) its partners who are liable for the debts, liabilities and other obligations of the limited partnership shall have the limitation on liability afforded to partners of limited liability partnerships under the Delaware Revised Uniform Partnership Act [Chapter 15 of this title], and (ii) no limited partner of the limited partnership shall have any liability for the obligations of the limited partnership under § 17-303(a) of this title.

...

A limited partnership must file a document with the state to register as an LLLP.

For federal income tax purposes, LLLPs are not subject to income tax at the entity level. Rather, the partnership's income/loss is allocated to the partners in accordance with the partnership agreement. The LLLP files a Form 1065 return each year with the IRS and provides each partner a Schedule K-1 informing the partner of the partner's share of the partnership's income/loss. The partner then transfers the information from the Schedule K-1 to the partner's Form 1040 (if the partner is an individual) on the appropriate line.

F. Limited Liability Company

A **limited liability company** (LLC) is an entity that gives the owners (called "members") liability protection from the debts of the LLC and allows the members very flexible management arrangements. Members of the LLC can generally choose to have the LLC "manager-managed" or "member-managed." This choice is typically made when the LLC files its "**Certificate of Organization**" (or "Certificate of Formation" or "Articles of Organization" depending on the state) with the appropriate state agency. Of course, if the LLC is member-managed, then typically each member has the right to be involved in the management of the LLC and can legally bind the LLC contractually. If the LLC is manager-managed, then typically the members are not involved in the management of the LLC unless the manager is also a member. In a manager-managed LLC, of course, the LLC is bound by the acts of the manager.[4] The members typically set forth their business relationship (e.g., voting rights, profit and loss sharing, etc.) by adopting an **operating agreement** (or "limited liability company agreement") that all members sign.

> **Delaware Code**
> **Title 6. Commerce and Trade**
> **Subtitle II. Other Laws Relating to Commerce and Trade**
> **Chapter 18. Limited Liability Company Act**
>
> **§ 18-402. Management of limited liability company**
>
> Unless otherwise provided in a limited liability company agreement, the management of a limited liability company shall be vested in its members in proportion to the then current percentage or other interest of members in the profits of the limited liability company owned by all of the members, the decision of members owning more than 50 percent of the said percentage or other interest in the profits controlling; provided however, that if a limited liability company agreement provides for the management, in whole or in part, of a limited liability company by a manager, the management of the limited liability company, to the extent so provided, shall be vested in the manager who shall be chosen in the manner provided in the limited liability company agreement. The manager shall also hold the offices and have the responsibilities accorded to the manager by or in the manner provided in a limited liability company agreement. A limited liability company may have more than 1 manager. Unless otherwise provided in a limited liability company agreement, each member and manager has the authority to bind the limited liability company.

[4] The acts of the *members* may also still bind the LLC unless the operating agreement provides that members cannot bind the LLC. Care should be taken by the members in this regard.

As mentioned, an LLC provides liability protection to its owners.

Delaware Code
Title 6. Commerce and Trade
Subtitle II. Other Laws Relating to Commerce and Trade
Chapter 18. Limited Liability Company Act

§ 18-303. Liability to third parties

(a) Except as otherwise provided by this chapter, the debts, obligations and liabilities of a limited liability company, whether arising in contract, tort or otherwise, shall be solely the debts, obligations and liabilities of the limited liability company, and no member or manager of a limited liability company shall be obligated personally for any such debt, obligation or liability of the limited liability company solely by reason of being a member or acting as a manager of the limited liability company.

. . .

Well-established principles of "piercing-the-corporate-veil" still apply to an LLC, however, if the member(s) do not respect the separateness of the entity (e.g., members commingle personal funds with LLC funds, enter into contracts personally rather than in the LLC's name, engage in fraudulent activities via the LLC, etc.).

rzvmuR /Shutterstock.com

For a court case analyzing the piercing of an LLC veil, see *GreenHunter Energy, Inc. v. Western Ecosystems Technology, Inc.*, 2014 WY 144. Excerpts of the *GreenHunter* case are included at the end of this chapter.

What if a *member* of the LLC is being sued or declares bankruptcy? Are the assets inside the LLC reachable by creditors of the member? Court cases have generally held that a single-member LLC's assets are reachable by the creditors of the sole member.[5]

[5] This is sometimes referred to as a "reverse" piercing of the LLC's veil. If an LLC has more than one member, typically courts will not conclude that a creditor can directly reach the assets of the LLC; rather, the court imposes a "charging order" against the debtor-member allowing the creditor to receive the profits of the LLC allocable to the debtor-member.

rzvmuR /Shutterstock.com

For a court case analyzing the bankruptcy of the member of a single-member LLC, see *In re Albright*, 291 B.R. 538 (Bankr. D. Colo. 2003). Excerpts of the *Albright* case are included at the end of this chapter.

A relatively new variation on LLCs is the creation of **series LLCs** under state law. Not all states have adopted series LLC legislation, however. Basically, series LLC laws allow one main LLC to have separate "mini" LLCs or "cells" inside of it. Each mini LLC inside the main LLC may, for example, hold just a few assets or operate one part of the overall business while other series LLCs hold other assets or operate another part of the overall business. Popular purposes for doing this are to isolate potential liability exposure and to reduce administrative costs that would otherwise apply in an organizational structure with multiple traditional LLCs. An excerpt from Delaware state law illustrates the point.

Delaware Code
Title 6. Commerce and Trade
Subtitle II. Other Laws Relating to Commerce and Trade
Chapter 18. Limited Liability Company Act

§ 18-215. Series of members, managers, limited liability company interests or assets

(a) A limited liability company agreement may establish or provide for the establishment of 1 or more designated series of members, managers, limited liability company interests or assets. Any such series may have separate rights, powers or duties with respect to specified property or obligations of the limited liability company or profits and losses associated with specified property or obligations, and any such series may have a separate business purpose or investment objective.

(b) Notwithstanding anything to the contrary set forth in this chapter or under other applicable law, in the event that a limited liability company agreement establishes or provides for the establishment of 1 or more series, and if the records maintained for any such series account for the assets associated with such series separately from the other assets of the limited liability company, or any other series thereof, and if the limited liability company agreement so provides, and if notice of the limitation on liabilities of a series as referenced in this subsection is set forth in the certificate of formation of the limited liability company, then the debts, liabilities, obligations and expenses incurred, contracted for or otherwise existing with respect to a particular series shall be enforceable against the assets of such series only, and not against the assets of the limited liability company generally or any other series thereof, and, unless otherwise provided in the limited liability company agreement, none of the debts, liabilities, obligations and expenses incurred, contracted for or otherwise existing with respect to the limited liability company generally or any other series thereof shall be enforceable against the assets of such series. Assets associated with a series may be held directly or indirectly, including in the name of such series, in the name of the limited liability company, through a nominee or otherwise. Records maintained for a series that reasonably identify its assets, including by specific listing, category, type, quantity, computational or allocational formula or procedure (including a percentage or share of any asset or assets) or by any other method where the identity of such assets is objectively determinable, will be deemed to account for the assets associated with such series separately from the other assets of the limited liability company, or any other series thereof. Notice in a certificate of formation of the limitation on liabilities of a series as referenced in this subsection shall be sufficient for all purposes of this subsection whether or not the limited liability company has established any series when such notice is included in the certificate of formation, and there shall be no requirement that any specific series of the limited liability company be referenced in such notice. The fact that a certificate of formation that contains the foregoing notice of the limitation on liabilities of a series is on file in the office of the Secretary of State shall constitute notice of such limitation on liabilities of a series.

(c) A series established in accordance with subsection (b) of this section may carry on any lawful business, purpose or activity, whether or not for profit, with the exception of the business of banking as defined in §126 of Title 8. Unless otherwise provided in a limited liability company agreement, a series established in accordance with subsection (b) of this section shall have the power and capacity to, in its own name, contract, hold title to assets (including real, personal and intangible property), grant liens and security interests, and sue and be sued.

...

For federal income tax purposes, LLCs with more than one member (multimember LLCs or "MMLLCs") are pass-through entities (like partnerships) and not subject to income tax at the entity level. An LLC's income/loss is allocated to the members in accordance with the operating agreement. A multimember LLC files a Form 1065 return each year with the IRS and provides each member a Schedule K-1 informing the member of the member's share of the LLC's income/loss. The member then transfers the information from the Schedule K-1 to the member's Form 1040 (if the member is an individual) on the appropriate line.

LLCs with only one member (single-member LLCs or "SMLLCs") are *disregarded entities* and all income, gain, loss, expense, credit, etc., of the LLC is reported directly on the income tax return of the SMLLC's owner (see additional discussion under the "Tax Treatment of Business Entities Under the Check-the-Box Regulations" section later in the chapter).

G. Corporation

Corporations, of course, have been a recognized form of doing business for a long time. State law provides liability protection to the shareholders from the debts of the corporation.

> **Delaware Code**
> **Title 8. Corporations**
> **Chapter 1. General Corporation Law**
>
> **§ 102. Contents of certificate of incorporation**
>
> . . .
>
> (b) In addition to the matters required to be set forth in the certificate of incorporation by subsection (a) of this section, the certificate of incorporation may also contain any or all of the following matters:
>
> . . .
>
> (6) A provision imposing personal liability for the debts of the corporation on its stockholders to a specified extent and upon specified conditions; otherwise, the stockholders of a corporation shall not be personally liable for the payment of the corporation's debts except as they may be liable by reason of their own conduct or acts;
>
> . . .

The management structure of a corporation is a bit more rigid than for partnerships and LLCs given that shareholders elect a board of directors and the directors then hire officers that perform certain functions. Shareholders in a corporation also often find it challenging to arrange profit and loss sharing in a manner other than pro-rata according to the number of shares owned. Corporations are created by filing **Articles of Incorporation** with the appropriate state agency. The corporation adopts **bylaws** that set forth the duties and responsibilities of the board of directors and officers, among other things. The shareholders of closely held corporations will often enter into a **shareholders'**

agreement to govern the relationship among them (e.g., right to sell or transfer stock, admission of new shareholders, etc.).

From a federal income tax standpoint, a corporation that does not make an "S" election is considered a "C" corporation and is subject to taxation separate from its shareholders. The shareholders then are typically taxed on subsequent dividends that the corporation distributes from the corporation's earnings and profits. Thus, "C" corporations are subject to a "double-tax" regime. A corporation can eliminate taxation at the entity level if the corporation meets the strict requirements for "S" status and makes an "S" corporation election.

H. Tax Treatment of Business Entities under the Check-the-Box Regulations

The Treasury Department has issued detailed regulations regarding the tax treatment of the various business entities we have discussed in this chapter. These regulations are often called the **"check-the-box" regulations**. The regulations have this unique name because they allow **"eligible entities"** to choose how to be treated for income tax purposes by checking a box on an IRS form (Form 8832). We now look at a couple of provisions in the check-the-box regulations.

Treas. Reg. § 301.7701-1. Classification of organizations for federal tax purposes

(a) Organizations for federal tax purposes.

(1) In general. The Internal Revenue Code prescribes the classification of various organizations for federal tax purposes. Whether an organization is an entity separate from its owners for federal tax purposes s a matter of federal tax law and does not depend on whether the organization is recognized as an entity under local law.

. . .

(4) Single owner organizations. Under Sections 301.7701-2 and 301.7701-3, certain organizations that have a single owner can choose to be recognized or disregarded as entities separate from their owners.

. . .

Treas. Reg. § 301.7701-2. Business entities; definitions

(a) Business entities... A business entity with two or more members is classified for federal tax purposes as either a corporation or a partnership. A business entity with only one owner is classified as a corporation or is disregarded; if the entity is disregarded, its activities are treated in the same manner as a sole proprietorship, branch, or division of the owner.

...

Treas. Reg. § 301.7701-3. Classification of certain business entities

(a) In general. A business entity that is not classified as a corporation under §301.7701-2(b)(1), (3), (4), (5), (6), (7), or (8) (an *eligible entity*) can elect its classification for federal tax purposes as provided in this section. An eligible entity with at least two members can elect to be classified as either an association (and thus a corporation under §301.7701-2(b)(2)) or a partnership, and an eligible entity with a single owner can elect to be classified as an association or to be disregarded as an entity separate from its owner. Paragraph (b) of this section provides a default classification for an eligible entity that does not make an election. Thus, elections are necessary only when an eligible entity chooses to be classified initially as other than the default classification or when an eligible entity chooses to change its classification. ...

(b) Classification of eligible entities that do not file an election.

(1) Domestic eligible entities. [U]nless the entity elects otherwise, a domestic eligible entity is—

(i) a partnership if it has two or more members; or

(ii) disregarded as an entity separate from its owner if it has a single owner.

...

(c) Elections.

(1) Time and place for filing.

(i) In general. [A]n eligible entity may elect to be classified other than as provided under paragraph (b) of this section, or to change its classification, by filing Form 8832 Entity Classification Election, with the service center designated on Form 8832...

...

(v) Deemed elections.

...

(C) S corporations. An eligible entity that timely elects to be an S corporation under Section 1362(a)(1) is treated as having made an election under this section to be classified as an association, provided that (as of the effective date of the election under Section 1362(a)(1)) the entity meets all other requirements to qualify as a small business corporation under Section 1361(b).

...

In short, an "eligible entity" may elect to be treated differently than its default classification. Entities formed as corporations under state law are not eligible entities. Partnerships and LLCs with more than one member are eligible entities and are treated as partnerships by default, but can elect to be treated as a corporation. Eligible entities with only one owner (e.g., single-member LLCs), are treated as disregarded entities by default, but can elect to be treated as a corporation. The election is made on Form 8832. One additional note: An eligible entity may elect "S" corporation status in accordance with Subchapter S without first checking the box to be treated as a corporation as long as the eligible entity meets the eligibility requirements governing "S" corporations. To accomplish the "S" election, an entity files IRS Form 2553 (*not* IRS Form 8832).

As mentioned, LLCs are treated as pass-through entities (or disregarded entities if the LLC has only one member) by default for federal income tax purposes. But how is a *series* LLC treated? While the Internal Revenue Code does not specifically address how to treat series LLCs, the Treasury Department has issued Proposed Regulations that give some guidance.

Prop. Treas. Reg. § 301.7701-1. Classification of organizations for federal tax purposes

(a) Organizations for federal tax purposes.

...

(5) Series and series organizations.

(i) Entity status of a domestic series. For federal tax purposes except as provided in ... this section, a series ... organized or established under the laws of the United States or of any State, whether or not a juridical person for local law purposes, is treated as an entity formed under local law.

...

(iii) Recognition of entity status. Whether a series that is treated as a local law entity under paragraph (a)(5)(i) ... is recognized as a separate entity for federal tax purposes is determined under this section and general tax principles.

...

(x) Examples. The following examples illustrate the principles of this paragraph (a)(5):

Example (1). Domestic series LLC.

(i) Facts. Series LLC is a series organization .... Series LLC has three members (1, 2, and 3). Series LLC establishes two series (A and B) pursuant to the LLC statute of state Y... Under general tax principles, Members 1 and 2 are the owners of Series A, and Member 3 is the owner of Series B...

(ii) Analysis. Under paragraph (a)(5)(i) of this section, Series A and series B are each treated as an entity formed under local law. The classification of Series A and Series B is determined under paragraph (b) of this section. The default classification under §301.7701-3 of Series A is a partnership and of Series B is a disregarded entity...

(b) Classification of organizations. The classification of organizations that are recognized as separate entities is determined under §§301.7701-2, 301.7701-3, and 301.7701-4 unless a provision of the Internal Revenue Code ... provides for special treatment of that organization...

The example in the regulations can be illustrated as follows:

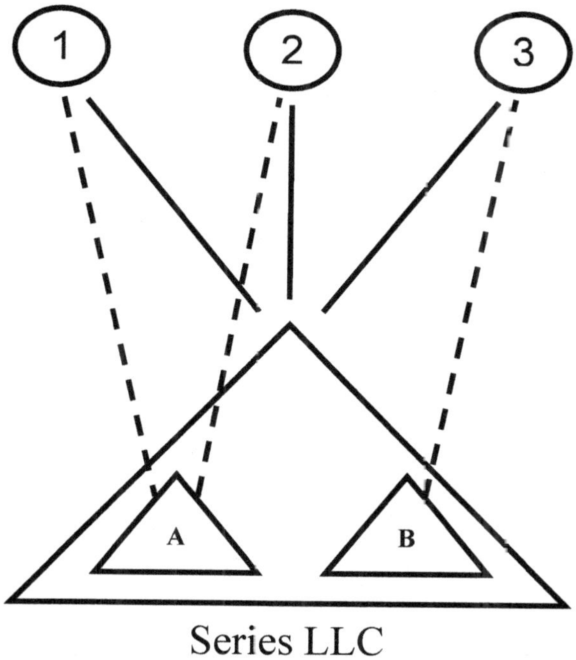

Source: Ryan H. Pace

Thus, according to the proposed regulations each series within the main LLC must be analyzed to determine whether, by default, it is a partnership or disregarded entity. Either way, each series may elect to be treated as a corporation for income tax purposes in accordance with the check-the-box rules or make an S corporation election.

I. Qualified Joint Ventures between Married Persons

A common situation encountered by a tax consultant is a business operated by married individuals. If no formal entity has been formed (e.g., corporation, LLC, etc.) by the married individuals, then the business is presumed to be a partnership by default. Nevertheless, the spouses may elect to treat the business as a **qualified joint venture** (QJV) if certain requirements are met.

Section 761. Terms defined

...

(f) Qualified joint venture.—

(1) In general. In the case of a qualified joint venture conducted by a husband and wife who file a joint return for the taxable year, for purposes of this title—

(A) such joint venture shall not be treated as a partnership,

(B) all items of income, gain, loss, deduction, and credit shall be divided between the spouses in accordance with their respective interests in the venture, and

(C) each spouse shall take into account such spouse's respective share of such items as if they were attributable to a trade or business conducted by such spouse as a sole proprietor.

(2) Qualified joint venture. For purposes of paragraph (1), the term 'qualified joint venture' means any joint venture involving the conduct of a trade or business if—

(A) the only members of such joint venture are a husband or wife,

(B) both spouses materially participate (within the meaning of Section 469(h) without regard to paragraph (5) thereof) in such trade or business, and

(C) both spouses elect the application of this subsection.

...

Notice that if a married couple conducts a business together and elects to <u>not</u> be treated as a partnership, then they are treated as two sole proprietors. This generally means that each spouse will report his or her share of the income and expenses of the business on a separate Schedule C on the couple's jointly filed IRS Form 1040. Filing the return in this manner effectively notifies the IRS that the couple elects to be treated as a QJV for income tax purposes rather than a partnership. Remember, QJV status is not available if the spouses have formed a separate entity under state law (e.g., corporation, LLC, etc.) in which to operate the business. One reason a married couple may desire to make the QJV election is so that each spouse gets credit for the social security taxes paid on the self-employment income from the business. (Note: the Code refers to *husband* and *wife* in the QJV context, but the QJV provisions also apply to same-sex couples that are legally married.)

J. Obtaining an Employer Identification Number (EIN)

Most new business will need to obtain an employer identification number. Financial institutions typically require the business to provide an EIN in order to open a checking account. An EIN is also needed for tax return reporting purposes (income tax, employment tax, excise tax, etc.). Obtaining an EIN is now quite streamlined. IRS Form SS-4 is the applicable form, but the SS-4 information can be submitted to the IRS entirely online at the IRS website (www.irs.gov). Once the SS-4 information is submitted to the IRS online, the business usually obtains its EIN electronically the same day.

CHAPTER 1 QUESTIONS FOR REVIEW

1. *Choice of entity.* Compare and contrast the non-tax characteristics (e.g., liability protection, formation, management structure, etc.) of the various business entities available under state law.

2. *Choice of entity.* Explain how an LLP differs from a general partnership.

3. *Choice of entity.* Explain how an LLLP differs from a limited partnership.

4. *Tax classification of entities.* What is an "eligible entity" under the check-the-box regulations?

5. *Tax classification of entities.* What is the default tax classification of an eligible entity with two or more owners?

6. *Tax classification of entities.* What is the default tax classification of an eligible entity with only one owner?

7. *Tax classification of entities.* R and J, both individuals, own LLC-1. LLC-1 owns 100% of LLC-2, LLC-3, LLC-4, LLC-5, and LLC-6. How will you treat this arrangement for federal income tax purposes? Why would R and J choose to structure their business(es) like this?

8. *Tax classification of entities.* R and J, both individuals, own LLC-1. LLC-1 owns 100% of LLC-2. LLC-2 owns 2% of LP-1 and LLC-1 owns 98% of LP-1. How will you treat this arrangement for federal income tax purposes? Why might R and J structure their business(es) like this?

9. *Tax classification of entities.* Evaluate the diagram below and indicate how each entity will be treated in accordance with their default income tax classification (i.e., partnership, corporation, or disregarded entity).

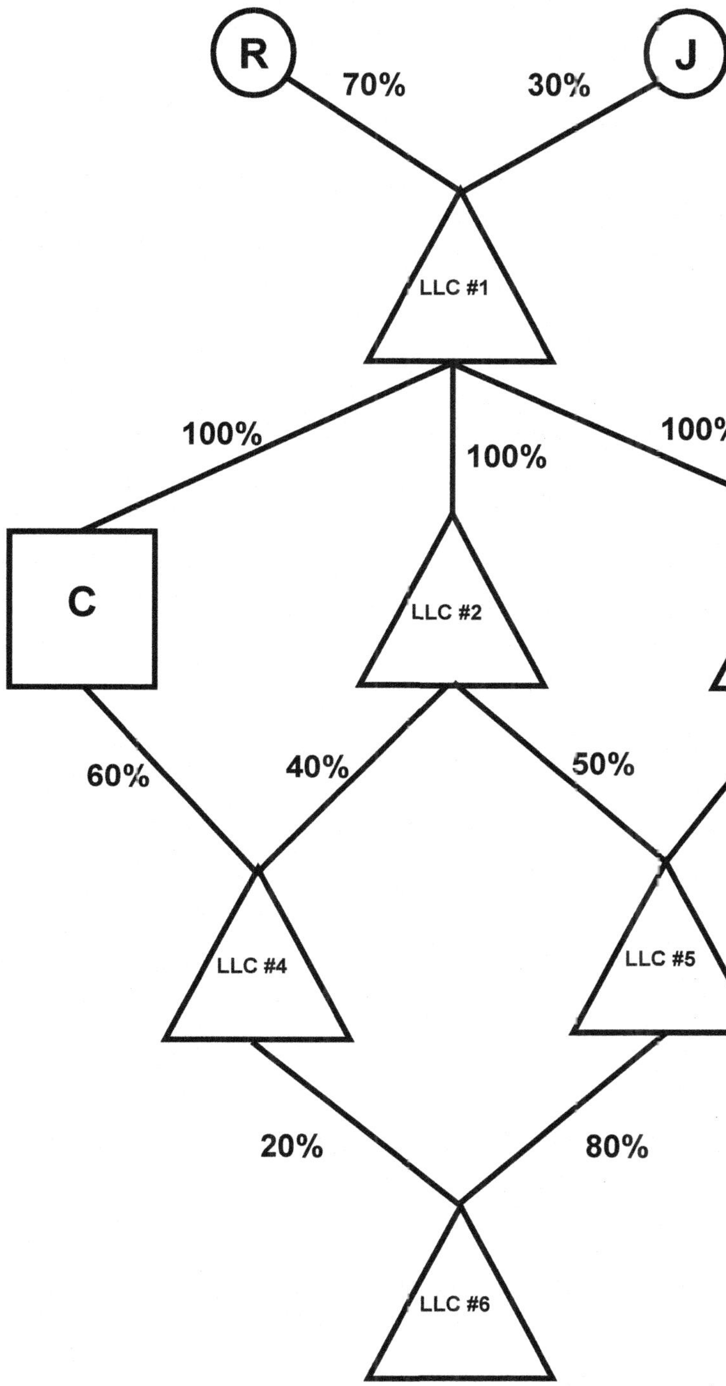

Source: Ryan H. Pace

10. *Piercing the LLC veil.* Summarize the facts in the *GreenHunter* case. What was the issue? What did the court conclude?

11. *Single-member LLCs—reverse veil piercing*. Summarize the facts in the *In re Albright* case. What was the issue? What did the court conclude?

12. *Tax classification of entities*. Is it possible for a limited liability company organized under state law to be treated as an "S" corporation for federal income tax purposes? If so, how does the LLC make the "S" election?

13. *Tax classification of entities*. On which IRS form does an eligible entity make an election to be treated as a different entity under the check-the-box-regulations?

14. *Series LLCs*. Explain the non-tax characteristics of a series LLC. How is a series LLC treated for federal income tax purposes?

15. *Qualified joint ventures*. How are businesses owned only by a married couple treated for income tax purposes by default if the couple has not created a separate entity under state law?

16. *Qualified joint ventures*. What are the eligibility requirements for a qualified joint venture election?

17. *Qualified joint ventures*. How is a qualified joint venture election made?

18. *Qualified joint ventures*. Why would a married couple make the QJV election?

GreenHunter Energy, Inc. v. Western Ecosystems Technology, Inc.

Supreme Court of Wyoming
2014 WY 144

DAVIS, Justice.

[¶1] Appellant GreenHunter Energy, Inc. is the sole member of a limited liability company, GreenHunter Wind Energy, LLC (LLC). It appeals from a district court decision piercing the LLC's veil to hold it liable for the LLC's contractual obligations to Appellee Western Ecosystems Technology, Inc. (Western). We conclude that under the specific circumstances of this case, the evidence supports the use of this extraordinary equitable remedy. We therefore affirm.

ISSUES

[¶2] Appellant presents the following issues, which we have rephrased somewhat:

1. Did the district court err as a matter of law by applying incorrect factors to determine whether the LLC's veil of limited liability should be pierced?

2. If the district court consulted the appropriate factors in determining whether to pierce the veil of the LLC, were its factual findings clearly erroneous and misapplied to the law?

FACTS

[¶3] In 2009, Appellee Western and the LLC [footnotes and citations omitted throughout] entered into a contract whereby Western undertook to provide the LLC consulting services related to the potential development of a wind turbine farm in Platte County, Wyoming. While Western performed under the contract, the LLC paid nothing for Western's services. Western consequently brought a breach of contract action against the LLC and obtained a judgment in the amount of $43,646.10...The district court also granted judgment in favor of Western in the amount of $2,161.84 for attorney's fees incurred in bringing a motion to compel discovery. The judgments cannot be satisfied because the LLC has no assets upon which Western can execute.

[¶4] After learning that it could not collect on its judgments against the LLC, Western brought this action against Appellant, the sole member of the LLC, seeking to pierce the LLC's veil and hold Appellant liable for the LLC's contractual obligations. After discovery was complete and dispositive motions were denied, the case proceeded to a bench trial.

[¶5] At trial, Western argued that Appellant was the LLC's alter ego and presented evidence, much of it uncontroverted, that it felt proved as much. Western was able to demonstrate that the LLC is a wholly-owned subsidiary of Appellant, the latter being the sole member and manager of the former. The LLC consistently carried an operating capital balance which was insufficient to cover its debts, and on numerous occasions its account had a balance of zero. Western showed that Appellant decided when and how much money to advance to the LLC to allow it to pay its accounts payable. Therefore Appellant, as the sole source of operating funds for the LLC, decided which of its creditors would be paid. Although Appellant advanced funds to permit the LLC to pay some creditors, it did not transfer any funds to allow the LLC to pay Western.

[¶6] Western was also able to show that the LLC did not have employees of its own, but that employees of Appellant performed services for and on behalf of the LLC, including negotiation of wind farm leases and other agreements. The LLC's chairman and general counsel held the same positions with Appellant.

[¶7] Western also established that Appellant and the LLC have the same business address. All bookkeeping and financial management of the LLC were performed by employees of Appellant, including maintenance of accounts receivable and accounts payable for the LLC. The tax returns of the LLC were consolidated with those of Appellant because the LLC had only a single member, and federal tax law permitted it to be treated as a disregarded entity. By this means, Appellant was able to deduct $884,092.00 in expenses and claim a loss of $61,047.00 for the LLC's activities on the Platte County wind farm project.

...

[¶9] The district court found in favor of Western. It pierced the LLC's veil and awarded a judgment of $45,807.94 against Appellant for the amount the LLC had not paid under its contract with Western and for the sanctions incurred during the underlying action.

[¶10] Appellant timely perfected this appeal. Additional evidence from the bench trial, as well as the district court's findings of fact and conclusions of law, will be discussed as necessary below.

...

DISCUSSION

Factors to determine whether the LLC's veil of limited liability should be pierced

[¶12] Certain legally recognized entities, such as corporations and limited liability companies, are separate and distinct from their owners... The fundamental feature of these business entities is limited liability, although that protection does not extend to behavior resulting in injustice...

[¶13] The common law therefore allowed courts to pierce the veil of limited liability and disregard the putatively separate entity under certain exceptional circumstances...

[¶14] With the advent of different types of business entities, including limited liability companies, the circumstances under which courts may properly pierce the veil have become even more difficult to understand. However, with the benefit of time and experience, this equitable remedy must begin to be applied with greater consistency and more predictability.

[¶15] In order to determine how to approach piercing in this case involving a limited liability company, we begin by studying the development of the law governing business organizations. Early on, the corporation was conceived to assure continuity of existence and to provide a means for shareholders to invest without incurring personal liability which might threaten their private wealth for the acts of the business... The concept of limited liability for corporations stimulated commerce and industrial growth throughout the years, and "[t]his incentive to business investment has been called the most important legal development of the nineteenth century." ...

...

[¶17] While the limited liability provided by corporations has served an important purpose in the development of our economy, there have been instances when exacting adherence to the concept that shareholders will not be liable for corporate debt led to injustice. As a result, courts began piercing the corporate veil. We long ago explained "[t]hat the legal entity of a corporation will be disregarded whenever the recognition thereof in a particular case will lead to injustice, has been announced so frequently that it is hardly necessary to cite the authorities." As the years passed, we continued to summarize circumstances under which a corporate veil would be pierced pursuant to Wyoming law:
Before a corporation's acts and obligations can be legally recognized as those of a particular person, and vice versa, it must be made to appear that the corporation is not only influenced and governed by that person, but that there is such a unity of interest and ownership that the individuality, or separateness, of such person and corporation has ceased, and that the facts are such that an adherence to the fiction of the separate existence of the corporation would, under the particular circumstances, sanction a fraud or promote injustice. Over time, we have provided a comprehensive list of factors for courts to consider when they are asked to pierce a corporation's veil.

[¶18] Because of the formalities required of corporations, and the tax treatment of their earnings, new types of business entities were conceived. In 1977, Wyoming enacted a statute that allowed the creation of limited liability companies... Limited liability companies provide the limited personal liability associated with corporations, but they are taxed like a partnership for federal income tax purposes and thus avoid double taxation...

[¶19] A limited liability company's "operation is intended to be much more flexible than a corporation's." ... The original Act, for example, required that a limited liability company be comprised of at least two members, unless the organizer elected "flexible limited liability company" status, which allowed for a single member...

[¶20] Since the Wyoming Legislature passed the original Act, we have had occasion to consider whether and when the veil of a limited liability company may be pierced or disregarded. Over a decade ago, we held that even in the absence of fraud, the veil of a limited liability company can be pierced as that of a corporation can... We recognized that piercing of a limited liability company veil was possible under certain circumstances even though Wyo. Stat. Ann. § 17-15-113 (2005) (repealed 2010) stated that "the members of a limited liability company... are [not] liable under a judgment, decree or order of a court, or in any other manner, for a debt, obligation or liability of the limited liability company." ... This Court observed, however, that "[c]ertainly, the various factors which would justify piercing an LLC veil would not be identical to the corporate situation for the obvious reason that many of the organizational formalities applicable to corporations do not apply to LLCs." ... This is so because limited liability companies are intended to be much more flexible than a corporation...

[¶21] In *Gasstop Two, LLC v. Seatwo, LLC*, this Court further defined the rules which govern whether the veil of a limited liability company may be pierced... Drawing upon factors utilized in the corporate context as a starting point, we refined the requirements for piercing the veil of a limited liability company, focusing on four factors: 1) fraud; 2) inadequate capitalization; 3) failure to observe company formalities; and 4) intermingling the business and finances of the company and the member to such an extent that there is no distinction between them. *Gasstop* also held that with the exception of fraud, no single factor is sufficient or required to pierce the limited liability company's veil, and that our courts must analyze all of these factors when asked to impose liability on an limited liability company's members... Applying these factors, we affirmed the district court's refusal to pierce the limited liability company's veil to make its members personally liable under the circumstances of that case...

[¶22] Five days after our opinion in *Gasstop* was issued, the Governor of the State of Wyoming signed the 2010 Wyoming Limited Liability Company Act into law... The 2010 Act has been described as "a comprehensive update" to the law governing limited liability companies... The 2010 Act came about because as the "sophistication and needs of businesses increased, the [original act] became quite outdated after more than three decades." ...

[¶23] The new Act provides limited liability companies w th even more flexibility. For example, it eliminated prior provisions dealing with a one-member "flexible limited liability company," and it allowed any limited liability company to simply be formed with a single member... The single member is allowed to manage the company by statutory design....

[¶24] The 2010 Act also repealed § 17-15-113 (2009) and recognized that the veil of limited liability companies may be pierced in certain circumstances:

(a) The debts, obligations or other liabilities of a limited liability company, whether arising in contract, tort or otherwise:

(i) Are solely the debts, obligations or other liabilities of the company; and

(ii) Do not become the debts, obligations or other liabilities of a member or manager solely by reason of the member acting as a member or manager acting as a manager.

(b) *The failure of a limited liability company to observe any particular formalities relating to the exercise of its powers or management of its activities is not a ground for imposing liability on the members or managers for the debts, obligations or other liabilities of the company.*

Wyo. Stat. Ann. § 17-29-304 (emphasis added).

[¶25] The language of § 17-29-304 is clear... Failure of a limited liability company to adhere to the formalities required of a corporation is not a basis for disregarding the company in an action seeking to pierce its veil. By passing the 2010 Act, the legislature determined that even greater flexibility and informality are acceptable features of a limited liability company. Additional provisions of the 2010 Act confirm that there are relatively few statutorily mandated formalities in order to allow significant freedom and flexibility in the management structure and operation of the company...

[¶26] While the 2010 Act alters the piercing analysis set forth in *Gasstop* to some extent, the essence of the original Act has been preserved, and our holding in *Kaycee* still controls; that is, the new Act continues to allow a limited liability company's veil to be pierced under certain extraordinary circumstances... We must now determine what test should be applied under the 2010 Act, and what factors may be considered in determining whether to pierce the veil of a limited liability company, which "is an entity distinct from its members." ...

[¶27] After a solicitous study of this Court's precedent, the legislative developments, and authority outside our borders, we conclude that a refinement and restatement of the test set forth in *Gasstop* is in order. The veil of a limited liability company may be pierced under exceptional circumstances when: (1) the limited liability company is not only owned, influenced and governed by its members, but the required separateness has ceased to exist due to misuse of the limited liability company; and (2) the facts are such that an adherence to the fiction of its separate existence would, under the particular circumstances, lead to injustice, fundamental unfairness, or inequity...

[¶28] This test is fact-driven and flexible, and it focuses on whether the limited liability company has been operated as a separate entity as contemplated by statute, or whether the member has instead misused the entity in an inequitable manner to injure the plaintiff. "We have made clear that[] [e]ach case involving the disregard of the separate entity doctrine must be governed by the special facts of that case ... [and] [t]he district court must complete a fact-intensive inquiry and exercise its equitable powers to determine whether piercing the veil is appropriate under the circumstances presented...."

[¶29] In determining whether both prongs of this test have been met, courts can usually apply several factors. The first is whether there has been fraud... We have advised, however, that in certain cases, "[a]lthough fraud in the classic sense requires an affirmative misrepresentation, this court has recognized that fraud may be perpetrated by silence as well as by affirmative representations; and when one has a duty to speak, the failure to speak may constitute fraud." ... We have further explained that "[e]ven in the absence of a duty to speak, if a person does speak, he must speak the truth and make a full and fair disclosure, as half the truth may be a lie in effect." ...

[¶30] Constructive fraud may be an alternative to actual fraud in certain circumstances. It "has been defined as consisting of all acts, omissions, and concealments involving breaches of a legal or equitable duty resulting in damage to another, and exists where such conduct, although not actually fraudulent, ought to be so treated when it has the same consequence and legal effects."....

[¶31] Second, inadequate capitalization, if there is evidence of it, may be considered. It is important to note, however, that undercapitalization alone will not suffice to pierce the veil... Basic business practice and societal policy call for a limited liability company to be financially responsible and require that it attempt to arrange for enough capital to reasonably cover its potential liabilities at various points of its existence...

[¶32] In determining whether a limited liability company is undercapitalized, courts must compare the amount of capital to the amount of business to be conducted and the obligations which must be satisfied... If the LLC is undercapitalized, or if its members have never attempted to make arrangements to secure sufficient capital, these facts may be evidence that the company was used to screen members from legitimate debt because it is not in reality an autonomous company capable of carrying on its own business. Undercapitalization is a relative concept, and the weight to be given to this factor is dependent on the particular circumstances of the case... As one commentator has explained, "[s]ome businesses need a great deal of capital, others very little, and of course there are the in-betweens."

[¶33] A third factor to consider is the degree to which the business and finances of the company and the member are intermingled. This factor may have numerous aspects which must be analyzed. Funds and assets should be separated and not commingled... Failure to maintain an arm's-length relationship between the member and company, as by not keeping separate bank accounts and bookkeeping records, may be weighed along with other factors... If the member treats limited liability company property as if it were that person's or company's personal property, a court should consider also this fact... Manipulation of assets and liabilities between the member and company so as to concentrate the assets in the former and the liabilities in the latter can be suggestive of improper use of the LLC as well.

...

[¶37] After having carefully examined the district court's Judgment and Order After Trial, we disagree with Appellant's assessment. The district court made it clear that it was well aware of § 17-29-304, and that in deciding whether to pierce the LLC's veil, it had

> not considered the "failure of a limited liability company to observe any particular formalities relating to the exercise of its powers or management of its activities," pursuant to § 17-29-304(b). In addition, the Court has not found that LLC's [] veil should be pierced "solely by reason of Defendant acting as a member or [] manager" consistent with § 17-29-304(a).

Conforming its analysis accordingly, it considered (1) the LLC's undercapitalization and absence of assets, (2) the LLC's and Appellant's intermingling of finances and business, including commingling of funds and concentration of benefits in the member and liabilities in the LLC, (3) the lack of any separateness between the two, and (4) Appellant's course of conduct in engaging and contracting with Western in the name of the LLC for services when it knew that it could not or would not provide funds to pay Western's bills, which it found to be fraudulent and not protected by the veil of limited liability.

[¶38] We are satisfied that the district court applied the correct law as set forth above...

Evidence supporting piercing the LLC's veil

[¶39] It bears repeating that limited liability is the rule, and piercing is the rare exception to be applied only in cases involving exceptional circumstances... This is one of those rare situations, although we must concede that it is a close call.

Undercapitalization

[¶40] Appellant first complains that the weight the district court gave to undercapitalization contradicts our direction in *Gasstop*, and that its findings are not supported by the evidence. We disagree. The district court did not rely solely on undercapitalization to determine that piercing the veil was warranted... Rather, undercapitalization was one of several factors it considered in the totality of the circumstances of this case, as was done in *Gasstop*...

[¶41] Our review of the record confirms the accuracy of the district court's finding that during the periods when Western's invoices were submitted to the LLC, it often had no money in its operating account, and that it received periodic money transfers from Appellant, which decided how much money would be transferred to the LLC to pay specific bills it decided to pay, and when.

...

[¶42] Based upon these facts, and other evidence introduced at trial, the district court correctly concluded that Appellant "failed to adequately capitalize LLC, that LLC was undercapitalized at all times relevant to this suit, and that LLC lacks corporate assets."

...

Intermingling of business and finances

[¶44] Appellant also asserts that the district court misunderstood the factor of intermingling business and finances between it and the LLC, and the court therefore misapplied the law to the evidence. It contends the district court should have focused solely on "whether or not Appellant and the LLC maintained separate accounting, bank accounts, accounts payable, accounts receivable, and could clearly demonstrate such distinction."

[¶45] Appellant and the LLC did maintain separate bank accounts and business records. If the analysis could end there, Appellant would have a convincing case. However, Appellant's argument ignores other facets of this factor which must be considered, as we explained above... In actions seeking to pierce the veil of a limited liability company, each case must be governed by its own facts... There is no rigid formula to which a court's analysis must conform; instead, each case requires a fact-intensive inquiry that must address the particular circumstances. Here, based upon the evidence presented at trial, the district court found the following with respect to intermingling:

• The overlap between the LLC's and Appellant's ownership, membership and management was considerable and to an extent such that, when considered with other factors, piercing was appropriate. Appellant and the LLC utilized

Appellant's accounting department, and in fact the same accountants managed the finances of both entities. They had the same business address and creditors of the LLC mailed their invoice to Appellant's address for processing. The LLC's tax returns were consolidated with the tax returns of Appellant.

. . .

• The LLC had no revenue separate from Appellant. Funds were commingled in the sense that the LLC's bills that Appellant wanted paid were settled with Appellant's funds which were "passed through" the LLC by periodic transfers. A particular bill was paid only if and when Appellant decided to transfer funds to pay it.

. . .

• Appellant manipulated the assets and liabilities in a manner such that Appellant improperly reaped all of the rewards and benefits of the LLC's activities, while simultaneously saddling the LLC with all of its losses and liabilities, including the unpaid bills for services rendered by Western. Appellant has enjoyed significant tax breaks attributable to the LLC's losses, without bearing any responsibility for the LLC's debt and obligations that contributed to such losses. Such a disparity in the risks and rewards resulting from this manipulation would lead to injustice.

[¶46] Based upon this, and other evidence in the record, the LLC was not only owned, influenced and governed by Appellant, but the entities had ceased to be separate due to Appellant's misuse of the LLC. Furthermore, the facts are such that adherence to the fiction of the LLC's separate existence would, under these particular circumstances, lead to an unjust and inequitable result. We conclude that the district court's findings of fact were not clearly erroneous and did not otherwise err in applying those findings to the law.

[¶47] However, Appellant makes several reasonable observations which temper these findings as they relate to a single-member limited liability company. The first involves the district court's consideration of federal tax filings. Appellant properly points out that as a single-member limited liability company, the LLC can properly be taxed as a disregarded entity... Federal tax law allows the LLC's losses to be attributed to Appellant and a consolidated tax return filed. As one commentator explains:

> With the advent of check-the-box, the tax treatment of single-member LLCs injects a new concept of "disregarded entity." A trend, however, is not to treat the LLC as disregarded for all purposes. A single-member LLC is a "disregarded entity." The term "disregarded entity' is defined by IRC §7701 and the regulations thereunder as any single-member entity that is not a corporation. The owner of a

> single-member entity can be a natural person or any other entity including a corporation.
>
> Natural persons who own single-member LLCs [disregarded entities] do not file any federal income tax forms for the entity. The disregarded entity owner reports the profits and losses of the company on the individual's personal Schedule C on the 1040 form. Single-member LLCs whose owners are corporations are treated as divisions of the corporate owner and the profits and losses are reflected on the corporate owner's returns...

[¶48] For that reason, while consideration of Appellant's consolidated tax return and the losses of the LLC reported therein may have been relevant to the district court's piercing analysis, the amount of weight given to this evidence must be balanced by the fact that this practice is permitted under our nation's tax laws. Stated differently, courts should not create a scenario in which a single-member limited liability company would be confronted with a catch 22: either follow federal tax law and risk losing limited liability, or forego advantages available under federal tax law to assure limited liability. The district court's ruling does not create that dilemma. Instead, it considered Appellant's tax filings as only one of many relevant pieces of evidence demonstrating that Appellant directed benefits from the LLC to itself, while at the same time it concentrated wind farm project debts it decided would not to be paid in the LLC. The district court did not err in doing so.

[¶49] Appellant also raises a reasonable policy concern regarding the operational and management structure of a single-member limited liability company. A single-member company is owned and by default often managed by its sole member as expressly permitted by the 2010 Act... Because of the minimal requirements for creating and operating a single-member limited liability company, this form of business organization can be utilized by many different types of members, from an individual starting a business out of her home to a large corporation... The flexibility allowed in the operation of such an entity does not conflict with the use of a home address as the business's address in some cases. Nor is it inconceivable that the sole member may manage the company's finances as well as its own or be responsible for entering into agreements on the company's behalf. Indeed, that will likely be the case when the sole member manages the company. While the district court noted that the LLC's address was the same as Appellant's and that all finances and negotiations were handled by the latter, under the circumstances of this case, it did not assign inappropriate weight to this evidence in its overall analysis.

[¶50] Finally, Appellant argues that Western should have protected itself by requiring Appellant to guarantee the LLC's obligation or require a retainer. As a matter of policy, Appellant posits, Western "was doing work at its own risk" by not taking "any commercially reasonable and available method to protect itself."

While it may be true, as Appellant suggests, that it is commonplace for lenders to seek personal guarantees from limited liability companies, other contract creditors that are not in such an advantageous position to insist on such guarantees or other protections should not be left holding the bag due to a member's misuse of the limited liability company...

...

[¶51] It makes good business sense for a contract creditor to try to obtain a guarantee from the member or retainer from the limited liability company itself. But we are mindful of the reality of the marketplace that many businesses are not in a position—competitively or economically—to insist on guarantees. For that reason, we decline Appellant's invitation to find piercing inappropriate in this case because Western did not protect itself from Appellant's misuse of the LLC by attempting to obtain a guarantee or other form of security. To do so would invite abuse of entities, as is the case here.

Fraud

[¶52] We have made it clear that a showing of fraud or an intent to defraud is not necessary to disregard the legal fiction of a separate entity... Our analysis could therefore stop here. However, the district court also found that Appellant's "course of conduct, which was executed in the name of the LLC, wherein it engaged and contracted with [Western] for valuable services knowing that it could not or would not pay [Western's] bill when received, constitutes a fraud that should not enjoy protection" behind the veil of limited liability. It reasoned that the instant case was "a far cry from cases such as that in *Gasstop*, where a claim of fraud was found to be inappropriate where the evidence showed that the [limited liability company] was not intentionally made insolvent to serve as a 'judgment-proof shell' that allowed the owner to avoid liabilities, but rather became insolvent due to an unforeseen and undesired economic recession."

[¶53] While not a prerequisite for piercing a limited liability company's veil, fraud can be a powerful reason to do so. "It is in the public interest to disregard the legal fiction of a separate entity, whether that be a corporation or LLC, when those benefiting from that fiction commit fraudulent conduct." ...
[¶54] Appellant argues, inter alia, that Western failed to present any evidence of fraud, or the intention by Appellant to commit any fraud, and the district court erred by inferring fraud from the facts of the case. We agree with Appellant on this point.

[¶55] The elements of fraud have been clearly set forth by this Court, and we have explained that the facts supporting those elements must be alleged clearly and distinctly, and proven by clear and convincing evidence.

> The elements of a claim for relief for fraud are a false representation made by the defendant which is relied upon

> by the plaintiff to his damage, the asserted false representation must be made to induce action, and the plaintiff must reasonably believe the representation to be true. A plaintiff who alleges fraud must do so clearly and distinctly, and fraud will not be imputed to any party when the facts and circumstances out of which it is alleged to arise are consistent with honesty and purity of intention. Fraud must be established by clear, unequivocal and convincing evidence, and will never be presumed.

...

[¶56] There is no evidence that Appellant made false statements that Western relied upon in entering into the contract with the LLC or in continuing to perform services thereunder. There is likewise no evidence that Appellant's employees made statements which were only partially truthful and therefore fraudulent... Finally, there is no evidence that either the LLC or Appellant assumed and violated any fiduciary duties which might support a claim of constructive fraud. ... The parties simply entered into an agreement that Western trusted would be performed by the LLC, and it was not.

[¶57] However, we believe the district court instinctively applied the test we have set forth above, although it used the term "fraud." It found that Appellant misused the LLC in order to improperly manipulate the situation to avoid paying for services which benefitted it, that it failed to maintain adequate separation, and that to allow it to do so would be unjust and inequitable. Thus, even though there was no fraud in the classic and technical sense, the district court's decision to pierce the LLC's veil to hold Appellant responsible for a debt for services which benefitted it was legally correct and not clearly erroneous.

CONCLUSION

[¶58] We conclude that the district court correctly applied the applicable law and that its findings of fact were not clearly erroneous. Based upon the totality of the circumstances, the evidence supports the determination that the LLC was not only owned, influenced and governed by Appellant, but that the LLC had ceased to be a separate entity due to Appellant's misuse of it in this transaction. Adherence to the fiction of the LLC's separate existence would, under these particular circumstances, lead to an unjust and inequitable result. Accordingly, we affirm the district court's judgment piercing the LLC's veil and imposing liability on Appellant for its debt to Western.

In re Ashley Albright

United States Bankruptcy Court
291 B.R. 538 (Bankr. D. Colo. 2003)

Ashley Albright, the debtor in this Chapter 7 case ("Debtor"), is the sole member and manager of a Colorado limited liability company named Western Blue Sky LLC. The LLC owns certain real property located in Saguache County, Colorado (the "Real Property"). The LLC is not a debtor in bankruptcy.

The Chapter 7 Trustee contends that because the Debtor was the sole member and manager of the LLC at the time she filed bankruptcy, he now controls the LLC and he may cause the LLC to sell the Real Property and distribute the net sales proceeds to his bankruptcy estate. The Debtor maintains that, at best, the Trustee is entitled to a charging order and cannot assume management of the LLC or cause the LLC to sell the Real Property.

Pursuant to the Colorado limited liability company statute, the Debtor's membership interest constitutes the personal property of the member. Upon the debtor's bankruptcy filing, she effectively transferred her membership interest to the estate. [Citation omitted.] Because there are no other members in the LLC, the entire membership interest passed to the bankruptcy estate, and the Trustee has become a "substituted member."

Section 7-80-702 of the [Colorado] Limited Liability Company Act requires the unanimous consent of "other members' in order to allow a transferee to participate in the management of the LLC. Because there are no other members in the LLC, no written unanimous approval of the transfer was necessary. Consequently, the Debtor's bankruptcy filing effectively assigned her entire membership interest in the LLC to the bankruptcy estate, and the Trustee obtained all her rights, including the right to control the management of the LLC.

The Debtor argues that the Trustee acts merely for her creditors and is only entitled to a charging order against distributions made on account of her LLC member interest. However, the charging order, as set forth in Section 703 of the Colorado Limited Liability Company Act, exists to protect other members of an LLC from having involuntarily to share governance responsibilities with someone they did not choose, or from having to accept a creditor of another member as a co-manager. A charging order protects the autonomy of the original members, and their ability to manage their own enterprise. In a single-member entity, there are no non-debtor members to protect. The charging order limitation serves no purpose in a single member limited liability company, because there are no other parties' interests affected.

The Colorado limited liability company statute provides that the members, including the sole member of a single member limited liability company, have the power to elect and change managers. Because the Trustee became the sole member of Western Blue Sky LLC upon the debtor's bankruptcy filing, the Trustee now controls, directly or indirectly, all governance of that entity, including decisions regarding liquidation of the entity's assets.

...

Based on the foregoing, it is hereby:

ORDERED that the Trustee, as sole member, controls the Western Blue Sky LLC and may cause the LLC to sell its property and distribute net proceeds to his estate. Alternatively, the Trustee may elect to distribute the LLC's property to the bankruptcy estate, and, in turn, liquidate that property himself; ...

...

Chapter 2

Transfer of Property to a Partnership

A. Nonrecognition of Gain or Loss
B. Partner's Initial Tax Basis in Partnership Interest
C. Partner's Holding Period in Partnership Interest
D. Partnership's Initial Tax Basis in Partnership Assets
E. Special Rules Relating to Character of Property Contributed
F. Partnership's Holding Period in Partnership Assets
G. A Partner's Capital Account
H. Contribution of Depreciable Assets
I. Exception to Nonrecognition: "Investment Companies"
J. Partnership Formation Example

When a taxpayer sells, exchanges, or otherwise disposes of an asset, the taxpayer has engaged in a **realization event**. Consequently, an analysis of the income tax consequences of the event is necessary. Code Section 1001 informs us how to calculate gain or loss upon the sale or exchange of property.

Section 1001. Determination of amount of and recognition of gain or loss

(a) Computation of gain or loss. The gain from the sale or other disposition of property shall be the excess of the amount realized therefrom over the adjusted basis provided in Section 1011 for determining gain, and the loss shall be the excess of the adjusted basis provided in such section for determining loss over the amount realized.

(b) Amount realized. The amount realized from the sale or other disposition of property shall be the sum of any money received plus the fair market value of the property (other than money) received.

...

(c) Recognition of gain or loss. Except as otherwise provided in this subtitle, the entire amount of the gain or loss, determined under this section, on the sale or exchange of property shall be recognized.

...

In sum, Section 1001 provides that the **amount realized** minus the **adjusted basis** (frequently referred to as "tax basis") in the property transferred generates a **gain (or loss) realized**. This gain (or loss) must be **recognized** unless some other provision of the Code provides otherwise. The amount realized includes money and the fair market value of any other property received. We should note here that if a transferor of property is relieved of debt as part of the transaction, the relief of the debt is also included in the transferor's amount realized.[1]

A. Nonrecognition of Gain or Loss

The transfer of property to a partnership is a realization event. Thus, in accordance with Section 1001, the gain or loss *realized* on the transfer must be *recognized* by the transferring partner unless the Code provides otherwise. In this case, the Code does provide otherwise. Section 721 allows for nonrecognition of gain to both the partner and the partnership upon a partner's transfer of property to the partnership in return for a partnership interest.

Section 721. Nonrecognition of gain or loss on contribution

(a) General rule. No gain or loss shall be recognized to a partnership or to any of its partners in the case of a contribution of property to the partnership in exchange for an interest in the partnership.

. . .

In accordance with Section 721(a), then, if a partner transfers property to the partnership, the partner recognizes no gain or loss. The term "property" is interpreted broadly and includes personal, real, and intangible property. The term "property" does not include the provision of *services* contributed by the partner, however.[2]

rzvmuR /Shutterstock.com

For a court case analyzing the definition of "property," see *United States v. Stafford*, 727 F.2d 1043 (11th Cir. 1984). Excerpts of the *Stafford* case are included at the end of this chapter.

[1] See, e.g., *Commissioner v. Tufts*, 461 U.S. 300 (1983).

[2] See Chapter 3 for a discussion on receiving a partnership interest in return for services provided by a partner.

A few narrow exceptions apply to the nonrecognition provision in Section 721(a) even in situations where the partner transfers property to the partnership. Among the exceptions are the following:

- When the transfer of property to the partnership is deemed a "disguised sale"[3];
- When the transfer of property is to a "partnership investment company"[4]; and
- When the property transferred to the partnership is subject to a liability or the partnership assumes a liability of the partner as part of the transaction.[5]

Importantly, Section 721(a) provides that the *partnership* also does not recognize gain or loss on the transfer of property by a partner to the partnership in exchange for an interest in the partnership.

B. Partner's Initial Tax Basis in Partnership Interest

Every individual and business entity has a tax basis (i.e., "adjusted" basis) in every asset they own. This includes both business assets and personal assets. When a partner transfers property to a partnership in return for a partnership interest, the partner must determine the partner's tax basis in the partnership interest received in the exchange. Section 722 provides the law in this regard.

Section 722. Basis of contributing partner's interest

The basis of an interest in a partnership acquired by a contribution of property, including money, to the partnership shall be the amount of such money and the adjusted basis of such property to the contributing partner at the time of the contribution increased by the amount (if any) of gain recognized under Section 721(b) to the contributing partner at such time.

Basically, then, according to Section 722 the partner's tax basis in his partnership interest is equal to the amount of money contributed plus the tax basis of other property contributed to the partnership.[6] ***Important note***: A partner's tax basis in

---

[3] See Code Sec. 707(a); see Chapter 11 for a discussion of disguised sales.

[4] See Code Sec. 721(b); see also Section I in this chapter for a discussion of partnership investment companies.

[5] See Chapter 5 regarding the impact of liabilities on a partner's outside basis and potential gain recognition on the contribution of property subject to a liability.

[6] Code Section 722 also provides that gain recognized under Section 721(b) should be included in the partner's initial outside basis. Code Section 721(b) is discussed in Section I of this chapter. If a partner contributes personal-use property to a partnership where the tax basis exceeds the fair market value, the

his partnership interest is frequently referred to as the partner's **"outside basis"** even though the Code itself does not use this term.

C. Partner's Holding Period in Partnership Interest

When a taxpayer sells a capital asset that has been held for longer than one year, the taxpayer recognizes a *long-term* capital gain (or loss).[7] Individual taxpayers benefit from the lower tax rates that apply to long-term capital gains compared to ordinary income.[8] Generally speaking, an interest in a partnership is considered a capital asset.[9] Thus, upon selling a partnership interest, the partner needs to know his or her **holding period** in the partnership interest to determine if the gain (or loss) is long term or short term.

> **Section 1223. Holding period of property**
>
> For purposes of this subtitle—
>
> (1) In determining the period for which the taxpayer has held property received in an exchange, there shall be included in the period for which he held the property exchanged if, under this chapter, the property has, for the purpose of determining gain or loss from a sale or exchange, the same basis in whole or in part in his hands as the property exchanged, and, in the case of such exchanges after March 1, 1954, the property exchanged at the time of such exchange was a capital asset as defined in Section 1221 or property described in Section 1231.
>
> . . .

Notice that if the partner transfers a capital asset[10] or a Section 1231 asset to the partnership, the partner's holding period in the partnership interest includes the amount of time the partner held the transferred property (or in tax jargon, the holding period **"tacks"**). If the partner transfers an ordinary asset (e.g., inventory and accounts receivable) to the partnership in return for the partnership interest, then the partner's holding period in their partnership interest is "new" (i.e., starts the day after the exchange).

---

partner's tax basis in the partnership is likely the fair market value of the property instead of the tax basis so that a partner cannot convert what would otherwise be a nondeductible loss into a deductible loss.

[7] Code Sec. 1222(3)-(4).

[8] Code Sec. 1(h).

[9] Code Sec. 741.

[10] See Code Section 1221 for the definition of capital asset. See also Section 741 (generally, the sale of a partnership interest generates capital gain to the seller).

D. Partnership's Initial Tax Basis in Partnership Assets

A partnership has a tax basis in every asset it owns. One reason the partnership must know this tax basis is that when the partnership sells or otherwise disposes of the asset, gain or loss can be determined.

> **Section 723. Basis of property contributed to partnership**
>
> The basis of property contributed to a partnership by a partner shall be the adjusted basis of such property to the contributing partner at the time of the contribution increased by the amount (if any) of gain recognized under Section 721(b) to the contributing partner.

The partnership's tax basis in the property contributed, then, is the same as the tax basis of the property to the partner at the time of the contribution (increased by any gain under Section 721(b)).[11] *Important note*: A partnership's tax basis in each of its assets is frequently referred to as the partnership's **"inside basis"** even though the Code itself does not use this term. Notice that a *partner* has an outside basis in the partnership and the *partnership* has an inside basis in its assets. If the property contributed to a partnership has an adjusted basis in excess of its fair market value and the property is nonbusiness property, the partnership's tax basis in the property is its fair market value.[12]

E. Special Rules Relating to Character of Property Contributed

Three special rules regarding the *character* of property contributed by a partner are important to discuss here:

1. If a partner transfers "unrealized receivables"[13] then the character of the receivables in the hands of the partnership remains as an ordinary asset until the receivables are recognized into income.

---

[11] Code Section 721(b) is discussed in Section I in this chapter. The calculation of a partner's initial outside basis is also impacted if the property transferred by the partner is subject to a liability or if other partners contribute property subject to a liability (discussed later in this chapter).

[12] See *Au v. Commissioner*, 330 F.2d 1008 (9th Cir. 1964) (relating to the contribution of a personal automobile by a partner).

[13] See Code Section 751(c) for the definition of "unrealized receivables" in this context.

Section 724. Character of gain or loss on contributed unrealized receivables, inventory items, and capital loss property

(a) Contributions of unrealized receivables. In the case of any property which—

(1) was contributed to the partnership by a partner, and

(2) was an unrealized receivable in the hands of such partner immediately before such contribution,

any gain or loss recognized by the partnership on the disposition of such property shall be treated as ordinary income or ordinary loss, as the case may be.

. . .

(d) Definitions. For purposes of this section—

(1) Unrealized receivable. The term "unrealized receivable" has the meaning given such term by Section 751(c) (determined by treating any reference to the partnership as referring to the partner).

. . .

2. If a partner transfers an "inventory item,"[14] then the character of the inventory in the hands of the partnership remains as an ordinary asset for five years. After five years, the character of the assets contributed as inventory may change depending upon how the partnership is employing the assets (e.g., Section 1231 asset, capital asset, or still an ordinary asset).

Section 724. Character of gain or loss on contributed unrealized receivables, inventory items, and capital loss property

. . .

(b) Contributions of inventory items. In the case of any property which—

(1) was contributed to the partnership by a partner, and

[14] See Code Section 751(d) for the definition of "inventory item" in this context.

(2) was an inventory item in the hands of such partner immediately before such contribution,

any gain or loss recognized by the partnership on the disposition of such property during the five-year period beginning on the date of such contribution shall be treated as ordinary income or ordinary loss, as the case may be.

...

(d) Definitions. For purposes of this section—

...

(2) Inventory item. The term "inventory item" has the meaning given such term by Section 751(d) (determined by treating any reference to the partnership as referring to the partner and by applying Section 1231 without regard to any holding period therein provided).

...

3. If a partner contributes property with a built-in capital loss (i.e., "capital loss" property), and if the partnership disposes of property within five years, the character of the loss to the partnership will be a capital loss (but only to the extent of the loss that existed at the time of the contribution of the property; the character of any additional loss would be determined by how the partnership is using the property at the time the loss is recognized).

Section 724. Character of gain or loss on contributed unrealized receivables, inventory items, and capital loss property

...

(c) Contributions of capital loss property. In the case of any property which—

(1) was contributed by a partner to the partnership, and

(2) was a capital asset in the hands of such partner immediately before such contribution,

any loss recognized by the partnership on the disposition of such property during the five-year period beginning on the date of such contribution shall be treated as a loss from the sale of a capital asset to the extent that, immediately before such contribution, the adjusted basis of such property in the hands of the partner exceeded the fair market value of such property.

. . .

F. Partnership's Holding Period in Partnership Assets

A partnership must also determine its holding period in each asset.

Section 1223. Holding period of property

For purposes of this subtitle—

. . .

(2) In determining the period for which the taxpayer has held property however acquired there shall be included the period for which such property was held by any other person, if under this chapter such property has, for the purpose of determining gain or loss from a sale or exchange, the same basis in whole or in part in his hands as it would have in the hands of such other person.

. . .

Notice that a *partnership's* holding period in property "tacks" regardless of whether the asset transferred is a capital asset, Section 1231 asset, or ordinary asset.[15]

Treas. Reg. § 1.723-1. Basis of property contributed to partnership

The basis to the partnership of property contributed to it by a partner is the adjusted basis of such property to the contributing partner at the time of the contribution. Since such property has the same basis in the hands of the partnership as it had in the hands of the contributing partner, the holding period of such property for the partnership includes the period during which it was held by the partner. See Section 1223(2)....

[15] Recall that a *partner's* holding period in the partnership interest tacks only if the partner transfers a capital asset or Section 1231 asset. See the discussion in Section C of this chapter.

G. A Partner's Capital Account

A partner's equity in the partnership is reflected in the partner's **capital account.** Of course, each of the partners' capital account balances in aggregate will equal the capital account total on the partnership's balance sheet. In short, a partner's capital account balance represents the amount a partner should receive if the partnership were to liquidate, pay its debts, and distribute the remaining assets to the partners.

As a practical matter, it is important to remember that throughout this chapter we discuss a partner's capital account as determined by complying with the Treasury Regulations and not necessarily by reference to financial accounting principles (e.g., GAAP).

Treas. Reg. § 1.704-1. Partner's distributive share

. . .

(b) Determination of partner's distributive share

. . .

(2) Substantial economic effect

. . .

(iv) Maintenance of capital accounts

. . .

(b) Basic rules. Except as otherwise provided in this paragraph (b)(2)(iv), the partners' capital accounts will be considered to be determined and maintained in accordance with the rules of this paragraph (b)(2)(iv) if, and only if, each partner's capital account is increased by

(1) the amount of money contributed by him to the partnership,

(2) the fair market value of property contributed by him to the partnership (net of liabilities secured by such contributed property that the partnership is considered to assume or take subject to under Section 752), and

(3) allocations to him of partnership income and gain (or items thereof), including income and gain exempt from tax . . . ;

and is decreased by

(4) the amount of money distributed to him by the partnership,

(5) the fair market value of property distributed to him by the partnership (net of liabilities secured by such distributed property that such partner is considered to assume or take subject to under Section 752),

(6) allocations to him of expenditures of the partnership described in Section 705(a)(2)(B), and

(7) allocations of partnership loss and deduction (or item thereof), ...; and is otherwise adjusted in accordance with the additional rules set forth in this paragraph (b)(2)(iv).

...

We will be working with these capital account rules throughout the chapter. _Important note_: Remember to differentiate between a partner's *outside basis* and a partner's *capital account*! For example, if a partner transfers to the partnership an asset with a tax basis of $70 and a fair market value of $100, the partner's initial outside basis in the partnership interest acquired is $70[16] and the partner's initial capital account balance is $100.[17] Of course, consistent with crediting a partner's capital account by the fair market value of property contributed, the partnership would also debit the corresponding asset account by the fair market value of the property contributed. These capital account maintenance rules originate from the Treasury Regulations related to Section 704. Consequently, a partnership's "books" are often referred to as being kept in accordance with Section 704(b). Thus, a partnership will need to keep at least two sets of books (perhaps *three* if there is a need to maintain books strictly in accordance with generally accepted accounting principles). These two sets of books are (1) the "tax basis" books (i.e., inside basis of each asset) and (2) the "Section 704(b)" books (i.e., compliance with the capital account maintenance regulations).

H. Contribution of Depreciable Assets

If a partner contributes a depreciable asset to the partnership, the partnership continues the same depreciation method and recovery period the partner was using (i.e., the partnership "steps into the shoes" of the partner). Any potential

[16] Code Sec. 722.
[17] Reg. §1.704-1(b)(2)(iv)(b).

depreciation recapture on a later disposition of the depreciable property also carries over to the partnership.[18]

I. Exception to Nonrecognition: "Investment Companies"

Remember that Section 721(a) generally provides that no gain or loss is recognized to a partner when the partner transfers property to a partnership.[19] This general rule does not apply with respect to realized gains, however, if the partnership is an "investment company."

Section 721. Nonrecognition of gain or loss on contribution

…

(b) Special rule. Subsection (a) shall not apply to gain realized on a transfer of property to a partnership which would be treated as an investment company (within the meaning of Section 351) if the partnership were incorporated.

…

Notice the cross-reference in Section 721(b) to Section 351 for the definition of "investment company." The Treasury Regulations related to Section 351 provide additional insight.

Treas. Reg. § 1.351-1. Transfer to corporation controlled by transferor

…

(c)

(1) The general rule of Section 351 [and 721] does not apply, and consequently gain or loss will be recognized, where property is transferred to an investment company after June 30, 1967. A transfer of property after June 30, 1967, will be considered to be a transfer to an investment company if—

(i) The transfer results, directly or indirectly, in diversification of the transferors' interests, and

[18] Reg. §1.1245-2(c)(2); See also Reg. §1.1250-3(c)(3).
[19] See Section A of this chapter.

> (ii) The transferee is (a) a regulated investment company, (b) a real estate investment trust, or (c) a corporation [partnership] more than 80 percent of the value of whose assets (excluding cash and non-convertible debt obligations from consideration) are held for investment and are readily marketable stocks or securities, or interests in regulated investment companies or real estate investment trusts.
>
> . . .

Thus, an investment company is a partnership that is a regulated investment company (RIC), a real estate investment trust (REIT), or has more than 80% of the value of its assets in marketable securities or interests in RICs or REITs and the transfer of property to such partnership results in "diversification" to the partners.[20] A wise tax adviser will keep in mind the "investment company" exception to the general nonrecognition rule of Section 721.

J. Partnership Formation Example

Brian, Chelsea, and Drew form BCD Partnership. They transfer the following properties to the partnership, respectively:

Partner	Property Description	Tax Basis to Partner	FMV
Brian	Parcel of land	$70	$100
Chelsea	Inventory	$40	$50
Drew	Copier	$10	$50

Assume that the partners agree that Brian will have a 50% interest in the partnership, and Chelsea and Drew will each have a 25% interest in the partnership. Brian purchased the land three years ago. The land is a capital asset in Brian's hands on the date of contribution. Chelsea purchased the inventory six months ago. The inventory is an ordinary asset in her hands on the date of contribution. Drew purchased the copier four years ago for $10. The copier is a Section 1231 asset in his hands on the date of contribution.

[20] Code Section 351 and the regulations thereunder contain details as to the definition of "marketable securities," "diversification," etc.

The following diagram illustrates the transaction:

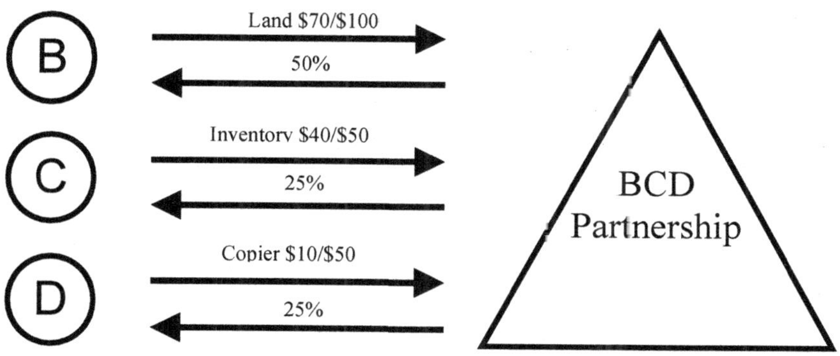

Source: Ryan H. Pace

Analysis:

Brian's gain realized is $30 ($100 – $70).[21]
Brian's gain recognized is $0.[22]
Brian's initial tax basis in his partnership interest (i.e., "outside basis") is $70.[23]
Brian's holding period in his partnership interest tacks (three years).[24]
Brian's initial book capital account is $100.[25]

Chelsea's gain realized is $10.
Chelsea's gain recognized is $0.
Chelsea's initial tax basis in her partnership interest is $40.
Chelsea's holding period in her partnership interest is new.
Chelsea's initial book capital account balance is $50.

Drew's gain realized is $40.
Drew's gain recognized is $0.
Drew's initial tax basis in her partnership interest is $10.
Drew's holding period in her partnership interest tacks (four years).
Drew's initial book capital account balance is $50.

BCD's gain or loss recognized is $0
BCD's initial tax basis in the land contributed by Brian is $70.[26]
BCD's initial tax basis in the inventory contributed by Chelsea is $40.

---

[21] Code Sec. 1001(a).
[22] Code Sec. 721(a).
[23] Code Sec. 722.
[24] Code Sec. 1223(1).
[25] Treas. Reg. §1.704-1(b)(2)(iv)(b).
[26] Code Sec. 723.

BCD's initial tax basis in the copier contributed by Drew is $10.[27]
BCD's holding period in each asset tacks.[28]
BCD's initial balance sheet:

BCD Partnership
Balance Sheet as of Formation Date

Assets	Tax	Book	Liabilities	Tax	Book
Inventory	$40	$50		$0	$0
Copier	$10	$50			
Land	$70	$100	Capital		
				Tax	Book
Total Assets	$120	$200			
			Brian	$70	$100
			Chelsea	$40	$50
			Drew	$10	$50
			Total Liabilities & Capital	$120	$200

In practice, most people refer to the numbers in the "Book" column in the capital section of the balance sheet as each respective partner's "capital account" even though technically it is each partner's *book* capital account. The "Tax" column in the capital section of the balance sheet, of course, reflects each partner's "tax capital account." (Notice that the difference between each partner's tax capital account and book capital account is the gain each partner *realized* but did not *recognize*.) *Important note*: Although sometimes a partner's book capital account or tax capital account may be the same amount as the partner's outside basis, the partnership's balance sheet does not specifically reflect what each partner's outside basis is.[29]

---

[27] The partnership continues to depreciate the copier using Drew's depreciation method and remaining recovery period.
[28] Code Sec. 1223(2).
[29] In this particular example, each respective partner's outside basis and tax capital account are the same, but this would likely not be so if the partnership had liabilities (see Chapter 5).

CHAPTER 2 QUESTIONS FOR REVIEW

1. *Realization event*. Is the transfer of property to a partnership a realization event? Why does it matter?

2. *Gain or loss realized*. How is gain or loss realized on the sale or exchange of property determined? What is your authority?

3. *Gain or loss recognized*. Does a partner recognize the partner's gain or loss realized on the transfer of property to a partnership? What is your authority?

4. *Gain or loss recognized*. Does the partnership recognize gain or loss on the receipt of property in exchange for an interest in the partnership? What is your authority?

5. *Exchange of property*. Summarize the facts in the *Stafford* case. What did the court conclude?

6. *Transfer of property to a partnership*. Manny, Noor, and Oscar form MNO Partnership. They transfer the following properties to the partnership:

Partner	Property Description	Tax Basis to Partner	FMV
Manny	Parcel of land	$160	$200
Noor	Inventory	$95	$100
Oscar	Copier	$20	$100

Assume that the partners agree that Manny will have a 50% interest in the partnership, and Noor and Oscar will each have a 25% interest in the partnership. Manny purchased the land ten years ago. The land is a capital asset in Manny's hands on the date of contribution. Noor purchased the inventory one month ago. The inventory is an ordinary asset in her hands on the date of contribution. Oscar purchased the copier six years ago for $20. The copier is a Section 1231 asset in his hands on the date of contribution.

With respect to these facts, please answer the following questions:

a. What is Manny's gain or loss realized? What is your authority?

b. What is Manny's gain or loss recognized? What is your authority?

c. What is Manny's outside basis in his MNO Partnership interest? What is your authority?

d. What is Manny's holding period in his MNO Partnership interest? What is your authority?

e. What is Manny's initial capital account in MNO Partnership? What is your authority?

f. What is MNO Partnership's inside basis in the land contributed by Manny? What is your authority?

g. What is MNO Partnership's holding period in the land contributed by Manny? What is your authority?

h. What is Noor's gain or loss realized? What is your authority?

i. What is Noor's gain or loss recognized? What is your authority?

j. What is Noor's outside basis in her MNO Partnership interest? What is your authority?

k. What is Noor's holding period in her MNO Partnership interest? What is your authority?

l. What is Noor's initial capital account in MNO Partnership? What is your authority?

m. What is MNO Partnership's inside basis in the inventory contributed by Noor? What is your authority?

n. What is MNO Partnership's holding period in the inventory contributed by Noor? What is your authority?

o. What is Oscar's gain or loss realized? What is your authority?

p. What is Oscar's gain or loss recognized? What is your authority?

q. What is Oscar's outside basis in his MNO Partnership interest? What is your authority?

r. What is Oscar's holding period in his MNO Partnership interest? What is your authority?

s. What is Oscar's initial capital account in MNO Partnership? What is your authority?

t. What is MNO Partnership's inside basis in the copier contributed by Oscar? What is your authority?

u. What is MNO Partnership's holding period in the copier contributed by Oscar? What is your authority?

v. Construct a balance sheet for MNO Partnership as of the date of formation. Be sure to show both the "tax basis" balance sheet and the "book" balance sheet (i.e., in compliance with the capital account maintenance rules).

w. Is MNO Partnership allowed to continue depreciating the copy machine that was contributed by Oscar? If so, how?

x. If MNO Partnership eventually sells the copy machine for a gain, does depreciation recapture apply? Explain.

7. *Character of property—unrealized receivables.* If a partner contributes unrealized receivables to a partnership, how long are the receivables considered an ordinary asset in the hands of the partnership.

8. *Character of property—inventory.* If a partner contributes property that was inventory in his hands, but the partnership employs the property as a capital asset or Section 1231 asset, how long is the property "tainted" with ordinary asset status?

9. *Character of property—capital loss property*. If a partner contributes "capital loss property," explain how the partnership determines the character of any loss on the future sale of the property even if the property is not employed as a capital asset in the hands of the partnership.

10. *Investment companies*. What is an "investment company?" What are the consequences to the partners on the contribution of property to a partnership if the partnership meets the investment company definition? What is your authority?

United States v. Stafford

727 F.2d 1043 (11th Cir. 1984)

Taxpayers DeNean and Flora Stafford appeal the district court's summary judgment in favor of the government on their refund action for allegedly overpaid taxes. The refund action involves the Staffords' 1969 tax return, in which they did not account for their receipt of a limited partnership interest valued at $100,000. The taxpayers argue that the partnership share qualified for nonrecognition treatment under I.R.C. Sec. 721(a) because it was received in "exchange" for "property" they contributed to the partnership. [Endnotes omitted throughout.] The district court held that nonrecognition was not available because the taxpayers' contribution of a letter of intent to the partnership did not meet the exchange and property requirements of the statute. We conclude that the district court applied an improper legal standard and under the proper legal test several issues should have been decided in favor of the taxpayers. With regard to additional issues, we conclude that genuine issues of fact remain such that summary judgment for the government was inappropriate. We therefore reverse and remand.

I. HISTORY OF THE CASE

The commercial transaction that underlies the current tax dispute has been discussed in previous opinions.... Nevertheless, the resolution of this case requires a detailed analysis of the facts. We therefore discuss the relevant aspects of the transaction.

Throughout the 1960's, DeNean Stafford worked as a real estate developer, often in projects involving hotel property. At least two of Stafford's projects had used financing from the Life Insurance Company of Georgia ("LOG"). The business relationship between Stafford and LOG had taken various forms depending on the project. The hotel development involved in the present case, however, was somewhat unique.

In the early 1960's, LOG acquired property in Atlanta and constructed its corporate headquarters. LOG also owned the land adjacent to the headquarters, which at the time was undeveloped. LOG officials, in particular Mr. H. Talmadge Dobbs, who was then an executive vice president and member of the finance committee, approached Stafford and began negotiations for construction of a hotel complex on the unused land. In February of 1967, the LOG finance committee officially authorized continued discussions with Stafford on the hotel development.

Negotiations between Stafford and LOG led to a July 2, 1968, letter from Mr. Dobbs to Stafford, setting forth the numerous points of agreement as of that date and additional details in need of future resolution. In particular, the letter promised 6¾% interest on the loan financing for the hotel and it specified lease terms; both the interest rate and lease terms were very favorable to Stafford given then existing market conditions. Mr. Dobbs sent additional correspondence to Stafford on July 3, 1968, indicating that the favorable conditions described in the July 2 letter would be open for Stafford's consideration for a period of 60 days.

Under the terms of the July 2 letter, Stafford or his designee were to provide 25% equity for the hotel development. With letter in hand, Stafford contacted attorneys and business acquaintances and investigated the formation of a limited partnership to provide that equity share. On August 30, 1968, he responded to the LOG letter of July 2, accepting the general terms set forth in the letter and proposing further negotiation on additional details.

On October 30, 1968, Mr. A.F. Irby, a business associate of Stafford's, contacted potential investors with a draft of a limited partnership agreement and details regarding the proposed development. The letter stated:

You will note in this file that Mr. Stafford is delivering the lease, which is highly economic, the construction loan and the permanent financing to the partners for what amounts to $100,000 of additional participation. The cost in the open market of procuring these three items would be in excess of $250,000 * * *

The Life of Georgia will supply all of the construction funds but will require that $2,000,000 of equity be invested prior to their own advancement of construction monies.

When you consider the fact that this is a very favorable tax arrangement, that the permanent loan is for 30 years at an interest of 6¾% and that the cost of the development is at least $1,500,000 less than it would be under ordinary circumstances this would appear to be an excellent deal.

In January of 1969, Stafford and a number of investors formed Center Investments, Ltd., a Georgia limited partnership, to pursue the development. Stafford was designated the sole general partner. He purchased two $100,000 shares and received a third limited partnership share for contributing to the partnership the letter of intent and the agreement with LOG contained therein. In all, the partnership sold 20 units for $100,000 each, which together with the unit Stafford received for his capital contribution made a total of 21 units. Some eighteen months later, the partnership voted to amend the partnership agreement to provide Stafford a salary for his duties as general manager.

By mid-1970 the necessary capital had been raised and plans for the hotel development were set and approved. LOG and Center Investments executed formal lease and loan documents. The hotel project had expanded to a 550 room facility. This expansion, and unforeseen construction problems, had escalated the cost to over $9,000,000. LOG increased the amount of its loan to $7,127,500, but it substantially abided by the terms set forth in the July 2, 1968, letter to DeNean Stafford. LOG maintained the 6¾% interest rate on the first $5,000,000 it loaned to Center Investments. (The remaining $2,127,500 was financed at 9¾% interest, the market rate in 1970.) LOG and Center Investments also followed the formula set forth in the July 2 letter as the method for calculating lease payments. These terms had become even more favorable to Center Investments than when first proposed, owing to changed market conditions.

On their 1969 joint federal tax return, the Staffords did not report as income their receipt of the third partnership share. The Commissioner audited that return and determined that the Staffords should have treated the partnership share as compensation for services that Stafford rendered to the partnership in negotiating and developing the investment. The Commissioner thus concluded that the nonrecognition principles of Sec. 721 did not apply to the third partnership share and assessed a deficiency of $64,000 plus interest. The Staffords paid the assessment and filed a claim for a refund.

After the Internal Revenue Service denied the refund claim, the taxpayers filed the present action in January of 1976. In 1977, after considering summary judgment motions by the government and the Staffords, the district court granted summary judgment to the Staffords on grounds that the taxpayers' 1969 receipt of the third limited partnership share qualified for nonrecognition treatment under I.R.C. Sec. 721....

On remand, the parties supplemented the record in a June 24, 1981, evidentiary hearing. The district court, after considering cross-motions for summary judgment, granted summary judgment in favor of the government. The taxpayers appealed to this court.

II. ISSUES ON APPEAL AND STANDARD OF REVIEW

The issues we now consider are easily stated. We must determine the proper tax characterization of the third partnership interest Stafford received. As was the situation when this case was last on appeal, we also consider the narrower issue of whether the district court properly granted a summary judgment.

With regard to this narrower issue, we cannot affirm the district court's summary judgment unless there are no remaining disputes of material fact: [W]here ... the parties disagree as to the facts and take inconsistent legal theories, the mere filing of cross-motions for summary judgment does not warrant the entry of such judgment....

We conclude that the government has not met this high burden.

III. EXCHANGE AND PROPERTY REQUIREMENTS

To qualify for nonrecognition treatment on the receipt of a partnership share, the partner must establish that he made a contribution of "property" in "exchange" for that share. I.R.C. Sec. 721(a). Contrary to the district court's holding that the exchange and property requirements were not met, we conclude that these issues should have been decided in the taxpayers' favor. We will first state the proper resolution of the issues at hand. In the final section of the opinion, we highlight the remaining factual issues that must be decided on remand.

A. The Exchange Requirement

1. Generally

The district court held that Stafford's contribution of the letter of intent to the limited partnership was not an "exchange" for purposes of Sec. 721. The court defined exchange as "a mutual or reciprocal transfer of one thing for another" and suggested that each side to the transaction must have a choice as to whether or not they desire the transfer.... Because transfer of the letter of intent to the partnership was part of the partnership agreement as drafted by the taxpayers' attorneys, the court found that the limited partners never had a choice as to whether or not the transfer would take place.

The district court's opinion on this element lacks support in the language and principles of Sec. 721. The regulations under Sec. 721 specify that each partner "is entitled to be repaid his contributions of money or other property to the partnership (at the value placed upon such property by the partnership at the time of the contribution) whether made at the formation of the partnership or subsequent thereto." Treas. Reg. Sec. 1.721-1(b)(1). That Stafford's contribution of the letter of intent was part of the partnership agreement at formation in no way undermines his argument that the contribution was part of an exchange with the partnership under Sec. 721.

Furthermore, the purpose of Sec. 721 is to facilitate the flow of property from individuals to partnerships that will use the property productively.... By analogy, Sec. 351 of the Internal Revenue Code allows nonrecognition for individuals transferring property to corporations. Indeed, post-transfer control of the transferee corporation by the contributing shareholder is a prerequisite to tax-free treatment under Sec. 351. We therefore reject the district court's assumption that individual members of the transferee limited partnership must agree to the transfer before an exchange can occur under Sec. 721.

The district court opinion focused on the lack of agreement between Stafford and the limited partners. Viewed properly, the exchange that took place was between

Stafford and the partnership, not the limited partners as individuals.... The assignment of January 21, 1969, tends to establish that such an exchange occurred. Stafford contributed the letter of intent and other items; the partnership issued the third share to Stafford. Again, that this exchange occurred at the formation of the partnership and without a formal partnership vote does not alter our conclusion that an exchange took place.

2. Whether Stafford Owned the Letter of Intent

The previous panel opinion noted another possible resolution of the exchange requirement in the present case. Relying primarily on the decision in *James v. Commissioner*, 53 T.C. 63 (1969), the court stated that a question arose as to "who had ownership rights in the letter of intent before the purported assignment, Stafford or the limited partnership?" .... If the partnership owned the letter of intent, Stafford could not be said to have contributed that letter because it was not his to give. Thus, Stafford would not be eligible for nonrecognition under Sec. 721 on his receipt of the third partnership share. A detailed examination of the record and application of the legal principles set forth in James leads us to conclude that Stafford owned the letter of intent and it was his property to contribute to the investment vehicle of his choice.

In James, the taxpayer entered into an agreement with Mr. and Mrs. Talbot whereby he agreed to secure the necessary legal and architectural work and to arrange for the financing of a rental apartment project on the Talbots' land. Upon completion of the project, the Talbots would transfer their land to a corporation, which would then issue stock to both the Talbots and the taxpayer. When James and the Talbots formed the corporation pursuant to the original agreement, James received 10 shares in the corporation in exchange for "property," described as a loan commitment from United Mortgage Servicing Corporation and an FHA commitment insuring the loan.

Two essential factors distinguish James from the instant case. First, the taxpayer in James was under agreement with the Talbots to perform the services that produced the loan commitments. By contrast, Stafford was under agreement to no one; when Stafford negotiated the terms embodied in the letter of intent, and when LOG issued the letter, Stafford was working on his own behalf. [Citation omitted.] Second, the loan commitment and the FHA commitment in James ran in favor of the corporation rather than the taxpayer individually, because the FHA regulations relevant to the transaction in James permitted commitments only to corporations and not to individuals. The James court thus held that the commitments belonged to the corporation and were not the taxpayer's to transfer.... In contrast, the letter of intent in the present case expressly ran in favor of Stafford or his designee.

The government's reliance in the present case on United States v. Frazell, ..., is similarly misplaced. As in James, the taxpayer in Frazell was under an agreement with other parties to perform personal services, i.e., Frazell was to locate potentially productive oil and gas properties for a partnership. In return for these services, Frazell received a salary and specified interest in the properties acquired. Conversely, when Stafford obtained the letter of intent in 1968 he was working on his own behalf.

The facts in the record are not in dispute and compel a holding that Stafford owned the letter and was free to contribute it to the investment vehicle of his choice. Having thus concluded that Stafford owned the letter of intent and that his assignment of it met the exchange requirement of Sec. 721, we turn to a discussion of the property requirement.

B. The Property Requirement

The district court alternatively held that Stafford had not received his third partnership share as the result of a contribution of "property." The court correctly stated that "the key to the benefit of nonrecognition afforded by I.R.C. Sec. 721(a) is that property must be exchanged for an interest in the partnership." ...The district court then stated as its test for property under Sec. 721:

After having carefully considered the arguments of counsel in conjunction with the opinion of the court of appeals, it is the opinion of the court that both value and enforceability are necessary to a conclusion that a document is "property" for purposes of Sec. 721.

Finding as a matter of law that the letter of intent was not enforceable, the court concluded that it was not property and the taxpayers were not eligible for nonrecognition under Sec. 721.

We agree with the district court's conclusion that the letter of intent was not enforceable. Under Georgia law an agreement becomes enforceable when there is a meeting of the parties' minds "at the same time, upon the same subject matter, and in the same sense." ...In the present case, the July 2 letter of intent and Stafford's subsequent acceptance on August 30 did reflect an agreement on many essential terms; in particular, the parties were in agreement on the interest rate for the loan and the formula for calculating lease terms. However, the July 2, 1968, letter of intent acknowledged that "there were many details to be worked out" and stated only that "we [LOG] would like to continue our negotiations along the following general lines." The July 3 letter from LOG may have converted the proposal to negotiate to a firm proposal of major terms, but Stafford's response again made the execution of final lease and loan agreements expressly "subject to further negotiations" on several items. "Where it is evident from a written instrument, that the parties contemplated that it was incomplete, and that a binding agreement would be made subsequently, there is no agreement." ...

The agreement in the present case unambiguously contemplated resolution of additional items before execution of the final contract. "An agreement to reach an agreement is a contradiction in terms and imposes no obligations on the parties thereto"; ...as such, the agreement between Stafford and LOG embodied in the letter of intent and acceptance letter was unenforceable.... Stafford's contention that the parties intended to carry through with the terms of agreement set forth in the letter of intent is unavailing. Where, as here, the parties' written documents clearly and definitely make final agreement subject to mutually satisfactory future negotiations, we must decide as a matter of Georgia law that "the parties did not intend the letter agreement to be a binding, enforceable contract." ...

Nevertheless, notwithstanding its lack of legal enforceability, we still must determine whether the letter of intent was "property" within the meaning of Sec. 721. The previous panel opinion stated that "enforceability of any agreement evidenced by the letter of intent, while perhaps not dispositive of the question, is important and material." ...We agree. An enforceable contract would perhaps be assured of property status; but the absence of enforceability does not necessarily preclude a finding that a document, substantially committing the parties to the major terms of a development project, is property.

Several nonenforceable obligations may rise to the level of property for purposes of Sec. 721 or Sec. 351. Unpatented know-how, which results from services and is not enforceable, nevertheless can be deemed property....

The instant transfer of the letter of intent outlining the major terms of a proposed loan and lease agreement to which both parties felt morally bound is closely analogous to a transfer of goodwill, which, although clearly unenforceable, nevertheless has been treated as property....

Thus, we conclude that the district court's requirement of legal enforceability as an absolute prerequisite to finding property status under Sec. 721 was improper.

For purposes of our discussion as to whether the instant letter of intent is "property," we will assume arguendo that the factfinder on remand determines that the letter had value. Under the appropriate legal standard and under the circumstances peculiar to this case, we conclude that the letter of intent encompassed a sufficient bundle of rights to constitute "property" within the meaning of Sec. 721.

Although the Internal Revenue Code does not define property for purposes of Sec. 721 or Sec. 351, the courts have given the term rather broad application. ...

The transfer of a taxpayer's full interest in a venture further supports a conclusion that the transferred item was property....

As noted in the previous panel opinion, a taxpayer can create property by his provision of personal services....

Finally, we have held that legal enforceability of the rights asserted as property is important, but not dispositive....

In the present case, the letter of intent of July 2 played a unique role. LOG officials have testified that it is the only commitment of this type the company has ever issued and that the letter was part of what they viewed to be a special project. Because the hotel was adjacent to LOG headquarters, officials of the company were willing to provide both construction financing, a permanent mortgage, and a lease for land and airspace, all at terms very favorable to the developer. When Stafford and LOG had reached agreement on these terms, the company offered the letter of intent because "this was a very peculiar transaction and I think because the way it developed, and the way the negotiations went on, this was a proper instrument to put the intent of the parties into something that would be--that we could rely on." ...

Although not enforceable in a strict legal sense, the written documents--i.e., the terms of the July 2 letter, together with the July 3 letter limiting availability of those terms to acceptance within 60 days, and Stafford's August 30 letter of acceptance wherein he agreed to the essential terms of the letter of intent, including the interest on the loan and the lease terms--represented an agreement on the major terms that was quite firm in the view of the parties. Both of the principals have testified that they felt bound by the terms of the letter.... Two years subsequent to the letter, when market conditions made those terms very favorable to the partnership, the parties substantially adhered to the terms stated in the letter of intent. The letter clearly was transferable. The letter itself evidenced a commitment to Stafford "or his designee." The principals have testified that from the outset they anticipated Stafford would transfer the letter to an investment group formed to develop the hotel. LOG officials attended meetings of the prospective partners and were aware that the letter would be transferred. Again, we note that even though Stafford transferred the letter to the partnership, LOG officials were willing to abide by the terms of the letter in subsequent dealing. If property "encompasses whatever may be transferred," ...then the letter of intent meets this test. In addition, the letter of intent that Stafford transferred to the partnership embodied his entire interest in the hotel development venture; he held nothing back.

A conclusion that the letter of intent is "property" under the instant circumstances comports with the purpose of Sec. 721. Stafford exerted personal efforts on his own behalf in negotiating with LOG. When LOG and Stafford exchanged the letter of intent and acceptance in 1968, the government had not suggested that Stafford recognized taxable income. He could have completed the project as a sole proprietor without recognition of income based on his receipt of the letter. The purpose of Secs. 721 and 351 is to permit the taxpayer to change his individual business into partnership or corporate form; the Code is designed to prevent the mere change in form from precipitating taxation. In keeping with this purpose, we can discern no reason to exclude Stafford's transfer of the letter of intent from the protective characterization as "property."

Stafford through his business reputation and work efforts was able to negotiate a very promising development project with LOG. He obtained from LOG officials a written document, morally, if not legally, committing LOG to the major terms of a proposed loan and lease. The transferability of the letter is undisputed and Stafford transferred his full interest in the project to the partnership. We conclude that the letter encompassed a sufficient bundle of rights and obligations to be deemed property for purposes of Sec. 721.

For the foregoing reasons, we have concluded that Stafford's transfer of the letter of intent to the partnership met both the "exchange" and "property" requirements of Sec. 721. However, the factual dispute identified by the previous panel remains unresolved on the record before us and, accordingly, we must remand.

IV. THE QUID PRO QUO FOR STAFFORD'S RECEIPT OF THE PARTNERSHIP SHARE

The previous panel remanded for the factfinder to determine: "what was the quid pro quo for Stafford's receipt of the twenty-first partnership interest?" ...The panel was concerned that a jury might find that Stafford received the partnership share wholly or partially in exchange for the services he was to provide as general partner. Thus, even though Stafford contributed the letter to the partnership, the panel was unable to conclude that Stafford's contribution of the letter was responsible for his receipt of the third partnership share. This dispute remains; from the record we cannot ascertain whether the partnership was compensating Stafford for services to be rendered or for contribution of the letter of intent, or partially for both.

On remand the factfinder could determine that Stafford received the partnership share wholly in exchange for the letter of intent he contributed to the partnership. If so, the nonrecognition principles of Sec. 721 apply and Stafford is entitled to his refund.... To support such a finding in this case, the jury necessarily must conclude that the letter of intent was worth at least $100,000 to the partnership.

On the other hand, it might be determined on remand that Stafford received the partnership share wholly as compensation for services, in which case the government's tax assessment was proper. See Treas. Reg. Sec. 1.721-1(b)(1) ("the value of an interest in such partnership capital so transferred to a partner as compensation for services constitutes income to the partner under Sec. 61").

Finally, the factfinder might conclude that Stafford's receipt of the partnership share was partly in compensation for services and partly in exchange for property. If this is the case, the factfinder should determine the value of the property element (i.e., the letter of intent) and the value of the services element (i.e., the services to be rendered to the partnership by Stafford after formation of the partnership, including any value inherent in Stafford's continuing service obligation due to LOG's confidence in him but excluding any salary paid to Stafford for such services), and allocate the $100,000 value of the third partnership share accordingly.... Thus, if the factfinder determines that Stafford's receipt of the partnership share was partly in exchange for the letter and partly as service compensation, then he should prevail in his refund claim as to so much of the $100,000 share as was properly allocable to his letter of intent.

The district court's summary judgment in favor of the government is reversed and remanded for disposition not inconsistent with this opinion.

REVERSED and REMANDED.

Chapter 3

Transfer of Services to a Partnership

A. Performing Services in Return for Property in General
B. Performing Services in Return for an Interest in the Partnership
C. Special Rule Relating to Substantially Nonvested Profits Interests Received by a Partner in Return for the Performance of Services

---

Sometimes instead of transferring property to a partnership a partner will perform services for the partnership in return for a partnership interest. This chapter addresses issues related to a partner's receiving an interest in a partnership in return for services.

A. Performing Services in Return for Property in General

Before we analyze the specific tax consequences to a partner when the partner performs services to a partnership in return for a partnership interest, we turn our attention to the fundamental principles of tax law that apply generally in situations when a taxpayer receives property in return for services performed.

Section 83. Property transferred in connection with performance of services

(a) General rule. If, in connection with the performance of services, property is transferred to any person other than the person for whom such services are performed, the excess of—

(1) the fair market value of such property … at the first time the rights of the person having the beneficial interest in such property are transferable or are not subject to a substantial risk of forfeiture, whichever occurs earlier, over

(2) the amount (if any) paid for such property, shall be included in the gross income of the person who performed the services in the first taxable year in which the rights of the person having the beneficial interest in such property are

transferable or are not subject to a substantial risk of forfeiture, whichever is applicable...

...

Notice that according to Section 83(a) the person receiving property in return for providing services does not include the value of such "restricted" property (minus the amount paid, if any, for such property) into gross income if the property received is nontransferable or subject to a substantial risk of forfeiture.[1] Once the property becomes transferable or not subject to the substantial risk of forfeiture (i.e., the restriction lapses), then the value of the property is included in the person's gross income at such time.

Notwithstanding the general rule, the Code does allow a person to *elect* to include into gross income the value of restricted property when received rather than at the time the restriction is removed. This is called a **Section 83(b) election**.

Section 83. Property transferred in connection with performance of services

...

(b) Election to include in gross income in year of transfer.—

(1) In general. Any person who performs services in connection with which property is transferred to any person may elect to include in his gross income, for the taxable year in which such property is transferred, the excess of—

(A) the fair market value of such property at the time of transfer ..., over

(B) the amount (if any) paid for such property.

If such election is made, subsection (a) shall not apply with respect to the transfer of such property, and if such property is subsequently forfeited, no deduction shall be allowed in respect of such forfeiture.

[1] Stated another way, a service-provider *does* include into gross income at the time of receipt the value of property received in return for performing the services if the property is transferable or there is no substantial risk of forfeiture.

(2) Election. An election under paragraph (1) with respect to any transfer of property shall be made in such manner as the Secretary prescribes and shall be made not later than 30 days after the date of such transfer. Such election may not be revoked except with the consent of the Secretary.

...

If a taxpayer makes a Section 83(b) election with respect to restricted property, the taxpayer includes the value of the property into gross income in the year the property is received rather than in the year the restrictions lapse. Notice, however, that this can be somewhat risky in that no deduction is allowed if the individual includes the amount in gross income but then later forfeits the property. On the other hand, a Section 83(b) election may be worthwhile if the value of the property now is relatively low and the individual anticipates that the value of the property will be quite high when the restrictions lapse or if the partner currently is in a low tax bracket and anticipates being in a high tax bracket when the restrictions lapse.

IRS Revenue Procedure 2012-29 provides information about making a Section 83(b) election.

Revenue Procedure 2012-29

Section 1. Purpose

This revenue procedure contains sample language that may be used (but is not required to be used) for making an election under § 83(b) of the Internal Revenue Code...

Section 2. Background

...

.02 Under § 1.83-3(f) of the Income Tax Regulations, property is transferred in connection with the performance of services if it is transferred to an employee or independent contractor (or beneficiary thereof) in recognition of the performance of services, or refraining from performance of services... The transfer of property is subject to § 83 whether such transfer is in respect of past, present, or future services.

...

.05 Under § 83(b)(2), an election made under § 83(b) must be made in accordance with the regulations thereunder and must be filed with the Internal Revenue Service no later than 30 days after the date that the property is transferred to the service provider. In accordance with § 7503, if the thirtieth day following the transfer of property falls on a Saturday, Sunday or legal holiday, the election will be considered timely filed if it is postmarked by the next business day.

.06 Under § 1.83-2(c), an election under § 83(b) is made by filing a copy of a written statement with the Internal Revenue Service office with which the person who performed the service files his return. In addition, the person who performed the services is required to submit a copy of such statement with his or her income tax return for the taxable year in which such property was transferred. Section 1.83-2(d) requires that the person who performed the services also submit a copy of the § 83(b) election to the person for whom the services were performed.

...

Section 3. Scope

This revenue procedure applies to taxpayers who receive substantially nonvested property in connection with the performance of services and wish to file an election under § 83(b).

...

Section 6. Sample election

.01 The sample election in this section, if properly completed and executed by an individual taxpayer, would satisfy the requirements of § 1.83-2 regarding the required content of a § 83(b) election with respect to shares of common stock subject to a substantial risk of forfeiture. For the election to be valid, the service provider must in addition satisfy all other applicable requirements, including the requirements discussed above relating to the time for filing the election, filing the election with the Internal Revenue Service, attaching a copy of the election to the tax return, and providing a copy to the service recipient. An election under § 83(b) must contain all the information required by § 1.83-2(e), but need not use the exact format or language of the sample election set forth below. In the sample election below, bracketed items and blanks should be replaced with the applicable information for the taxpayer. An election with respect to property other than common stock should include an appropriate description of the property in item 2 and modifications to items 5 and 6 as necessary.

.02 The text of the sample election follows.

Section 83(b) Election

The undersigned taxpayer hereby elects, pursuant to § 83(b) of the Internal Revenue Code of 1986, as amended, to include in gross income as compensation for services the excess (if any) of the fair market value of the shares described below over the amount paid for those shares.

1. *The name, taxpayer identification number, address of the undersigned, and the taxable year for which this election is being made are:*

   TAXPAYER'S NAME: ______________________
   TAXPAYER'S SOCIAL SECURITY NUMBER: ______________
   ADDRESS: ______________________________
   TAXABLE YEAR: Calendar Year 20____

2. *The property which is the subject of this election is ________ shares of common stock of ______________________.*

3. *The property was transferred to the undersigned on* ***[DATE]****.*

4. *The property is subject to the following restrictions:* ***[Describe applicable restrictions here.]***

5. *The fair market value of the property at the time of transfer (determined without regard to any restriction other than a nonlapse restriction as defined in § 1.83-3(h) of the Income Tax Regulations) is: $__________ per share x ________ shares = $_______________.*

6. *For the property transferred, the undersigned paid $________ per share x __________ shares = $__________________.*

7. *The amount to include in gross income is $____________________.* ***[The result of the amount reported in item 5 minus the amount reported in Item 6.]***

The undersigned taxpayer will file this election with the Internal Revenue Service office with which taxpayer files his or her annual income tax return not later than 30 days after the date of transfer of the property. A copy of the election also will be furnished to the person for whom the services were performed. Additionally, the undersigned will include a copy of the election with his or her income tax return for the taxable year in which the property is transferred. The undersigned is the person performing the services in connection with which the property was transferred.

Dated: ________________________ ________________________________

Taxpayer

B. Performing Services in Return for an Interest in the Partnership

Perhaps the most critical issue to determine when a partner transfers services to a partnership in return for a partnership interest is whether the partner is receiving an interest in the partnership's *capital* or only in the partnership's future *profits*. Thus, the distinction between a capital interest and profits interest is worthy of discussion here. IRS Revenue Procedure 93-27 provides the fundamental rules distinguishing between a capital interest and a profits interest.

Revenue Procedure 93-27

1. Purpose

This revenue procedure provides guidance on the treatment of the receipt of a partnership profits interest for services provided to or for the benefit of the partnership.

2. Definitions

The following definitions apply for purposes of this revenue procedure.

.01. A capital interest is an interest that would give the holder a share of the proceeds if the partnership's assets were sold at fair market value and then the proceeds were distributed in a complete liquidation of the partnership. This determination generally is made at the time of receipt of the partnership interest.

.02. A profits interest is a partnership interest other than a capital interest.

3. Background

Under Section 1.721-1(b)(1) of the Income Tax Regulations, the receipt of a partnership capital interest for services provided to or for the benefit of the partnership is taxable as compensation. On the other hand, the issue of whether the receipt of a partnership profits interest for services is taxable has been the subject of litigation. ...

4. Application

.01. Other than as provided below, if a person receives a profits interest for the provision of services to or for the benefit of a partnership in a partner capacity or in anticipation of being a partner, the Internal Revenue Service will not treat the receipt of such an interest as a taxable event for the partner or the partnership.

.02. This revenue procedure does not apply:

(1) If the profits interest relates to a substantially certain and predictable stream of income from partnership assets, such as income from high-quality debt securities or a high-quality net lease;

(2) If within two years of receipt, the partner disposes of the profits interest; or

(3) If the profits interest is a limited partnership interest in a "publicly traded partnership" within the meaning of Section 7704(b) of the Internal Revenue Code.

. . .

1. Tax Treatment to the Partner

As mentioned in Rev. Proc. 93-27, if a partner receives an interest in the capital of the partnership in return for the partner's services, the partner recognizes ordinary income to the extent of the value of the partnership interest received (unless the interest is nontransferable and subject to a substantial risk of forfeiture). The Treasury Regulations make this clear.

Treas. Reg. § 1.721-1. Nonrecognition of gain or loss on contribution

. . .

(b)

(1) Normally, under local law, each partner is entitled to be repaid his contributions of money or other property to the partnership (at the value placed upon such property by the partnership at the time of the contribution) whether made at the formation of the partnership or subsequent thereto. To the extent that any of the partners gives up any part of his right to be repaid his contributions (as distinguished from a share in partnership profits) in favor of another partner as compensation for services (or in satisfaction of an obligation), Section 721 does not apply. The value of an interest in such partnership capital so transferred to a partner as compensation for services constitutes income to the partner under Section 61. The amount of such income is the fair market value of the interest in capital so transferred, either at the time the transfer is made for past services, or at the time the services have been rendered where the transfer is conditioned on the completion of the transferee's future services. The time when such income is realized depends on all the facts and circumstances,

including any substantial restrictions or conditions on the compensated partner's right to withdraw or otherwise dispose of such interest... .

...

The service partner's initial outside basis includes the amount the partner included in the partner's gross income. The Treasury Regulations address this issue as well.

Treas. Reg. § 1.722-1. Basis of contributing partner's interest

The basis to a partner of a partnership interest acquired by a contribution of property, including money, to the partnership shall be the amount of money contributed plus the adjusted basis at the time of contribution of any property contributed. If the acquisition of an interest in partnership capital results in taxable income to a partner, such income shall constitute an addition to the basis of the partner's interest... .

According to Rev. Proc. 93-27 (cited earlier) if a partner receives an interest in only the profits of the partnership in return for the partner's services, the partner does not recognize income until such profits are earned by the partnership.[2]

rzvmuR /Shutterstock.com

For a court case analyzing the receipt of a partnership interest in exchange for services, see *McDougal v. Commissioner*, 62 T.C. 720 (1974). Excerpts of the *McDougal* case are included at the end of this chapter.

2. Tax Treatment to the Partnership

If a partner receives an interest in the capital of the partnership in return for the partner's services, the partnership is entitled to a deduction equal to the amount that the partner includes in the partner's gross income.[3] Typically, the partnership's deduction is allocated to the partners other than the service provider. (Note: We are assuming here that the services provided by the partner are in the nature of *deductible* services rather than services that are required to be *capitalized* by the partnership.)

[2] Unless the arrangement meets one of the three exceptions explained in Rev. Proc. 93-27.

[3] Treas. Reg. §1.721-1(b)(2).

If a partner receives an interest in only the profits of the partnership in return for the partner's services, the partnership is not entitled to a deduction since the partner does not include any amount in the partner's gross income.

3. Examples

Example 3.1. Individuals M, N, and O form MNO Partnership. M contributes $15,000 in cash in return for a 1/3 interest in the partnership's profits and capital. N contributes $15,000 in cash in return for a 1/3 interest in the partnership's profits and capital. O contributes services in return for a 1/3 interest in the partnership's profits and capital. The services provided by O are in the nature of services that are deductible by MNO.

The facts are illustrated in the following diagram:

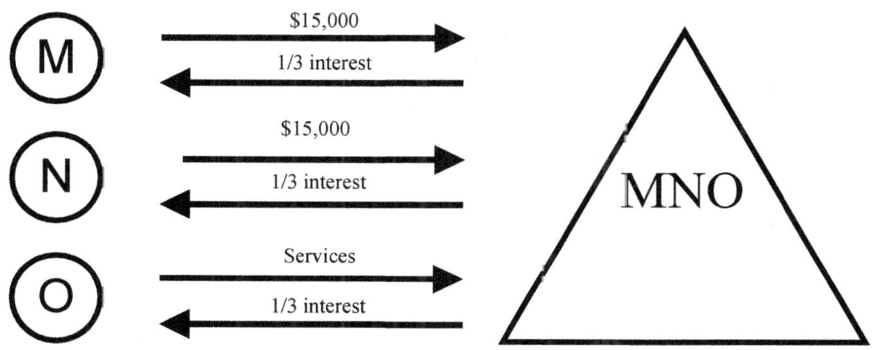

Source: Ryan H. Pace

Analysis:

O includes $10,000 into her gross income. This is because the partnership has $30,000 in total capital and O receives a 1/3 interest in the partnership's capital in return for the contribution of services.[4] Her capital account is $10,000 (as are M's and N's respective capital accounts), and thus she would be entitled to $10,000 if the partnership were to immediately liquidate. The partnership receives a $10,000 deduction and allocates this deduction between the other two partners, M and N.

Example 3.2. Individuals T, U, and V form TUV Partnership. T contributes $15,000 in cash in return for a one-half interest in the partnership's capital and a 1/3 interest in the partnership's profits. U contributes $15,000 in cash in return for a one-half interest in the partnership's capital and a 1/3 interest in the partnership's profits. V contributes services in return for no interest in the partnership's capital and a vested 1/3 interest in the partnership's profits.

[4] We will ignore here any possible argument that the fair market value of the partnership interest received by O is less than $10,000 because of certain factors such as a marketability discount or minority interest.

The facts are illustrated in the following diagram:

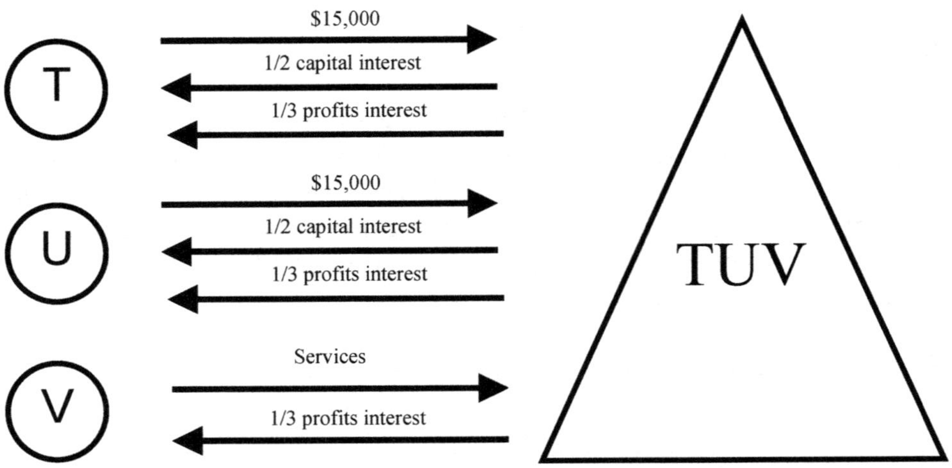

Source: Ryan H. Pace

Analysis:

Since V received only a profits interest in the partnership, V does not include any amount in his gross income.[5] Moreover, V has a $0 capital account balance. T and U each have a capital account balance of $15,000. The partnership receives no deduction since V did not include any amount in gross income.

C. Special Rule Relating to Substantially Nonvested Profits Interests Received by a Partner in Return for the Performance of Services

As discussed in Section A of this chapter, a service provider may receive a "restricted" interest in property in exchange for his or her services (i.e., the interest is nontransferable and subject to a substantial risk of forfeiture for a period of time). What if the property received by the service provider is a restricted interest in a partnership? This raises an issue as to whether the analysis determining whether the interest is a profits interest versus a capital interest should be undertaken at the time the interest is granted or at the time the restrictions lapse. Revenue Procedure 2001-43 addresses this issue.

[5] We will assume none of the three exceptions provided in Rev. Proc. 93-27 apply.

Revenue Procedure 2001-43

Section 1. Purpose

This revenue procedure clarifies Rev. Proc. 93-27 (1993-2 C.B. 343) by providing guidance on the treatment of the grant of a partnership profits interest that is substantially nonvested for the provision of services to or for the benefit of the partnership.

Section 2. Background

Rev. Proc. 93-27 provides that (except as otherwise provided in Section 4.02 of the revenue procedure), if a person receives a profits interest for the provision of services to or for the benefit of a partnership in a partner capacity or in anticipation of being a partner, the Internal Revenue Service will not treat the receipt of the interest as a taxable event for the partner or the partnership. For this purpose, Section 2.02 of Rev. Proc. 93-27 defines a profits interest as a partnership interest other than a capital interest. Section 2.01 of Rev. Proc. 93-27 defines a capital interest as an interest that would give the holder a share of the proceeds if the partnership's assets were sold at fair market value and then the proceeds were distributed in a complete liquidation of the partnership. Section 2.01 of Rev. Proc. 93-27 provides that the determination as to whether an interest is a capital interest generally is made at the time of receipt of the partnership interest.

Section 3. Scope

This revenue procedure clarifies Rev. Proc. 93-27 by providing that the determination under Rev. Proc. 93-27 of whether an interest granted to a service provider is a profits interest is, under the circumstances described below, tested at the time the interest is granted, even if, at that time, the interest is substantially nonvested (within the meaning of §1.83-3(b) of the Income Tax Regulations). Accordingly, where a partnership grants a profits interest to a service provider in a transaction meeting the requirements of this revenue procedure and Rev. Proc. 93-27, the Internal Revenue Service will not treat the grant of the interest or the event that causes the interest to become substantially vested (within the meaning of §1.83-3(b) of the Income Tax Regulations) as a taxable event for the partner or the partnership. Taxpayers to which this revenue procedure applies need not file an election under Section 83(b) of the Code.

Section 4. Application

This revenue procedure clarifies that, for purposes of Rev. Proc. 93-27, where a partnership grants an interest in the partnership that is substantially nonvested to a service provider, the service provider will be treated as receiving the interest on the date of its grant, provided that:

.01 The partnership and the service provider treat the service provider as the owner of the partnership interest from the date of its grant and the service provider takes into account the distributive share of partnership income, gain, loss, deduction, and credit associated with that interest in computing the service provider's income tax liability for the entire period during which the service provider has the interest;

.02 Upon the grant of the interest or at the time that the interest becomes substantially vested, neither the partnership nor any of the partners deducts any amount (as wages, compensation, or otherwise) for the fair market value of the interest; and

.03 All other conditions of Rev. Proc. 93-27 are satisfied.

...

Notice that Rev. Proc. 2001-43 clarifies that the nonvested (i.e., restricted) profits interest is treated as being received at the time of grant to the partner (if the specific requirements indicated in Rev. Proc. 2001-43 and Rev. Proc. 93-27 are met) rather than at the time the interest vests to the partner.

CHAPTER 3 QUESTIONS FOR REVIEW

1. *Property in exchange for services.* You repair your friend's roof. In return, your friend pays you with his baseball card collection. Must you include the value of the baseball cards in your gross income in the current year? What is your authority?

2. *Capital versus profits interest.* Explain the difference between a capital interest and profits interest in a partnership. What is your authority?

3. *Partnership interest in return for services.* You provide services to a partnership in return for a capital interest in the partnership. Do you have income to recognize right now? If so, how much? If not now, when? What is your authority?

4. *Partnership interest in return for services.* You provide services to a partnership in return for a capital interest in the partnership. As part of the agreement, if you fail to accomplish the promised services within three years, you must return the partnership interest to the partnership. Do you have income to recognize right now? If so, how much? What if you make a Section 83(b) election?

5. *Section 83(b) election.* How does a taxpayer make a Section 83(b) election?

6. *Partnership interest in return for services.* You provide services to a partnership in return for a profits interest in the partnership. Do you have income to recognize right now? If so, how much? What is your authority?

7. *Partnership deduction.* Assuming a partner provides services that are deductible by a partnership, how does the partnership typically allocate the deduction if the partnership transfers an interest in the partnership to the service provider?

8. *Formation of a partnership.* Individuals D, E, and F form DEF Partnership. D contributes $30,000 in cash in return for a 1/3 interest in the partnership's profits and capital. E contributes $30,000 in cash in return for a 1/3 interest in the partnership's profits and capital. F contributes services in return for a 1/3 interest in the partnership's profits and capital. The services provided by F are in the nature of services that are deductible by DEF.

   a. How much income does F recognize upon the formation of the partnership?

   b. What is F's outside basis in her partnership interest?

   c. What are the income tax consequences to D and E?

   d. What does the partnership's initial balance sheet look like?

9. *Formation of a partnership.* Individuals X, Y, and Z form XYZ Partnership. X contributes $30,000 in cash in return for a one-half interest in the partnership's capital and a 1/3 interest in the partnership's profits. Y contributes $30,000 in cash in return for a one-half interest in the partnership's capital and a 1/3 interest in the partnership's profits. Z contributes services in return for no interest in the partnership's capital and a 1/3 interest in the partnership's profits.

   a. How much income does Z recognize upon the formation of the partnership?

   b. What is Z's outside basis in his partnership interest?

   c. What are the income tax consequences to X and Y? What are their outside bases in their respective partnership interests?

   d. What does the partnership's initial balance sheet look like?

10. *Formation of a Partnership*. What is a nonvested partnership interest? At what time is the nonvested partnership profits interest generally treated as being received by the partner? What is your authority?

11. *Receiving property in exchange for services*. Summarize the facts in the *McDougal* case. What was the issue? What did the court conclude?

McDougal v. Commissioner

United States Tax Court
62 T.C. 720 (1974)

FAY, *Judge:*

...

Mutual concessions having been made, the following issues remain to be decided:

(1) Did the McDougals' transfer of one-half interest in the race-horse, Iron Card, to Gilbert McClanahan constitute a gift, or alternatively, did the aforesaid transfer constitute a contribution to an oral partnership or joint venture previously or contemporaneously formed by the McDougals and Gilbert McClanahan; ...

...

FINDINGS OF FACT

Certain facts have been stipulated by the parties and are found accordingly. The stipulation of facts and exhibits attached thereto are incorporated herein by this reference.

F.C. and Frankie McDougal are husband and wife, as are Gilbert and Jackie McClanahan. Each couple filed joint Federal income tax returns for the years 1968 and 1969 with the district director of internal revenue in Austin, Tex. Petitioners were all residents of Berino, N. Mex., when they filed their petitions with this Court.

F.C. and Frankie McDougal [footnotes omitted throughout] maintained farms at Lamesa, Tex., where they were engaged in the business of breeding and racing horses. Gilbert McClanahan was a licensed public horse trainer who rendered his services to various horse owners for a standard fee. He had numbered the McDougals among his clientele since 1965.

On February 21, 1965, a horse of exceptional pedigree, Iron Card, had been foaled at the Anthony Ranch in Florida. Title to Iron Card was acquired in January of 1967 by one Frank Ratliff, Jr., who in turn transferred title to himself, M.H. Ratliff, and John V. Burnett (Burnett). The Ratliffs and Burnett entered Iron Card in several races as a 2-year-old; and although the horse enjoyed some success in these contests, it soon became evident that he was suffering from a condition diagnosed by a veterinarian as a protein allergy.

When, due to a dispute among themselves, the Ratliffs and Burnett decided to sell Iron Card for whatever price he could attract, McClanahan (who had trained the horse for the Ratliffs and Burnett) advised the McDougals to make the purchase. He made this recommendation because, despite the veterinarian's prognosis to the contrary, McClanahan believed that by the use of home remedy Iron Card could be restored to full racing vigor. Furthermore, McClanahan felt that as Iron Card's allergy was not genetic and as his pedigree was impressive, he would be valuable in the future as a stud even if further attempts to race him proved unsuccessful.

The McDougals purchased Iron Card for $10,000 on January 1, 1968. At the time of the purchase McDougal promised that if McClanahan trained and attended to Iron Card, a half interest in the horse would be his once the McDougals had recovered the costs and expenses of acquisition. This promise was not made in lieu of payment of the standard trainer's fee; for from January 1, 1968, until the date of the transfer, McClanahan was paid $2,910 as compensation for services rendered as Iron Card's trainer.

McClanahan's home remedy proved so effective in relieving Iron Card of his allergy that the horse began to race with success, and his reputation consequently grew to such proportion that he attracted a succession of offers to purchase, one of which reached $60,000. The McDougals decided, however, to keep the horse and by October 4, 1968, had recovered out of their winnings the costs of acquiring him. It was therefore on that date that they transferred a half interest in the horse to McClanahan in accordance with the promise which McDougal had made to the trainer. A document entitled "Bill of Sale," wherein the transfer was described as a gift, was executed on the following day.

Iron Card continued to race well until very late in 1968 when, without warning and for an unascertained cause, he developed a condition called "hot ankle" which effectively terminated his racing career. From 1970 onward he was used exclusively for breeding purposes. That his value as a stud was no less than his value as a racehorse is attested to by the fact that in September of 1970 petitioners were offered $75,000 for him; but after considering the offer, the McDougals and McClanahan decided to refuse it, preferring to exploit Iron Card's earning potential as a stud to their own profit.

On November 1, 1968, petitioners had concluded a partnership agreement by parol to effectuate their design of racing the horse for as long as the proved feasible and of offering him out as a stud thereafter. Profits were to be shared equally by the McDougals and the McClanahans, while losses were to be allocated to the McDougals alone.

Though the partnership initially filed no return for its first brief taxable year ended December 31, 1968, petitioners did make the computations which such a return would show and reported the results in their individual returns. The partnership was considered to have earned $1,314, against which was deducted depreciation in the amount of $278. Other deductions left the partnership with taxable income for the year of $737, which was allocated to the extent of $405 to the McDougals and to the extent of $332 to the McClanahans.

On their joint return for the year 1968 the McDougals reported, inter alia, gross income of $22,891 from their Lamesa farms. Against this income they deducted $1,390 representing depreciation on Iron Card for the first 10 months of 1968 and $9,213 in training fees. The McDougals appear, however, to have initially claimed no deduction by reason of the transfer to McClanahan of the half interest in Iron Card.

In addition to their distributive share of partnership income referred to above, the McClanahans reported $5,000 of gross income which they identified as a gift interest in a racehorse.

We shall now turn our attention to those returns and amended returns filed in April of 1970. The McDougals explicitly claimed by way of amendment to have transferred the half interest in Iron Card to McClanahan as compensation for services rendered and thus to be entitled to a $30,000 business expense deduction, computed by reference to the last offer to purchase Iron Card received prior to October 4, 1968. Furthermore, the McDougals acknowledged that they had recognized a gain on the aforesaid transfer. By charging the entire depreciation deduction of $1,390 against the portion of their unadjusted cost basis allocable to the half interest in Iron Card which they retained, the McDougals computed this gain to be $25,000 and characterized it as a long-term capital gain under Section 1231(a) of the Internal Revenue Code of 1954.

The McClanahans simultaneously increased their income arising out of the transfer from $5,000 to $30,000. They could thus claim to have a tax cost basis of $30,000 in their half interest in the horse. Finally, purporting to have transferred the horse to a partnership in concert on November 1, 1968, petitioners computed the partnership's basis in the horse to be $33,610 under Section 723. This increase in basis led the partnership to claim a depreciation deduction of $934 for 1968 instead of $278 and to report only $81 of taxable income for that year. The McDougals thereupon reduced their distributive share of partnership income for 1968 from $405 to $40, while the McClanahans reduced their share from $332 to $41. For the year 1969 the partnership claimed a deduction for depreciation on Iron Card in the amount of $5,602, closing the year with a loss of $8,911. This loss was allocated in its entirety to the McDougals, pursuant to the partnership agreement.

. . .

ULTIMATE FINDINGS OF FACT

The transfer of October 4, 1968, gave rise to a joint venture to which the McDougals are deemed to have contributed Iron Card and in which they are deemed to have granted McClan[a]han an interest in the capital and profits thereof, equal to their own, as compensation for his having trained Iron Card.

. . .

OPINION

Respondent contends that the McDougals did not recognize a $25,000 gain on the transaction of October 4, 1968, and that they were not entitled to claim a $30,000 business expense deduction by reason thereof. He further contends that were Iron Card to be contributed to a partnership or joint venture under the circumstances obtaining in the instant case, its basis in Iron Card at the time of contribution would have been limited by the McDougals' cost basis in the horse, as adjusted. Respondent justifies these contentions by arguing that the transfer of October 4, 1968, constituted a gift.

In the alternative, respondent has urged us to find that at some point in time no later than the transfer of October 4, 1968, McDougal and McClanahan entered into a partnership or joint venture to which the McDougals contributed Iron Card and McClanahan contributed services. Respondent contends that such a finding would require our holding that the McDougals did not recognize a gain on the transfer of October 4, 1968, by reason of Section 721, and that under Section 723 the joint venture's basis in Iron Card at the time of the contribution was equal to the McDougals' adjusted basis in the horse as of that time.

We dismiss at the outset respondent's contention that the transfer of October 4, 1968, constituted a gift, and we are undeterred in so doing by the fact that petitioners originally characterized the transfer as a gift, [citations omitted throughout]. A gift has been defined as a transfer motivated by detached and disinterested generosity, ... The presence of such motivation is belied in this instance by two factors. The relationship of the parties concerned was essentially of a business nature, and the transfer itself was made conditional upon the outcome of an enterprise which McDougal had undertaken at McClanahan's suggestion and in reliance upon McClan[a]han's ability to render it profitable. These factors instead bespeak the presence of an arm's-length transaction.

With respect to respondent's alternative contention, we note firstly that the law provides no rule easy of application for making a determination as to whether a partnership or joint venture has been formed but rather directs our attention to a congeries of factors relevant to the issue, of which none is conclusive, ...

A joint venture is deemed to arise when two or more persons agree, expressly or impliedly, to enter actively upon a specific business enterprise, the purpose of which is the pursuit of profit; the ownership of whose productive assets and of the profits generated by them is shared; the parties to which all bear the burden of any loss; and the management of which is not confined to a single participant, ...

While in the case at bar the risk of loss was to be borne by the McDougals alone, all the other elements of a joint venture were present once the transfer of October 4, 1968, had been effected. Accordingly, we hold that the aforesaid transfer constituted the formation of a joint venture to which the McDougals contributed capital in the form of the horse, Iron Card, and in which they granted McClanahan an interest equal to their own in capital and profits as compensation for his having trained Iron Card. We further hold that the agreement formally entered into on November 1, 1968, and reduced to writing in April of 1970, constituted a continuation of the original joint venture under Section 708(b)(2)(A). Furthermore, that McClanahan continued to receive a fee for serving as Iron Card's trainer after October 4, 1968, in no way militates against the soundness of this holding... However, this holding does not result in the tax consequences which respondent has contended would follow from it...

When on the formation of a joint venture a party contributing appreciated assets satisfies an obligation by granting his obligee a capital interest in the venture, he is deemed first to have transferred to the obligee an undivided interest in the assets contributed, equal in value to the amount of the obligation so satisfied. He and the obligee are deemed thereafter and in concert to have contributed those assets to the joint venture.

The contributing obligor will recognize gain on the transaction to the extent that the value of the undivided interest which he is deemed to have transferred exceeds his basis therein. The obligee is considered to have realized an amount equal to the fair market value of the interest which he receives in the venture and will recognize income depending upon the character of the obligation satisfied. The joint venture's basis in the assets will be determined under Section 723 in accordance with the foregoing assumptions. Accordingly, we hold that the transaction under consideration constituted an exchange in which the McDougals realized $30,000, ...

In determining the basis offset to which the McDougals are entitled with respect to the transfer of October 4, 1968, we note the following: that the McDougals had an unadjusted cost basis in Iron Card of $10,000; that they had claimed $1,390 in depreciation on the entire horse for the period January 1 to October 31, 1968; and that after an agreement of partnership was concluded on November 1, 1968, depreciation on Iron Card was deducted by the partnership exclusively.

Section 704(c) allows partners and joint venturers some freedom in determining who is to claim the deductions for depreciation on contributed property. As is permissible under the statute, petitioners clearly intended the depreciation to be claimed by the common enterprise once it had come into existence, an event which they considered to have occurred on November 1. 1968. Consistent with their intent and with our own holding that a joint venture arose on October 4, 1968, we now further hold that the McDougals were entitled to claim depreciation on Iron Card only until the transfer of October 4, 1968. Thereafter depreciation on Iron Card ought to have been deducted by the joint venture in the computation of its taxable income.

In determining their adjusted basis in the portion of Iron Card on whose disposition they are required to recognize gain, the McDougals charged all the depreciation which they had taken on the horse against their basis in the half in which they retained an interest. This procedure was improper. As in accordance with Section 1.167(g)-1, Income Tax Regs., we have allowed the McDougals a depreciation deduction with respect to Iron Card for the period January 1 to October 4, 1968, computed on their entire cost basis in the horse of $10,000; so also do we require that the said deduction be charged against that entire cost basis under Section 1016(a)(2)(A).

As the McDougals were in the business of racing horses, any gain recognized by them on the exchange of Iron Card in satisfaction of a debt would be characterized under Section 1231(a) provided he had been held by them for the period requisite under Section 1231(b) as it applies to livestock acquired before 1970. In that as of October 4, 1968, Iron Card had been used by the McDougals exclusively for racing and not for breeding, we do now hold that they had held him for a period sufficiently long to make Section 1231(a) applicable to their gain on the transaction. This is the case although the McDougals may have intended eventually to use Iron Card for breeding purposes, ...

The joint venturer's basis in Iron Card as of October 4, 1968, must be determined under Section 723 in accordance with the principles of law set forth earlier in this opinion. In the half interest in the horse which it is deemed to have received from the McDougals, the joint venture had a basis equal to one-half of the McDougals' adjusted cost basis in Iron Card as of October 4, 1968, i.e., the excess of $5,000 over one-half of the depreciation which the McDougals were entitled to claim on Iron Card for the period January 1 to October 4, 1968. In the half interest which the venture is considered to have received from McClanahan, it can claim to have had a basis equal to the amount which McClanahan is considered to have realized on the transaction, $30,000. The joint venture's deductions for depreciation on Iron Card for the years 1968 and 1969 are to be determined on the basis computed in the above-described manner.

When an interest in a joint venture is transferred as compensation for services rendered, any deduction which may be authorized under Section 162(a)(1) by reason of that transfer is properly claimed by the party to whose benefit the services accrued, be that party the venture itself or one or more venturers ... Prior to McClanahan's receipt of his interest, a joint venture did not exist under the facts of the case at bar; the McDougals were the sole owners of Iron Card and recipients of his earnings. Therefore, they alone could have benefited from the services rendered by McClanahan prior to October 4, 1968, for which he was compensated by the transaction of that date. Accordingly, we hold that the McDougals are entitled to a business expense deduction of $30,000, that amount being the value of the interest which McClanahan received. Respondent has contended that a deduction of $30,000 would be unreasonable in amount in view of the nature of the services for which McClanahan was being compensated. But having found that the transaction under consideration was not a gift but rather was occasioned by a compensation arrangement which was entered upon at arm's length, we must reject his contention...

...

Decision will be entered under Rule 155.

Chapter 4

Other Partnership Formation Issues

A. Taxable Year
B. Method of Accounting
C. Costs Related to Partnership Formation
D. Electing Out of Subchapter K

Other issues that typically arise upon the formation of a partnership are the selection of a taxable year, selection of a method of accounting, and how to treat costs associated with forming the partnership. We discuss these issues in this chapter. We also briefly cover the narrow situations where a partnership may elect out of the provisions of Subchapter K.

A. Taxable Year

Although a partnership is a pass-through entity and is not itself subject to federal income taxes,[1] a partnership must determine its taxable year so as to be able to report the partnership's income, expense, gain, loss, etc., to the partners (and IRS).[2] Code Section 706 provides the law in this regard.

Section 706. Taxable years of partner and partnership

. . .

(b) Taxable year.—

(1) Partnership's taxable year.—

(A) Partnership treated as taxpayer. The taxable year of a partnership shall be determined as though the partnership were a taxpayer.

(B) Taxable year determined by reference to partners. Except as provided in subparagraph (C), a partnership shall not have a taxable year other than—

(i) the majority interest taxable year (as defined in paragraph 4),

[1] Code Sec. 701.

[2] Code Sec. 6031 requires a partnership to file an information return.

(ii) if there is no taxable year described in clause (i), the taxable year of all the principal partners of the partnership, or

(iii) if there is no taxable year described in clause (i) or (ii), the calendar year unless the Secretary by regulations prescribes another period.

(C) Business purpose. A partnership may have a taxable year not described in subparagraph (B) if it establishes, to the satisfaction of the Secretary, a business purpose therefor. For purposes of this subparagraph, any deferral of income to partners shall not be treated as a business purpose.

(2) Partner's taxable year. A partner may not change to a taxable year other than that of a partnership in which he is a principal partner unless he establishes, to the satisfaction of the Secretary, a business purpose therefor.

(3) Principal partner. For the purpose of this subsection, a principal partner is a partner having an interest of 5 percent or more in partnership profits or capital.

(4) Majority interest taxable year; limitation on required changes. For purposes of paragraph (1)(B)(i)—

(A) Majority interest taxable year defined.

(i) In general. The term "majority interest taxable year" means the taxable year (if any) which, on each testing day, constituted the taxable year of 1 or more partners having (on such day) an aggregate interest in partnership profits and capital of more than 50 percent.

(ii) Testing days. The testing days shall be—

(I) the 1st day of the partnership taxable year (determined without regard to clause (i)), or

(II) the days during such representative period as the Secretary may prescribe.

. . .

Notice in Section 706 that the partnership's taxable year is determined by reference to the partners' taxable years. More specifically, the partnership has the same taxable year as its **majority interest** (i.e., those partners having in aggregate an interest in more than 50% of the partnership's profits and capital) if the majority partners all have the same taxable year.

1. Majority interest test

Example 4.1. MNO, LLC is owned by the following members with the respective ownership percentages and taxable years indicated below:

Member	Ownership Percentage	Taxable Year
M, an individual	40%	December 31
N Corporation	30%	September 30
O Corporation	30%	September 30

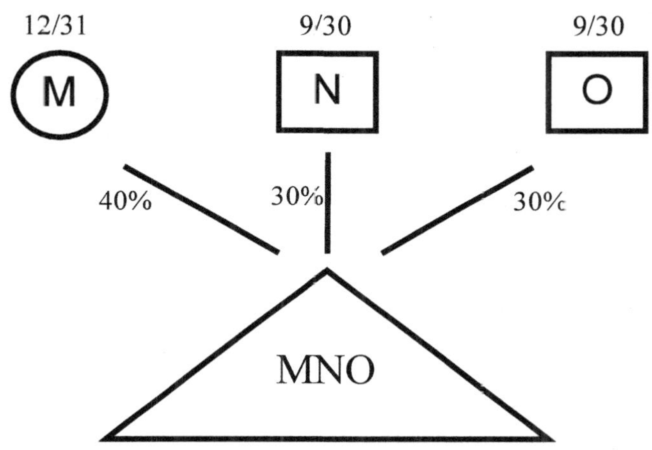

Source: Ryan H. Pace

What is MNO's required taxable year?

Analysis:

Since N and O both have the same taxable year and together they own more than 50% of the partnership's profits and capital, the partnership must adopt September 30 as its taxable year.

2. Principal partners test

If the partners have different taxable years so that the majority interest test cannot be applied, then the partnership must apply the **principal partners** test. Under this test, the partnership identifies each partner that has an interest of 5 percent or more in the partnership's profits or capital, and if each of these partners has the same taxable year, then the partnership adopts that same year.

Example 4.2. MNO, LLC is owned by the following members with the respective ownership percentages and taxable years indicated below:

Member	Ownership Percentage	Taxable Year
M Corporation	30%	June 30
N Corporation	10%	June 30
O Corporation	5%	June 30
P Corporation	4%	May 31
Q Corporation	4%	September 30
R Corporation	2%	September 30
45 individuals	1% each	December 31

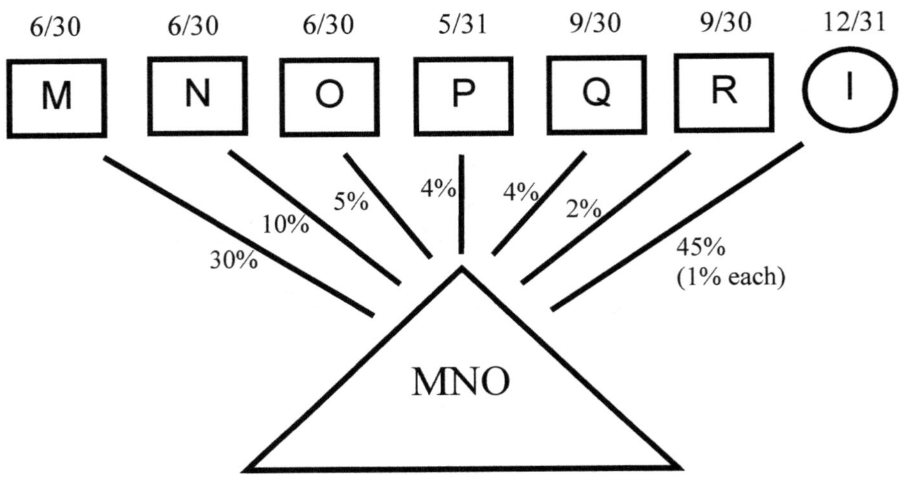

Source: Ryan H. Pace

What is MNO's required taxable year?

Analysis:

Since the majority interest test is not available (i.e., no partners with the same taxable year own more than 50% of partnership profits and capital), the principal partners test is applied. In this case, M, N, and O are the only principal partners (i.e., they each own at least 5%) and they each have the same taxable year. Thus, June 30 is the partnership's taxable year.

3. Least aggregate deferral test

If neither the majority interest test nor principal partners test can be applied, then Section 706 indicates the partnership's taxable year is the calendar year "unless the Secretary by regulations prescribes another period." The Secretary has, in fact, established by regulation another test to apply in these situations. This test is called the **least aggregate deferral** test.

Treas. Reg. § 1.706-1. Taxable years of partner and partnership

. . .

(b) Taxable year.—

(1) Partnership treated as a taxpayer. The taxable year of a partnership must be determined as though the partnership were a taxpayer.

(2) Partnership's taxable year.—

(i) Required taxable year. Except as provided in paragraph (b)(2)(ii) of this section, the taxable year of a partnership must be—

(A) The majority interest taxable year, as defined in Section 706(b)(4);

(B) If there is no majority interest taxable year, the taxable year of all the principal partners of the partnership, as defined in 706(b)(3) (the principal partners' taxable year); or

(C) If there is no majority interest taxable year or principal partners' taxable year, the taxable year that produces the least aggregate deferral of income as determined under paragraph (b)(3) of this section.

. . .

(3) Least aggregate deferral.—

(i) Taxable year that results in the least aggregate deferral of income. The taxable year that results in the least aggregate deferral of income will be the taxable year of one or more of the partners in the partnership which will result in the least aggregate deferral of income to the partners. The aggregate deferral for a particular year is equal to the sum of the products determined by multiplying the month(s) of deferral for each partner that would be generated by that year and each partner's interest in partnership profits for that year. The partner's taxable year that produces the lowest sum when compared to the other partner's taxable years is the taxable year that results in the least aggregate deferral of income to the partners. If the calculation results in more than one taxable year qualifying as the taxable year with the least aggregate deferral, the partnership may select any one of those taxable years as its taxable year. However, if one of the qualifying taxable years is also the partnership's existing taxable year, the partnership must maintain its existing taxable year. The determination of the taxable year that results in the least aggregate deferral of income generally must be made as of the beginning of the partnership's current taxable year.

. . .

The least aggregate deferral method is intended to determine which taxable year end the partnership is required to adopt so that the income reported by the partnership to the partners will be included in the partners' taxable years in the shortest amount of time.

Example 4.3. MNO, LLC is owned by the following members with the respective ownership percentages and taxable years indicated below:

Member	Ownership Percentage	Taxable Year
M Corporation	40%	January 31
N Corporation	30%	May 31
O Corporation	30%	October 31

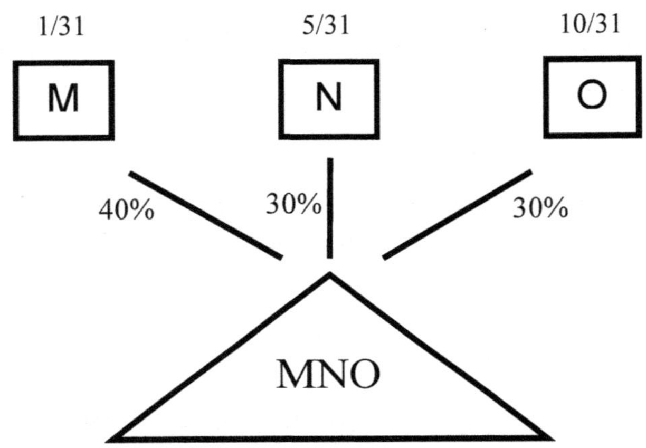

Source: Ryan H. Pace

What is the MNO's required taxable year?

Analysis: Three different taxable years must be analyzed.

*** January 31**

a Member	b Months of Deferral	c Profit %	d Product (b x c)
M	0	.40	0
N	4	.30	1.2
O	9	.30	2.7
			3.9

*** May 31**

a Member	*b* Months of Deferral	*c* Profit %	*d* Product (b x c)
M	8	.40	3.2
N	0	.30	0
O	5	.30	1.5
			4.7

*** October 31**

a Member	*b* Months of Deferral	*c* Profit %	*d* Product (b x c)
M	3	.40	1.2
N	7	.30	2.1
O	0	.30	0
			3.7

The taxable year with the least aggregate deferral is October 31.

In short, a partnership determines its taxable year by using one of the three tests just discussed (i.e., majority interest year, principal partners' year, or least aggregate deferral year). Nevertheless, some exceptions are available.

Treas. Reg. § 1.706-1. Taxable years of partner and partnership

...

(b) Taxable year.—

...

(2) Partnership's taxable year.

...

(ii) Exceptions. A partnership may have a taxable year other than its required taxable year if it makes an election under Section 444, elects to use a 52–53-week taxable year that ends with reference to its required taxable year or a taxable year elected under Section 444, or establishes a business purpose for such taxable year and obtains approval of the Commissioner under Section 442.

...

Thus, a partnership may adopt a 52–53 week taxable year,[3] a business-purpose taxable year if the partnership receives IRS approval,[4] or a taxable year allowed by Section 444.[5]

4. Partnership return due date

A partnership must file an IRS Form 1065 each year. Section 6072 sets forth the due date for partnership returns.

Section 6072. Time for filing income tax returns

...

(b) Returns of partnerships and S corporations. Returns of partnerships under Section 6031 and returns of S corporations under Section 6012 and 6037 made on the basis of the calendar year shall be filed on or before the 15th day of March following the close of the calendar year, and such returns made on the basis of a fiscal year shall be filed on or before the 15th day of the third month following the close of the fiscal year...

Notice that partnership returns for calendar-year partnerships are due by March 15 (or, for fiscal year partnerships, the 15th day of the third month). Partnerships can receive a six-month extension to file by filing IRS Form 7004.

B. Method of Accounting

Generally, a partnership can use either the cash or accrual method of accounting (or combination thereof).

[3] See Code Sec. 441(f); See also Reg. § 1.441-2.
[4] See Rev. Proc. 2002-39.
[5] Section 444 allows a partnership (and S corporation and personal service corporation) to elect a taxable year other than the required taxable year as long as the length of deferral is not more than three months and other requirements established by Section 444 are met. See also Temp. Reg. § 1.444-1T.

Section 446. General rule for methods of accounting

(a) General rule. Taxable income shall be computed under the method of accounting on the basis of which the taxpayer regularly computes his income in keeping his books.

(b) Exceptions. If no method of accounting has been regularly used by the taxpayer, or if the method used does not clearly reflect income, the computation of taxable income shall be made under such method, in the opinion of the Secretary, does clearly reflect income.

(c) Permissible methods. Subject to the provisions of subsections (a) and (b), a taxpayer may compute taxable income under any of the following methods of accounting—

(1) the cash receipts and disbursements method;

(2) an accrual method;

(3) any other method permitted by this chapter; or

(4) any combination of the foregoing methods permitted under regulations prescribed by the Secretary.

...

Notwithstanding the fact that Section 446 permits the use of various methods of accounting, the Code limits the use of the *cash* method in certain situations.

Section 448. Limitation on use of cash method of accounting

(a) General rule. Except as otherwise provided in this section, in the case of a—

(1) C corporation,

(2) partnership which has a C corporation as a partner, or

(3) tax shelter,

taxable income shall not be computed under the cash receipts and disbursements method of accounting.

(b) Exceptions.—

(1) Farming business. Paragraphs (1) and (2) of subsection (a) shall not apply to any farming business.

(2) Qualified personal service corporations. Paragraphs (1) and (2) of subsection (a) shall not apply to a qualified personal service corporation, and such a corporation shall be treated as an individual for purposes of determining whether paragraph (2) of subsection (a) applies to any partnership.

(3) Entities with gross receipts of not more than $5,000,000. Paragraphs (1) and (2) of subsection (a) shall not apply to any corporation or partnership for any taxable year if, for all prior taxable years beginning after December 31, 1985, such entity (or any predecessor) met the $5,000,000 gross receipts test of subsection (c).

(c) $5,000,000 gross receipts test. For purposes of this section—

(1) In general. A corporation or partnership meets the $5,000,000 gross receipts test of this subsection for any prior taxable year if the average annual gross receipts of such entity for the 3-taxable-year period ending with such prior taxable year does not exceed $5,000,000.

. . .

Thus, a partnership is allowed to use the cash method of accounting unless the partnership is (1) a "tax shelter" (as defined in Section 461(i)(3)) or (2) has a C corporation as a partner and the partnership has had more than $5 million in average annual gross receipts over the past three taxable years.[6]

Regardless of the method of accounting selected by the partnership, notice that Section 446(b) requires that the method "clearly reflects income."

[6] *See* Temp. Treas. Reg. § 1.448-1T.

C. Costs Related to Partnership Formation

Organizers of a partnership will often incur costs relating to the formation of the partnership. These costs can be categorized into three different types: (1) organizational expenses; (2) start-up expenses; and (3) syndication expenses.

1. Organizational expenses

Code Section 709 provides the tax treatment for organizational expenses and syndication fees.

> **Section 709. Treatment of organization and syndication fees**
>
> **(a) General rule**. Except as provided in subsection (b), no deduction shall be allowed under this chapter to the partnership or to any partner for any amounts paid or incurred to organize a partnership or to promote the sale of (or to sell) an interest in such partnership.
>
> **(b) Deduction of organization fees**.—
>
> (1) Allowance of deduction. If a partnership elects the application of this subsection (in accordance with regulations prescribed by the Secretary) with respect to any organizational expenses—
>
> (A) the partnership shall be allowed a deduction for the taxable year in which the partnership begins business in an amount equal to the lesser of—
>
> (i) the amount of organization expenses with respect to the partnership, or
>
> (ii) $5,000, reduced (but not below zero) by the amount by which such organizational expenses exceed $50,000, and
>
> (B) the remainder of such organizational expenses shall be allowed as a deduction ratably over the 180-month period beginning with the month in which the partnership begins business.
>
> . . .

Thus, a partnership may elect to deduct up to $5,000 of organizational expenses in the current year (reduced dollar for dollar for the amount over $50,000) and amortize the remainder over 180 months. The Treasury Regulations provide examples of organizational expenses that are eligible for the election under Section 709(b).

Treas. Reg. § 1.709-2. Definitions

(a) Organizational expenses.—

. . .

The following are examples of organizational expenses within the meaning of Section 709 and this section: Legal fees for services incident to the organization of the partnership, such as negotiation and preparation of a partnership agreement; accounting fees for services incident to the organization of the partnership; and filing fees. The following are examples of expense that are not organizational expenses within the meaning of Section 709 and this section (regardless of how the partnership characterizes them): Expenses connected with acquiring assets for the partnership or transferring assets to the partnership; expenses connected with the admission or removal of partners other than at the time the partnership is first organized; expenses connected with a contract relating to the operation of the partnership trade or business (even where the contract is between the partnership and one of its members); and syndication expenses.

. . .

2. Start-up expenses

The Code treats start-up expenses the same as organizational expenses.

Section 195. Start-up expenditures

(a) Capitalization of expenditures. Except as otherwise provided in this section, no deduction shall be allowed for start-up expenditures.

(b) Election to deduct.—

(1) Allowance of deduction. If a taxpayer elects the application of this subsection with respect to any start-up expenditures—

(A) the taxpayer shall be allowed a deduction for the taxable year in which the active trade or business begins in an amount equal to the lesser of—

(i) the amount of start-up expenditures with respect to the active trade or business, or

(ii) $5,000, reduced (but not below zero) by the amount by which such start-up expenditures exceed $50,000, and

(B) the remainder of such start-up expenditures shall be allowed as a deduction ratably over the 180-month period beginning with the month in which the active trade or business begins.

. . .

(c) Definitions. For purposes of this section—

(1) Start-up expenditures. The term "start-up expenditure" means any amount—

(A) paid or incurred in connection with—

(i) investigating the creation or acquisition of an active trade or business, or

(ii) creating an active trade or business, or

(iii) any activity engaged in for profit and for the production of income before the date on which the active trade or business begins, in anticipation of such activity becoming an active trade or business, and

(B) which, if paid or incurred in connection with the operation of an existing active trade or business (in the same field as the trade or business referred to in subparagraph (A)), would be allowable as a deduction for the taxable year in which paid or incurred.

. . .

3. Syndication expenses

The Treasury Regulations specifically provide that syndication expenses must be capitalized and are not eligible for the election to expense or amortize under Section 709.

Treas. Reg. § 1.709-2. Definitions

. . .

(b) Syndication expenses. Syndication expenses are expenses connected with the issuing and marketing of interests in the partnership. Examples of syndication expenses are brokerage fees; registration fees; legal fees of the underwriter or placement agent and the issuer (the general partner or the partnership) for securities advice and for advice pertaining to the adequacy of tax disclosures in the prospectus or placement memorandum for securities law purposes; accounting fees for preparation of representations to be included in the offering materials; and printing costs of the prospectus, placement memorandum, and other selling and promotional material. These expenses are not subject to the election under Section 709(b) and must be capitalized.

. . .

D. Electing Out of Subchapter K

Although an organization formed by two or more persons may technically fall within the definition of "partnership" in accordance with Subchapter K, the Code allows a partnership to elect out of the provisions of Subchapter K in some very narrow situations.

Section 761. Terms defined

(a) Partnership. For purposes of this subtitle, the term "partnership" includes a syndicate, group, pool, joint venture, or other unincorporated organization through or by means of which any business, financial operation, or venture is carried on, and which is not, within the meaning of this title, a corporation or a trust or estate. Under regulations the Secretary may, at the election of all the members of an unincorporated organization, exclude such organization from the application of all or part of this subchapter, if it is availed of—

(1) for investment purposes only and not for the active conduct of a business,

(2) for the joint production, extraction, or use of property, but not for the purpose of selling services or property produced or extracted, or

(3) by dealers in securities for a short period for the purpose of underwriting, selling, or distributing a particular issue of securities,

> if the income of the members of the organization may be adequately determined without the computation of partnership taxable income.
>
> ...

Notice that the Code specifically identifies three situations in which an organization may elect out of Subchapter K, but only if the income of the members can otherwise be adequately determined without applying partnership tax law.[7]

[7] LLCs taxed as partnerships are unlikely allowed to elect out of Subchapter K since the regulations require that the members of the organization own the property as co-owners. Most state LLC statutes provide that the LLC (and not the *members*) is treated as directly owning the property. See Treas. Reg. 1.761-2.

CHAPTER 4 QUESTIONS FOR REVIEW

1. *Taxable year.* M, N, and O are members of MNO, LLC. MNO is treated as a partnership for federal income tax purposes. M is an individual and has a taxable year of December 31. N is an individual and has a taxable year of December 31. O is a corporation and has a taxable year of May 31. M and N each have a 30% interest in MNO's profits and capital. O has a 40% interest in MNO's profits and capital. What is MNO's required taxable year?

2. *Taxable year.* W, U, and V are members of WUV, LLC. WUV is treated as a partnership for federal income tax purposes. W is an individual and has a taxable year of December 31. U is a corporation and has a taxable year of May 31. V is a corporation and has a taxable year of May 31. W and U each have a 30% interest in WUV's profits and capital. V has a 40% interest in WUV's profits and capital. What is WUV's required taxable year?

3. *Taxable year.* JKL, LLC is owned by the following members with the respective ownership percentages and taxable years indicated below:

Member	Ownership Percentage	Taxable Year
J Corporation	20%	July 31
K Corporation	15%	July 31
L Corporation	10%	July 31
D Corporation	4%	August 31
E Corporation	4%	March 31
F Corporation	2%	March 31
45 individuals	1% each	December 31

What is JKL's required taxable year?

4. *Taxable year*. PQR, LLC is owned by the following members with the respective ownership percentages and taxable years indicated below:

Member	Ownership Percentage	Taxable Year
P Corporation	25%	March 31
Q Corporation	35%	June 30
R Corporation	40%	November 30

What is LLC's required taxable year?

5. *Taxable year*. Identify some exceptions available for a partnership to adopt a taxable year other than the required taxable year.

6. *Method of accounting*. Under what circumstances is a partnership prohibited from using the cash method of accounting?

7. *Organizational expenses*. What are organizational expenses? Explain how a partnership's organizational costs are treated for income tax purposes.

8. *Start-up expenses*. What are start-up expenses? Explain how a partnership's start-up costs are treated for income tax purposes.

9. *Syndication fees*. What are syndication fees? Explain how such fees are treated by a partnership for income tax purposes.

10. *Election out of Subchapter K.* In what situations may an organization that may otherwise be classified as a partnership for income tax purposes elect out of Subchapter K?

Part II

Partnership Operations

Chapter 5	Ordinary Business Income and Loss, Separately Stated Items, and Adjustments to Outside Basis
Chapter 6	Limitations on Partnership Losses Deductible by Partners
Chapter 7	Guaranteed Payments and Other Nondistribution Transactions between Partners and the Partnership
Chapter 8	Allocations Attributable to Built-in Gain or Loss Property
Chapter 9	Special Allocations, Substantial Economic Effect, and Nonrecourse Deductions

Chapter 5

Ordinary Business Income and Loss, Separately Stated Items, and Adjustments to Outside Basis

---

A partnership is a pass-through entity.[1] As such, the partnership must report to each partner the partner's share of the partnership's income. Partners may be required to treat some income from the partnership (e.g., ordinary income) differently than other income (e.g., capital gain); consequently, the partnership must report the *character* of the income to the partners. This chapter explains the distinction between the partnership's ordinary business income (or loss) and items of partnership income (or loss) that are stated separately from the partnership's business income so that the partners can properly report the item on their own respective income tax returns.

A. Pass-Through Nature of a Partnership

Section 701 is the statutory authority that establishes a partnership as a pass-through entity.

Section 701. Partners, not partnership, subject to tax

A partnership as such shall not be subject to the income tax imposed by this chapter. Persons carrying on business as partners shall be liable for income tax only in their separate or individual capacities.

Although the partnership itself is not subject to income tax, the partnership does file an informational return (IRS Form 1065) on which it reports its ordinary business income and identifies its separately stated items.

---

[1] Code Sec. 701.

B. Partnership Ordinary Business Income

The Code requires a partnership to calculate its taxable income. (Remember, however, that just because the Code uses the term "taxable income," the partnership itself does not pay tax on the income.)

Section 703. Partnership computations

(a) Income and deductions. The taxable income of a partnership shall be computed in the same manner as in the case of an individual except that—

(1) the items described in Section 702(a) shall be separately stated, and

(2) the following deductions shall not be allowed to the partnership:

(A) the deductions for personal exemptions provided in Section 151,

(B) the deduction for taxes provided in Section 164(a) with respect to taxes, described in Section 901, paid or accrued to foreign countries and to possessions of the United States,

(C) the deduction for charitable contributions provided in Section 170,

(D) the net operating loss deduction provided in Section 172,

(E) the additional itemized deductions for individuals provided in part VII of subchapter B (sec. 211 and following), and

(F) the deduction for depletion under Section 611 with respect to oil and gas wells.

(b) Elections of the partnership. Any election affecting the computation of taxable income derived from a partnership shall be made by the partnership, except that any election under—

(1) subsection (b)(5) or (c)(3) of Section 108 (relating to income from discharge of indebtedness),

(2) Section 617 (relating to deduction and recapture of certain mining exploration expenditures), or

(3) Section 901 (relating to taxes of foreign countries and possessions of the United States),

shall be made by each partner separately.

Notice that the default rule is that a partnership calculates its taxable income in the same manner as an individual (e.g., the same Code provisions apply as to what constitutes income, exclusions, deductions, etc.) except as noted in Section 703. The Code disallows deductions for personal exemptions, deductions for foreign taxes paid, charitable contribution deductions, net operating losses, and itemized deductions such as medical expenses, alimony payments, moving expenses, deductions for interest on education loans, and qualified tuition expenses. These deductions, of course, are taken by partners directly.
A discussion of some terminology is in order at this point. A partnership's "ordinary business income (loss)" excludes separately stated items. A partnership's "taxable income (loss)" includes ordinary business income *and* the separately stated items.

C. Separately Stated Items

A partnership's capital gains, charitable contributions, dividends, etc., may ultimately impact each partner differently because of different tax rates that apply (e.g., long-term capital gains and qualified dividends) or limitations on deductibility (e.g., charitable contributions). The Code identifies these items that must be separated from the partnership's ordinary income so that partners know the character of the income or deduction.

Section 702. Income and credits of partner

(a) General rule. In determining his income tax, each partner shall take into account separately his distributive share of the partnership's—

(1) gains and losses from sales or exchanges of capital assets held for not more than 1 year,

(2) gains and losses from sales or exchanges of capital assets held for more than 1 year,

(3) gains and losses from sales or exchanges of property described in Section 1231 (relating to certain property used in a trade or business and involuntary conversions),

(4) charitable contributions (as defined in Section 170(c)),

(5) dividends with respect to which Section 1(h)(11) or part VIII of subchapter B applies,

(6) taxes, described in Section 901, paid or accrued to foreign countries and to possessions of the United States,

(7) other items of income, gain, loss, deduction, or credit, to the extent provided by regulations prescribed by the Secretary, and

(8) taxable income or loss, exclusive of items requiring separate computation under other paragraphs of this subsection.

(b) Character of items constituting distributive share. The character of any item of income, gain, or loss, deduction, or credit included in a partner's distributive share under paragraphs (1) through (7) of subsection (a) shall be determined as if such item were realized directly from the source from which realized by the partnership, or incurred in the same manner as incurred by the partnership.

...

The amount of income, loss, deduction, etc., that is allocated to a partner according to the partnership agreement (usually in terms of a percentage (e.g., 50%/50%, 70%/30%, etc.)) is called a partner's **distributive share**. The meaning of this term is often misunderstood because a partner's distributive share of the partnership's income, etc., *does not mean that the partnership has actually distributed the income to the partner!* It does mean, however, that the amount of income, loss, deduction, etc., constituting a partner's distributive share will be reflected in the partner's capital account balance.

Notice that the Code directly identifies the following as separately stated items:

- Short-term capital gains
- Short-term capital losses
- Long-term capital gains
- Long-term capital losses
- Section 1231 gains
- Section 1231 losses
- Charitable contributions
- Qualified dividends
- Foreign taxes

The Code provides that separately stated items retain their character as they are reported by the partners.[2] Thus, each partner will report as a long-term capital gain the partner's share of the partnership's long-term capital gain. The Treasury Regulations set forth other separately stated items.

Treas. Reg. § 1.702-1. Income and credits of partner

(a) General rule. Each partner is required to take into account separately in his return his distributive share, whether or not distributed, of each class or item of partnership income, gain, loss, deduction, or credit described in subparagraphs (1) through (9) of this paragraph. ...

...

(7) Each partner shall take into account ... his distributive share of ...tax-exempt interest received by the partnership....

(8)

(i) Each partner shall take into account separately, as part of any class of income, gain, loss, deduction, or credit, his distributive share of the following items: recoveries of bad debts ...; gains and losses from wagering transactions ...; nonbusiness expenses ...; medical, dental, etc., expenses ...; ... intangible drilling and development costs ...; exploration expenditures ...; certain mining exploration expenditures ...; and any items of income, gain, loss, deduction, or credit subject to a special allocation under the partnership agreement which differs from the allocation of partnership taxable income or loss generally.

(ii) Each partner must also take into account separately the partner's distributive share of any partnership item which, if separately taken into account by any partner, would result in an income tax liability for that partner, or for any other person, different from that which would result if that partner did not take the item into account separately.

...

D. Nature of Partnership Reporting (IRS Form 1065)

The partnership reports its taxable income and separately stated items on IRS Form 1065. Notice that the return is not identified as a "tax return." Rather it is an "information return." This is consistent with the fact that the partnership itself

[2] Code Sec. 702(b).

does not pay federal income taxes. The partnership's ordinary income is calculated on the first page. Separately stated items are identified on Schedule K. Each partner receives a Schedule K-1 showing the partner's distributive share of the partnership's ordinary income and the partner's distributive share of each separately stated item. The Schedule K-1 also shows the partner's capital account balance.

E. Adjustments to a Partner's Outside Basis Due to Partnership Operations (Excluding Liabilities)

In Chapter 2 we determined that a partner's initial tax basis in the partnership upon contributing property to the partnership is the amount of money contributed by the partner plus the adjusted basis in any other property contributed by the partner. (A service provider's initial outside basis is the fair market value of the partnership interest received in return for the services.) Unfortunately, for those who like simplicity, a partner's outside basis does not remain the same over time. Rather, the outside basis is adjusted upward and downward depending upon whether the partnership earns income, experiences losses, makes distributions, etc.

In this chapter we will cover the general rule and an alternative rule for determining a partner's outside basis due to partnership operations. We will ignore—for now—the impact that a partnership's liabilities have on a partner's outside basis. We will address the impact of liabilities later in the chapter.

1. General rule for outside basis adjustments

The Code provides the method for adjusting a partner's outside basis to reflect partnership operations.

Section 705. Determination of basis of partner's interest

(a) General rule. The adjusted basis of a partner's interest in a partnership shall, except as provided in subsection (b), be the basis of such interest determined under Section 722 (relating to contributions to a partnership) or Section 742 (relating to transfers of partnership interests)—

(1) increased by the sum of his distributive share for the taxable year and prior taxable years of—

(A) taxable income of the partnership as determined under Section 703(a),

(B) income of the partnership exempt from tax under this title, and

(C) the excess of the deductions for depletion over the basis of the property subject to depletion;

(2) decreased (but not below zero) by distributions by the partnership as provided in Section 733 and by the sum of his distributive share for the taxable year and prior taxable years of—

(A) losses of the partnership, and

(B) expenditures of the partnership not deductible in computing its taxable income and not properly chargeable to capital account; and

(3) decreased (but not below zero) by the amount of the partner's deduction for depletion for any partnership oil and gas property to the extent such deduction does not exceed the proportionate share of the adjusted basis of such property allocated to such partner under Section 613A(c)(7)(D).

. . .

In summary, adjustments to a partner's outside basis are as follows (we will ignore depletion deductions):

- Beginning outside basis as determined under Section 722 (contributing property to a partnership in return for a partnership interest) or Section 742 (purchasing a partnership interest)

Increased by:

- the adjusted basis of property contributed plus money contributed
- the partner's share of the partnership's taxable income
- the partner's share of the partnership's tax-exempt income

Decreased by:

- distributions to the partner by the partnership[3]
- the partner's share of the partnership's losses
- the partner's share of nondeductible partnership expenses

These increases and decreases include items in the partnership's calculation of its ordinary income or loss as well as separately stated items.

[3] Section 733 provides that a partner's outside basis is reduced by the amount of money distributed to the partner and, with some exceptions, by the adjusted basis of property distributed to the partner.

2. Alternative rule

In some situations, a partner may have no idea what the partner's tax basis in the partnership is. Moreover, it may be impracticable for the partner to review historical records to recreate the adjustments to the partner's initial tax basis. Consequently, the Code allows an alternative method to determining a partner's outside basis when the basis cannot be determined in accordance with the general rule.

Section 705. Determination of basis of partner's interest

...

(b) Alternative rule. The Secretary shall prescribe regulations the circumstances under which the adjusted basis of a partner's interest in a partnership may be determined by reference to his proportionate share of the adjusted basis of partnership property upon a termination of the partnersh p.

The Treasury Regulations provide a bit more guidance in this area.

Treas. Reg. § 1.705-1. Determination of basis of partner's interest

...

(b) Alternative rule. In certain cases, the adjusted basis of a partner's interest in a partnership may be determined by reference to the partner's share of the adjusted basis of partnership property which would be distributable upon termination of the partnership. The alternative rule may be used to determine the adjusted basis of a partner's interest where circumstances are such that the partner cannot practicably apply the general rule set forth in Section 705(a) ..., or where, from a consideration of all the facts, it is, in the opinion of the Commissioner, reasonable to conclude that the result produced will not vary substantially from the result obtainable under the general rule. Where the alternative rule is used, adjustments may be necessary in determining the adjusted basis of a partner's interest in a partnership. Adjustments would be required, for example, in order to reflect in a partner's share of the adjusted basis of partnership property any significant discrepancies arising as a result of contributed property, transfers of partnership interest, or distributions of property to the partners.

...

Thus, under the alternative rule, a partner can determine his/her outside basis by reference to the partner's share of the partnership's inside basis. As the regulation mentioned, however, this may not be as simple as taking the aggregate inside basis of the partnership's assets and dividing by the number of partners in the partnership. Nevertheless, the alternative approach may be the only practical approach in determining a partner's outside basis in some situations. Although a partner's outside basis is not required to be shown on a partnership return (Form 1065) or on the Schedule K-1 that a partner receives, a partner (or, more likely, the partner's tax adviser) would be wise to determine the partner's outside basis at least annually so that a significant amount of work is not necessary to recreate it.

rzvmuR /Shutterstock.com

For a court case analyzing the issue of determining a partner's outside basis, see *Coloman v. Commissioner*, 38 AFTR 2d 76-5523 (9th Cir.) Excerpts of the *Coloman* case are included at the end of this chapter.

F. Example

R and J are the only members of RJ, LLC. The LLC is treated as a partnership for federal income tax purposes. R and J have agreed to share profits and losses 70%/30%, respectively. During the year, RJ, LLC experienced the following items of income and expense:

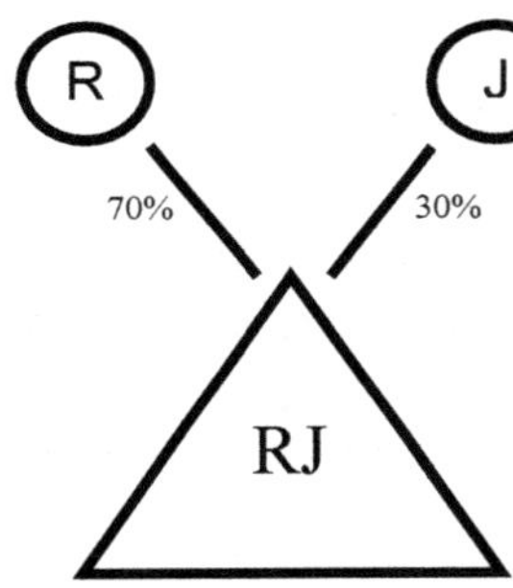

Source: Ryan H. Pace

Gross revenue	$80,000
Long-term capital gain	2,000
Tax-exempt income	1,000
Dividend income	3,000
Wages expense	40,000
Rent expense	10,000
Advertising expense	4,000
Bad debt expense	1,000
Charitable contribution	4,000

a. Identify each of RJ, LLC's separately stated items.
b. What is RJ, LLC's ordinary income?
c. What is R's distributive share of RJ, LLC's ordinary income and separately stated items?
d. What is J's distributive share of RJ, LLC's ordinary income and separately stated items?

Analysis:

a. RJ, LLC's separately stated items are: (1) long-term capital gain; (2) tax-exempt income; (3) dividend income; and (4) charitable contribution.[4]

b. RJ, LLC's ordinary income is $25,000 ($80,000 − $40,000 − $10,000 − $4,000 − $1,000).[5]

c. R's distributive share of the ordinary income is $17,500 ($25,000 × 70%). His distributive share of each separately stated item is 70% of each such item.

d. J's distributive share of RJ, LLC's ordinary income is $7,500 ($25,000 × 30%). Her distributive share of each separately stated item is 30% of each such item.

G. Adjustments to a Partner's Outside Basis Due to Partnership Liabilities

Earlier in this chapter we determined that a partner's outside basis is adjusted to reflect the partner's distributive share of income and deductions. We now look at how partnership-level liabilities impact a partner's outside basis.

1. Impact of Partnership Liabilities on a Partner's Outside Basis: In General

Suppose you are in the market to purchase a personal residence. You have $40,000 in your bank account and you obtain a $160,000 loan in order to purchase a residence for $200,000. What is your tax basis in the residence after you purchase it? The answer is $200,000. This means that under general principles of tax law, a person is able to include amounts borrowed in the person's tax basis in the property acquired with the loan proceeds. We need to relate this concept to partnership tax law.

If a partnership borrows money, the Code treats it as if the partners indirectly borrowed the money. Thus, the partners are entitled to an increase in their outside basis. Section 752 provides the law in this regard.

---

[4] Code Sec. 702(a); Treas. Reg. §1.702-1.
[5] Code Sec. 703.

Section 752. Treatment of certain liabilities

(a) Increase in partner's liabilities. Any increase in a partner's share of the liabilities of a partnership, or any increase in a partner's individual liabilities by reason of the assumption by such partner of partnership liabilities, shall be considered as a contribution of money by such partner to the partnership.

(b) Decrease in partner's liabilities. Any decrease in a partner's share of the liabilities of a partnership, or any decrease in a partner's individual liabilities by reason of the assumption by the partnership of such individual liabilities, shall be considered as a distribution of money to the partner by the partnership.

(c) Liability to which property is subject. For purposes of this section, a liability to which property is subject shall, to the extent of the fair market value of such property, be considered as a liability of the owner of the property.

. . .

Notice that an increase in a partner's "share" of partnership liabilities is treated as a contribution of money (which increases a partner's outside basis). A decrease in a partner's share of partnership liabilities is treated as a distribution of money (which decreases a partner's outside basis).

Now we just need to ascertain how to determine a partner's "share" of partnership liabilities. The methodology we use depends on whether a liability is a **recourse** liability or a **nonrecourse** liability. The Treasury Regulations provide definitions.

Treas. Reg. § 1.752-1. Treatment of partnership liabilities

(a) Definitions. For purposes of Section 752, the following definitions apply:

(1) Recourse liability defined. A partnership liability is a recourse liability to the extent that any partner or related person bears the economic risk of loss for that liability under § 1.752-2.

(2) Nonrecourse liability defined. A partnership liability is a nonrecourse liability to the extent that no partner or related person bears the economic risk of loss for that liability under § 1.752-2.

. . .

Thus, if no partner bears the economic risk of a partnership liability, then the liability is nonrecourse.

2. Recourse Liabilities

A partnership liability is a recourse liability to the extent that any partner or partners bear the economic risk of loss with respect to that liability. In other words, to the extent a partner would have to reach into the partner's own pocket to satisfy the lender, the partner bears an economic risk of loss relating to that liability.

Treas. Reg. § 1.752-2. Partner's share of recourse liabilities

(a) In general. A partner's share of a recourse partnership liability equals the portion of that liability, if any, for which the partner or related person bears the economic risk of loss. The determination of the extent to which a partner bears the economic risk of loss for a partnership liability is made under the rules in paragraphs (b) through (j) of this section.

(b) Obligation to make a payment.

(1) In general. Except as otherwise provided in this section, a partner bears the economic risk of loss for a partnership liability to the extent that, if the partnership constructively liquidated, the partner or related person would be obligated to make a payment to any person (or a contribution to the partnership) because that liability becomes due and payable and the partner or related person would not be entitled to reimbursement from another partner or person that is a related person to another partner. Upon a constructive liquidation, all of the following events are deemed to occur simultaneously:

(i) All of the partnership's liabilities become payable in full;

(ii) … [A]ll of the partnership's assets, including cash, have a value of zero;

(iii) The partnership disposes of all of its property in a fully taxable transaction for no consideration (except relief from liabilities for which the creditor's right to repayment is limited solely to one or more assets of the partnership);

(iv) All items of income, gain, loss, or deduction are allocated among the partners; and

(v) The partnership liquidates.

. . .

Notice that in determining a partner's share of a recourse partnership liability a "constructive" liquidation (also sometimes called a "hypothetical liquidation" or "doomsday scenario" or something similar) occurs where the partnership sells all its assets for zero. The resulting loss is then allocated among the partners according to their loss sharing ratios. To the extent a partner has a negative capital account after the allocation, the amount of the negative capital account is deemed to be the partner's share of the recourse liability.

3. Nonrecourse Liabilities

A different process is required to determine a partner's "share" of a nonrecourse liability.

Treas. Reg. § 1.752-3. Partner's share of nonrecourse liabilities

(a) In general. A partner's share of the nonrecourse liabilities of a partnership equals the sum of paragraphs (a)(1) through (a)(3) of this section as follows—

(1) The partner's share of partnership minimum gain determined in accordance with the rules of Section 704(b) and the regulations thereunder;

(2) The amount of any taxable gain that would be allocated to the partner under Section 704(c)(or in the same manner as Section 704(c) in connection with a revaluation of partnership property) if the partnership disposed of (in a taxable transaction) all partnership property subject to one or more nonrecourse liabilities of the partnership in full satisfaction of the liabilities and for no other consideration; and

(3) The partner's share of the excess nonrecourse liabilities (those not allocated under paragraphs (a)(1) and (a)(2) of this section) of the partnership as determined in accordance with the partner's share of partnership profits. ...

Thus, there is a three-tier process in determining a partner's share of partnership nonrecourse liabilities:

1. Determine the partner's share of partnership minimum gain;
2. Determine the partner's Section 704(c) minimum gain;
3. Determine the partner's share of excess nonrecourse liabilities

This three-tier process likely means nothing to a first-time reader (or even a multiple-time reader) without further explanation.

a. Partnership minimum gain

If a partnership nonrecourse liability exceeds the *book value* (adjusted for depreciation deductions) of the property to which the nonrecourse liability is attached, then the partnership would recognize gain if the lender foreclosed on the property as the sole consideration in satisfaction of the liability. The gain that would be recognized is called **partnership minimum gain** under tier one of the nonrecourse liability allocation process. Of course, the partners could allocate the partnership minimum gain among the partners in the same manner as their general profit sharing ratios. Partners can also allocate minimum gain in a manner that is consistent with other agreed-upon allocations that have substantial economic effect.

If the book value of an asset and the principal amount of the nonrecourse liability attached to that asset get further apart, partnership minimum gain *increases*. If the book value of an asset and the principal amount of the nonrecourse liability attached to that asset get closer, partnership minimum gain *decreases*.

[Note: Partners sometimes allocate deductions associated with property acquired with nonrecourse liabilities (e.g., depreciable real estate) in a unique manner. These deductions are called "nonrecourse deductions." In some cases a partner may benefit from a special deduction allocated to the partner because of how the partners agreed to allocate deductions relating to partnership minimum gain. If a partnership's minimum gain decreases, the partner may have a **minimum gain chargeback.** A detailed presentation of this topic is beyond the scope of our discussion here. We will discuss "partnership nonrecourse deductions" in Chapter 9, which will also cover the concept of partnership minimum gain and a partner's potential minimum gain chargeback in more detail.]

b. Section 704(c) minimum gain

If, at the time a partner contributes property to the partnership, the property is encumbered by a nonrecourse liability and that liability exceeds the *tax basis* of the property, then the liability is considered a **Section 704(c)-type** liability for purposes of tier two of the nonrecourse liability allocation process, *but only to the extent by which the principal amount of the liability exceeds the tax basis of the property*. This represents the tax gain that would be allocated to the contributing partner if the lender foreclosed on the property in satisfaction of the liability. If any part of this "built-in" gain was already allocated to a partner under tier one, only the remaining Section 704(c)-type gain is allocated in tier two.

c. Excess nonrecourse liabilities

A partner's share of the partnership's nonrecourse liabilities not allocated under tier one or tier two is considered **excess nonrecourse liabilities.** Excess nonrecourse liabilities are allocated among the partners in accordance with their profit sharing ratios.

4. Summary

Partnership liabilities impact the calculation of a partner's outside basis. The first step in determining the partner's "share" of the partnership's liabilities is to identify each liability as recourse or nonrecourse. To the extent the liability is nonrecourse, a partner's share of that liability is determined by undergoing a three-tier allocation process. The partnership provides a partner with the partner's share of nonrecourse liabilities (in addition to a partner's share of *recourse* liabilities) on the Schedule K-1 that the partnership sends to each partner.

H. Partnership Interest Created by Gift

A parent who is a partner in a partnership may try to shift some of the partnership's income to a family member who may be at a lower income tax rate bracket. Thus, the income is taxed at a lower rate, but the income still stays within the family. What if a parent transfers an interest in a partnership to a child as a gift? Is the child recognized as a partner for income tax purposes? Or is all the income still taxed to the parent? The Code addresses these issues.

Section 704. Partner's distributive share

...

(e) Partnership interest created by gift.—

(1) Distributive share of donee includible in gross income. In the case of any partnership interest created by gift, the distributive share of the donee under the partnership agreement shall be includible in his gross income, except to the extent that such share is determined without allowance of reasonable compensation for services rendered to the partnership by the donor, and except to the extent that the portion of such share attributable to donated capital is proportionately greater than the share of the donor attributable to the donor's capital. The distributive share of a partner in the earnings of the partnership shall not be diminished because of absence due to military service.

(2) Purchase of interest by member of family. For purposes of this subsection, an interest purchased by one member of a family from another shall be considered to be created by gift from the seller and the fair market value of the purchased interest shall be considered to be donated capital. The “family” of any individual shall include only his spouse, ancestors, and lineal descendants, and any trusts for the primary benefit of such persons.

. . .

Notice that the general rule is that distributive share of the donee of a partnership interest is recognized into income by the donee. If the donor provides services to the partnership and is not paid reasonable compensation for those services, however, the service-providing partner is deemed to be paid a reasonable amount.[6] Similarly, the partnership is not allowed to allocate disproportionately more income to the donee’s capital than to the donor’s capital.

[6] This would presumably be treated as a guaranteed payment to the service-providing partner and considered ordinary income to the service provider and a deduction for the partnership. Thus, the ordinary business income to be allocated among all partners would be less than if the service provider did not receive reasonable compensation.

CHAPTER 5 QUESTIONS FOR REVIEW

1. *Pass-through entity.* A client asks you how a partnership is treated for income tax purposes. You say that it is a "pass-through" entity. Your client then queries, "What do you mean by a 'pass-through' entity?" Explain. What is your authority?

2. *Partnership ordinary income.* How is "partnership ordinary income (loss)" calculated?

3. *Partnership taxable income.* What constitutes "partnership taxable income (loss)"?

4. *Separately stated items.* Why are some items of income, gain, loss, deduction, etc., stated separately from the partnership's ordinary income?

5. *Separately stated items.* Name at least six separately stated items.

6. *Distributive share.* Explain what a partner's "distributive share" is.

7. *Partnership reporting.* On what schedule of Form 1065 does a partnership report its separately stated items?

8. *Partnership reporting.* Explain how a partner knows what the partner's distributive share of the partnership's taxable income is so that the partner can properly complete the partner's income tax return.

9. *Determining a partner's outside basis.* Explain generally how a partner's outside basis is determined (ignoring the impact of liabilities and depletion).

10. *Determining a partner's outside basis.* If a partner is unable to determine his outside basis under the general rule, explain how the partner would determine his outside basis.

11. *Outside basis calculation.* R and J form an LLC, which is treated as a partnership for federal income tax purposes. R contributes $14,000 in cash in return for a 70% interest in the LLC's profits and capital. J contributes property with a tax basis of $3,500 and fair market value of $4,000. J also contributed municipal bonds with a tax basis of $2,000 and fair market value of $2,000. J receives a 30% interest in profits and capital. The following operations occurred during the year:

Sales revenue	$400,000	
COGS	$140,000	
Tax-exempt interest	$100	
Rent expense	$15,000	
Advertising expense	$15,000	
Transportation expense	$20,000	
Meals and entertainment	$20,000	(only 50% tax deductible)

At the end of the year the LLC distributes $70,000 in cash to R and $30,000 in cash to J.

a. What is R's outside basis at the end of the year?

b. What is J's outside basis at the end of the year?

12. *Coloman v. Commissioner.* Summarize the facts of the Coloman case. What was the issue? Summarize the court's analysis. How did the court rule?

13. *Partnership liabilities in general.* If partnership liabilities increase, how does this impact a partner's outside basis?

14. *Partnership liabilities in general.* If partnership liabilities decrease, how does this impact a partner's outside basis?

15. *Partnership recourse liability.* Explain the distinction between a partnership nonrecourse liability and a partnership recourse liability.

16. *Partner's share of partnership recourse liabilities.* R and J form an LLC. They agree to share profits and losses equally. R transfers cash of $100 and J transfers cash of $100. The partnership then acquires a parcel of land for $1,000, using the $200 cash contributed by the partners and by obtaining an $800 loan that both R and J personally guarantee.

    a. What is each partner's share of the recourse liability?
    b. What is each partner's outside basis after the partnership incurs the liability?

    Now assume the same facts, but R and J agree to share profits 50%/50% and losses 80%/20%.

    c. What is each partner's share of the recourse liability?
    d. What is each partner's outside basis after the partnership incurs the liability?

17. *Partnership nonrecourse liabilities.* How is a partner's "share" of partnership nonrecourse liabilities determined?

18. *Partnership minimum gain.* RJ partnership owns a building. The building's tax basis is $50 and its book value is $70. The building is encumbered by a nonrecourse liability of $80, however. The building was not contributed to the partnership by any partner; rather, the partnership acquired the building using its own cash and proceeds from the nonrecourse loan.

    a. What is the amount of the partnership's minimum gain?
    b. What is the amount of the partnership's Section 704(c)-type gain?
    c. What is the amount of the partnership's excess nonrecourse liabilities?

19. *Partnership Section 704(c) minimum gain.* R and J form RJ, LLC, which is treated as a partnership for federal income tax purposes. R transfers cash of $100, and J transfers property with a tax basis of $30 and a fair market value of $150. The property contributed by J is encumbered with a

nonrecourse liability of $50, which the LLC assumes. R and J are equal partners.

a. What is the amount of the partnership's minimum gain?
b. What is the amount of the partnership's Section 704(c) minimum gain?
c. What is the amount of the partnership's excess nonrecourse liabilities?
d. What is J's share of the partnership's nonrecourse liability?
e. What is J's outside basis immediately after formation of the LLC?
f. What is R's share of the partnership's nonrecourse liability?
g. What is R's outside basis immediately after formation of the LLC?

20. *Partnership liabilities: transfer of property to partnership.* R and J form RJ, LLC, which is treated as a partnership for federal income tax purposes. R and J agree to share profits and losses equally. Upon formation of the LLC, R transfers cash of $100. J transfers property with a tax basis of $70, fair market value of $130. The property is encumbered with a $30 nonrecourse liability, which the LLC assumes.

a. What is R's amount realized?
b. What is R's gain or loss realized?
c. What is R's gain or loss recognized?
d. What is J's amount realized?
e. What is J's gain or loss realized?
f. What is J's gain or loss recognized?
g. What is R's outside basis immediately after the LLC's formation?
h. What is J's outside basis immediately after the LLC's formation?
i. What does the LLC's balance sheet look like from both a tax basis standpoint and a book basis standpoint?

21. *Partnership interest created by gift.* Explain the rules applicable to allocating income to a donee of a partnership interest.

Coloman v. Commissioner

38 AFTR 2d 76-5523 (9th Cir.)

OPINION

These are consolidated appeals from the decision of the United States Tax Court [citation omitted] upholding the Commissioner's determination of deficiencies in appellants' income tax for the years 1967 through 1970. During those years taxpayers claimed on their tax returns loss deductions arising from certain corporate stock they held which they allege became worthless. The Tax Court held that the taxpayers had failed to establish any basis in the stock, that its basis was, therefore, zero, and by implication that the Commissioner's disallowance of the loss deductions taken, and the corresponding assessment of deficiencies, was correct. We affirm.

Taxpayers, husband and wife, with two others, formed a dry cleaning business in 1962 which they operated as a partnership until March, 1964, at which time they incorporated the business in California under the name of Village Valet, Inc. All assets and liabilities of the partnership were transferred to the corporation, and the partners took stock in the corporation in exchange. [Footnotes omitted throughout.]

In September 1970 the corporation was dissolved and liquidation begun. Taxpayers took possession of some of the corporation's equipment and reopened the business at a new location as a sole proprietorship. The taxpayers reported in 1970 a portion of the loss attributable to the stock's allegedly having become worthless; the remainder of the loss was carried back to 1967, 1968, and 1969 as a net operating loss.

Under Section 358(a) of the Internal Revenue Code, the basis of stock received from a corporation is equal to the basis of the property exchanged for that stock. Here, the taxpayers exchanged their partnership interest for the corporate stock; therefore, the basis of their stock would be the carryover basis of their partnership interest.

Taxpayers' basis in their partnership interest is determined by the provisions of subchapter K .... As a general rule, a partner's basis in a newly formed partnership will be the same as his adjusted basis in the property he exchanged for his interest, plus any money contributed. ... This initial basis is further adjusted for increases or decreases in partnership liabilities assumed by the individual partners. ... In addition, the initial basis is continually adjusted by virtue of the ordinary activities relating to the partnership vis-à-vis the individual partners; for example, Section 705(a) provides that the basis of a partner's interest is to be increased by his distributive share of the partnership's taxable income for each year, his distributive share of tax-exempt partnership income, and the excess of deductions for depletion over the basis of property subject to depletion. Similarly, basis is decreased (but not below zero) by distributions by the partnership to the partner as provided in Section 733, and by the sum of his distributive share for the current and prior taxable years of partnership losses, and non-deductible and non-capitalizable partnership expenditures. Furthermore, Section 704 provides, in determining the partner's distributive share for purposes of gain or loss, that such ratios and amounts shall be determined by the partnership agreement, and, if the agreement is not lacking in substance, the partners themselves can determine their distributive shares as to total gain or loss, or to individual items of income, gain, loss, deduction and credit. [Citation omitted.]

Thus, in order to establish the basis in the interest in the partnership at the time the corporation was formed (which in turn would be the basis in the corporate stock at the time of incorporation), the taxpayers had to establish to the Tax Court's satisfaction (1) the initial basis in the partnership interest at the time the partnership was formed, and (2) the amount of any adjustments thereto by virtue of the activities of the partnership, pursuant to Section 705(a), and/or by virtue of assumptions of liabilities by other partners, pursuant to Section 752.

The burden of so establishing rested on the taxpayers. [Citation omitted.] Establishing basis is a factual matter, [citation omitted], and the Commissioner's determination is accepted by the Tax Court as presumptively correct. [Citation omitted.] The fact that basis may be difficult to establish does not relieve a taxpayer from his burden. [Citation omitted.]

The testimony presented by the taxpayers did not, in the Tax Court's opinion, meet this burden. About the only evidence relevant on the basis issue was the husband's taxpayer's unverified statement that he had contributed property "worth" $28,000 to the partnership in the form of a second deed of trust. But, as the Service notes, the "worth" or value of a piece of property may be quite different from its basis in the taxpayer's hands, and this is the basis that the taxpayers failed to prove. Thus, the Tax Court concluded that the taxpayers had not established their initial basis in the partnership interest.

Moreover, there was insufficient evidence of what adjustments to this basis may have been necessary during the course of operations of the partnership, according to the provisions of Sections 705, 733 and 752. Thus, taxpayers failed in several important respects to establish the basis in the partnership interest at the termination of the partnership, so as to satisfy the general statutory requirements found in Sections 722, 733, 752 and 705(a).

However, taxpayers argue on appeal that the alternative rule of Section 705(b) should have been applied by the Tax Court, and should now be applied here. Under Section 705(b), the Commissioner is empowered to prescribe by regulations the circumstances under which the adjusted basis of a partner's interest in the partnership may be determined by reference to his proportionate share of the adjusted basis of partnership property upon a *termination of the partnership*. The rule promulgated to implement this section found in 26 CFR §1.705-1(b) and set forth in full in the margin, states that the alternative method may be used "where circumstances are such that the partner cannot practicably apply the general rule set forth in Section 705(a)." Even under the alternative rule, adjustments to basis may be necessary to reflect discrepancies arising as a result of contributed property, transfers of partnership interest, or distributions of property to the partners.

Presumably to bring themselves within Section 705(b), taxpayers presented evidence in the form of testimony by the corporation's accountant that at the time of incorporation, the accountant computed the taxpayers' basis in the partnership interest to be approximately $16,000. The Tax Court refused to accept the basis figure proposed by the taxpayers for the reason that it was based on figures supplied to the accountant by the taxpayers and not independently verified by the accountant.

We find no error in the lower court's refusal to accept the taxpayer's basis figure. Taxpayers had the burden of *establishing* basis, which burden was not met, in the Tax Court's view, by the taxpayers' simply stating that the basis was such and such, or by having an accountant come in to court to so state, in reliance upon figures supplied by the taxpayers. In essence, what the Tax Court held was that *even if* Section 705(b) could be said to be applicable, there was insufficient evidence of the partner' adjusted basis in the partnership interest at the termination of the partnership. The court might not point out, however, that no showing was made in the first instance that Section 705(b) was even applicable. That is, there was no testimony elicited by the taxpayers directed to the issue of whether circumstances were such that the taxpayers could not "practicably" apply the general rule of Section 705(a). Taxpayers did state that the books and records of the partnership were not available, but no reason was given for their unavailability. Whether under these circumstances Section 705(a) could not be "practicably" applied, as required by the regulation for the invocation of Section 705(b), is a question we need not answer at this time. It is sufficient to sustain the Tax Court's holding that the taxpayers did not sustain their burden of proving their adjusted basis in the partnership interest at the time of termination of the partnership.

In assessing the taxpayers' evidence on the issue of basis, the Tax Court concluded:

> In the present case ... petitioner failed to produce such evidence (of basis) other than his own testimony, which was imprecise and vague. Petitioner was unable to recall what amounts of cash and property were contributed to the

> partnership or the corporation. He was unable to establish precisely the amounts that the partnership invested in the various types of equipment it purchased. He failed to indicate with specificity the extent to which this equipment had depreciated at the time it was contributed to the corporation. Accordingly, we have no choice but to hold that petitioners have failed to establish that their stock had a basis in excess of zero and that they therefore have not proved that they realized a loss upon the liquidation of the corporation.

This factual finding is not so clearly erroneous as to compel us to set it aside on this appeal.

. . .

For the foregoing reasons, the decision of the Tax Court is affirmed.

Chapter 6

Limitations on Partnership Losses Deductible by Partners

A. Outside Basis Limitation
B. At-Risk Loss Limitation
C. Passive Loss Limitation

Since a partnership is a pass-through entity, income, gains, expenses, losses, credits, etc., recognized at the partnership level are reported on the partners' respective income tax returns. When a partnership recognizes losses, however, certain Code provisions may restrict the deductibility of such losses by the partners in the current year. This chapter discusses the three loss limitations that may apply to a partner's ability to deduct the distributive share of a partnership loss. These three limitations are (1) the outside basis limitation; (2) the at-risk loss limitation; and (3) the passive loss limitation.

A. Outside Basis Limitation

You may recall that losses of the partnership and distributions from the partnership cause a partner's outside basis to decrease. Nevertheless, a partner's outside basis cannot become negative.

Section 704. Partner's distributive share

...

(d) Limitation on allowance of losses. A partner's distributive share of partnership loss (including capital loss) shall be allowed only to the extent of the adjusted basis of such partner's interest in the partnership at the end of the partnership year in which such loss occurred. Any excess of such loss over such basis shall be allowed as a deduction at the end of the partnership year in which such excess is repaid to the partnership.

...

The Treasury Regulations go into a bit more detail on how to handle a partnership loss that passes through to a partner when the partner does not have sufficient outside basis.

Treasury Regulation §1.704-1. Partner's distributive share

. . .

(d) Limitation on allowance of losses

(1) A partner's distributive share of partnership loss will be allowed only to the extent of the adjusted basis (before reduction by current year's losses) of such partner's interest in the partnership at the end of the partnership taxable year in which such loss occurred. A partner's share of loss in excess of his adjusted basis at the end of the partnership taxable year will not be allowed for that year. However, any loss so disallowed shall be allowed as a deduction at the end of the first succeeding partnership taxable year, and subsequent partnership taxable years, to the extent that the partner's adjusted basis for his partnership interest at the end of any such year exceeds zero (before reduction by such loss for such year).

(2) In computing the adjusted basis of a partner's interest for the purpose of ascertaining the extent to which a partner's distributive share of partnership loss shall be allowed as a deduction for the taxable year, the basis shall first be increased under Section 705(a)(1) and decreased under Section 705(a)(2), except for losses of the taxable year and losses previously disallowed. If the partner's distributive share of the aggregate of items of loss specified in Section 702(a)(1), (2), (3), (8), and (9) exceeds the basis of the partner's interest computed under the preceding sentence, the limitation on losses under Section 704(d) must be allocated to his distributive share of each such loss. This allocation shall be determined by taking the proportion that each loss bears to the total of all such losses. For purposes of the preceding sentence, the total losses for the taxable year shall be the sum of his distributive share of losses for the current year and his losses disallowed and carried forward from prior years.

. . .

(4) The provisions of this paragraph may be illustrated by the following examples.

Example (1). At the end of the partnership taxable year 1955, partnership AB has a loss of $20,000. Partner A's distributive share of this loss is $10,000. At the end of such year, A's adjusted basis for his interest in the partnership (not taking into account his distributive share of the loss) is $6,000. Under Section 704(d), A's distributive share of partnership loss is allowed to him (in his taxable year within or with which the partnership taxable year ends) only to the extent of his adjusted basis of $6,000. The $6,000 loss allowed for 1955 decreases the adjusted basis of A's interest to zero. Assume that, at the end of partnership taxable year 1956, A's share of partnership income has increased the adjusted basis of A's interest in the partnership to $3,000 (not taking into account the $4,000 loss disallowed in 1955). Of the $4,000 loss disallowed for the partnership taxable year 1955, $3,000 is allowed A for the partnership taxable year 1956, thus again decreasing the adjusted basis of his interest to zero. If, at the end of partnership taxable year 1957, A has an adjusted basis of his interest of at least $1,000 (not taking into account the disallowed loss of $1,000), he will be allowed the $1,000 loss previously disallowed.

. . .

Example (3). At the end of partnership taxable year 1955, partner C has the following distributive share of partnership items described in Section 702(a): long-term capital loss, $4,000; short-term capital loss, $2,000; income as described in Section 702(a)(9), $4,000. Partner C's adjusted basis for his partnership interest at the end of 1955, before adjustment for any of the above items, is $1,000. As adjusted under Section 705(a)(1)(A), C's basis is increased from $1,000 to $5,000 at the end of the year. C's total distributive share of partnership loss is $6,000. Since without regard to losses, C has a basis of only $5,000, C is allowed only $5,000/$6,000 of each loss, that is, $3,333 of his long-term capital loss, and $1,667 of his short-term capital loss. C must carry forward to succeeding years $667 as a long-term capital loss and $333 as a short-term capital loss.

. . .

Section 705 (relating to calculating a partner's outside basis) and Section 733 (relating to distributions from a partnership to a partner) also make reference to the fact that a partner's outside basis cannot be reduced below zero. To the extent a partner's distributive share of partnership losses exceeds the partner's outside basis, the loss is carried forward until such time as the partner has sufficient outside basis to absorb the loss.

rzymuR /Shutterstock.com

For a court case analyzing the disallowance of losses due to a partner's zero outside basis, see *Minter v. Commissioner*, TC Memo 1991-448. Excerpts of the *Minter* case are included at the end of this chapter.

B. At-Risk Loss Limitation

A partner can deduct losses only to the extent that a partner is economically "at risk" with respect to those losses.

Section 465. Deductions limited to amount at risk

(a) Limitation to amount at risk.—

(1) In general. In the case of—

(A) an individual, and

(B) a C corporation with respect to which the stock ownership requirement of paragraph (2) of Section 542(a) is met,

engaged in an activity to which this section applies, any loss from such activity for the taxable year shall be allowed only to the extent of the aggregate amount with respect to which the taxpayer is at risk (within the meaning of subsection (b)) for such activity at the close of the taxable year.

(2) Deduction in succeeding year. Any loss from an activity to which this section applies not allowed under this section for the taxable year shall be treated as a deduction allocable to such activity in the first succeeding taxable year.

...

(b) Amounts considered at risk.—

(1) In general. For purposes of this section, a taxpayer shall be considered at risk for an activity with respect to amounts including—

(A) the amount of money and the adjusted basis of other property contributed by the taxpayer to the activity, and

(B) amounts borrowed with respect to such activity (as determined under paragraph (2)).

(2) Borrowed amounts. For purposes of this section, a taxpayer shall be considered at risk with respect to amounts borrowed for use in an activity to the extent that he—

(A) is personally liable for the repayment of such amounts, or

(B) has pledged property, other than property used in such activity, as security for such borrowed amount (to the extent of the net fair market value of the taxpayer's interest in such property).

...

(c) Activities to which section applies.—

(1) Types of activities. This section applies to any taxpayer engaged in the activity of—

(A) holding, producing, or distributing motion picture films or video tapes,

(B) farming (as defined in Section 464(e)),

(C) leasing any Section 1245 property (as defined in section 1245(a)(3)),

(D) exploring for, or exploiting, oil and gas resources as a trade or business or for the production of income, or

(E) exploring for, or exploiting, geothermal deposits (as defined in Section 613(e)(2)).

...

(3) Extension to other activities.—

(A) In general. In the case of taxable years beginning after December 31, 1978, this section also applies to each activity—

(i) engaged in by the taxpayer in carrying on a trade or business or for the production of income, and

(ii) which is not described in paragraph (1).

...

Although Section 465 does not specifically address partners in partnerships, it does indicate that the at-risk rules apply to individuals. This includes individuals who are partners in partnerships. Notice a partner's amount considered at risk is money contributed to the partnership, the adjusted basis of property contributed to the partnership, and any borrowing for which the partner is obligated to repay (e.g., recourse liabilities). Thus, any losses allocated to a partner in excess of this amount at risk is carried forward until the partner has sufficient amount at risk.

rzymuR /Shutterstock.com

For a court case analyzing the at-risk limitation applied to a partner in a partnership, see *Pritchett v. Commissioner*, 827 F.2d 644 (9th Cir. 1987). Excerpts of the *Pritchett* case are included at the end of this chapter.

For purposes of the at-risk rules a partner's share of the partnership's "qualified nonrecourse financing" is also considered at risk even though the loan may be nonrecourse. Qualified nonrecourse financing basically is financing incurred to obtain real property, and the real property secures the debt.

Section 465. Deductions limited to amount at risk

...

(b) Amounts considered at risk.—

...

(6) Qualified nonrecourse financing treated as amount at risk. For purposes of this section—

(A) In general. Notwithstanding any other provision of this subsection, in the case of an activity of holding real property, a taxpayer shall be considered at risk with respect to the taxpayer's share of any qualified nonrecourse financing which is secured by real property used in such activity.

(B) Qualified nonrecourse financing. For purposes of this paragraph, the term "qualified nonrecourse financing" means any financing—

(i) which is borrowed by the taxpayer with respect to the activity of holding real property,

(ii) which is borrowed by the taxpayer from a qualified person or represents a loan from any Federal., State, or local government or instrumentality thereof, or is guaranteed by any Federal, State, or local government,

(iii) except to the extent provided in regulations, with respect to which no person is personally liable for repayment, and

(iv) which is not convertible debt.

(C) Special rule for partnership. In the case of a partnership, a partner's share of any qualified nonrecourse financing of such partnership shall be determined on the basis of the partner's share of liabilities of such partnership incurred in connection with such financing (within the meaning of Section 752).

...

C. Passive Loss Limitation

Passive losses are deductible only against passive income (and not active income or portfolio income). Net passive losses are not deductible and are carried forward until there is passive income to absorb the passive losses. A passive loss is no longer considered passive when the taxpayer disposes of the activity. Thus, any remaining passive losses can be deducted at that time.

Section 469. Passive activity losses and credits limited

(a) Disallowance.—

(1) In general. If for any taxable year the taxpayer is described in paragraph (2), neither—

(A) the passive activity loss, nor

(B) the passive activity credit,

for the taxable year shall be allowed.

(2) Persons described. The following are described in this paragraph:

(A) any individual, estate, or trust,

(B) any closely held C corporation, and

(C) any personal service corporation.

(b) Disallowed loss or credit carried to next year. Except as otherwise provided in this section, any loss or credit from an activity which is disallowed under subsection (a) shall be treated as a deduction or credit allocable to such activity in the next taxable year.

(c) Passive activity defined. For purposes of this section—

(1) In general. The term "passive activity" means any activity—

(A) which involves the conduct of any trade or business, and

(B) in which the taxpayer does not materially participate.

. . .

(h) Material participation defined. For purposes of this section—

(1) In general. A taxpayer shall be treated as materially participating in an activity only if the taxpayer is involved in the operations of the activity on a basis which is—

(A) regular,

(B) continuous, and

(C) substantial.

. . .

In the partnership context, the "material participation" test applies at the partner level.[1] Thus, even if the partnership's activity is not passive, any losses flowing through from the partnership will be passive losses to a partner who does not materially participate with respect to the activity.

The Treasury Regulations provide seven ways in which a person can meet the material participation test.

Treas. Reg. § 1.469-5T. Material participation

(a) In general. Except as provided in paragraphs (e) and (h)(2) of this section, an individual shall be treated, for purposes of Section 469 and the regulations thereunder, as materially participating in an activity for the taxable year if and only if—

(1) The individual participates in the activity for more than 500 hours during such year;

(2) The individual's participation in the activity for the taxable year constitutes substantially all of the participation in such activity of all individuals (including individuals who are not owners of interests in the activity) for such year;

(3) The individual participates in the activity for more than 100 hours during the taxable year, and such individual's participation in the activity for the taxable year is not less than the participation in the activity of any other individual (including individuals who are not owners of interests in the activity) for such year;

[1] Temp. Reg. §1.469-2T(e)(1).

> (4) The activity is a significant participation activity… for the taxable year, and the individual's aggregate participation in all significant participation activities during such year exceeds 500 hours.
>
> (5) The individual materially participated in the activity… for any five taxable years (whether or not consecutive) during the ten taxable years that immediately precede the taxable year;
>
> (6) The activity is a personal service activity… and the individual materially participated in the activity for any three taxable years (whether or not consecutive) preceding the taxable year; or
>
> (7) Based on all of the facts and circumstances… the individual participates in the activity on a regular, continuous, and substantial basis during such year.
>
> …

In sum, if a partner survives all three potential loss limitations (i.e., outside basis limitation, at-risk loss limitation, and passive loss limitation), the partner's distributive share of the partnership's loss is deductible to the partner.

CHAPTER 6 QUESTIONS FOR REVIEW

1. *Outside basis limitation.* R and J are equal partners in the RJ Partnership, a consulting business. R's outside basis at the beginning of the year was $100. During the year, the partnership's activities produced the following:

Consulting revenue	$2,000
Guaranteed payment to R	$700
Guaranteed payment to J	$700
Advertising expense	$300
Utilities expense	$200
Rent expense	$500

   a. What is the partnership's net income or loss for the year?
   b. What is R's distributive share of the partnership's income or loss for the year?
   c. What is R's outside basis at the end of the year?
   d. If, in fact, R's distributive share from the partnership is a loss, does the loss exceed R's outside basis? If so, by how much? How much of the loss allocated to R can R deduct (assuming the at-risk and passive loss limitations do not apply) for the current year?

2. *Minter v. Commissioner.* Summarize the facts of the *Minter* case. What was the issue? What was the court's conclusion?

3. *At-risk loss limitation.* Who is subject to the at-risk loss limitation?

4. *At-risk loss limitation.* What is considered an amount at risk?

5. *Pritchett v. Commissioner.* Summarize the facts of the *Pritchett* case. What was the issue? What was the court's conclusion?

6. *Passive loss limitation.* Who is subject to the passive loss limitation?

7. *Passive loss limitation.* Name three ways a partner is considered to materially participate in the partnership's business activity.

Minter v. Commissioner

United States Tax Court
TC Memo 1991-448

MEMORANDUM OPINION

PARR, *Judge*:

. . .

The issues for decision are: (1)...; (6) whether petitioner sustained deductible partnership losses in the years 1983 through 1985 from his interest in a real estate partnership;...

A. Background

Petitioners were married in 1984. Mr. Minter filed a Federal income tax return for 1983, in which he reported the filing status of "single." He reported adjusted gross income of $0 after deducting losses from operation of his accounting, tax return preparation, and notary service business; from the rental real estate he owned individually; and from a pass-through loss from a real estate partnership in which he owned a 50-percent interest. ...

Petitioners filed Federal income tax returns for 1984 and 1985 in which they reported the filing status of "married, filing joint return." They reported adjusted gross income of $0 and $14,068, respectively, after deducting losses from operation of petitioner's accounting, tax return preparation, and notary service business; from the rental real estate he owned individually; and from a pass-through loss from a real estate partnership in which he owned a 50-percent interest....

. . .

G. Partnership Loss

Petitioner deducted his distributive share of the losses incurred by Minter-Clayvon Company (the partnership) for 1983 through 1985 in the amounts of $4,250, $4,850, and $4,043, respectively. Respondent disallowed these deductions on the theory that petitioner's basis in the partnership was zero.

Petitioner testified that each partner originally contributed $35,000 to the partnership's capital, but his statement is inconsistent with the settlement statement.

Petitioner presented no credible evidence of amounts he contributed to the partnership's capital since the property was purchased. His protestations to the contrary, the partnership information returns do not reflect sufficient information to prove petitioner's basis, as they are replete with mathematical errors and inconsistencies. For each year, the amount reflected in the balance sheet as "Partners' Capital Accounts" does not equal the balance reflected in the "Reconciliation of Partners' Capital Accounts" section of the information return. In fact, the balance sheet reflects a positive balance in the capital accounts, whereas the reconciliation reflects a negative balance; no explanation was given in any of the 3 years for this inconsistency.

On each 1983 Schedule K-1, on which the partnership was to report transactions in each partner's capital account, the reconciliation of the total partnership capital is copied. No detail is reported as to the amount of capital contributed by each partner.

The closing balance sheet on the 1984 partnership information return is completely different from the opening balance sheet on the 1985 partnership information return. Petitioner, as an accountant, should have known that the closing balance from one year should equal the opening balance of the next.

Section 704(d) limits the deduction of a partner's distributive share of partnership loss to the partner's adjusted basis in the partnership at the end of the partnership year. Sec. 1.704-1(d)(1), Income Tax Regs. The partner's adjusted basis in his or her partnership interest is comprised of his or her adjusted basis in property contributed to the partnership. Secs. 705(a) and 722. A liability to which partnership property is subject, to the extent of the property's fair market value, is considered a liability of the owner. Sec. 752(c). Any partnership liabilities to which a partner is liable shall be considered a capital contribution by such partner to the partnership. Sec. 752(a). Moreover, a partner's adjusted basis in the partnership is increased, inter alia, by the partner's distributive share of the partnership's taxable income, since he or she became a partner, Section 705(a)(1)(A); and decreased, inter alia, by the partner's distributive share of partnership losses since he or she became a partner. Sec. 705(a)(2)(A). Any loss in excess of the taxpayer's adjusted basis will be allowed in the year in which such excess is repaid to the partnership. Sec. 704(d).

Petitioner contributed no more than $3,738 to the partnership when it was formed in 1977. He presented no evidence of any capital contributions since then. Petitioner's share of the partnership's liability at December 31, 1983, 1984, and 1985 was $12,075, $12,495, and $12,240, respectively. He testified that the partnership consistently lost approximately $4,000 per year. At that rate, his adjusted basis in the partnership was less than zero by 1981.

. . .

[The Tax Court ruled in favor of the IRS and disallowed the pass-through losses to the partner.]

Pritchett v. Commissioner

Ninth Circuit Court of Appeals
827 F.2d 644 (9th Cir. 1987)

OPINION

SKOPIL, CIRCUIT JUDGE

We must decide in this case whether taxpayers, limited partners in five similar partnerships engaged in oil and gas drilling operations, were "at risk" pursuant to 26 U.S.C. Section 465 on certain recourse notes and thus entitled to deduct distributive shares of non-cash partnership losses. The Tax Court in a reviewed, split decision held that each taxpayer was at risk only to the extent of actual cash contribution. [Citation omitted.] We reject the Tax Court's rationale in holding that taxpayers were not at risk on the recourse debt....

FACTS AND PROCEEDINGS BELOW

Taxpayers are each members in similar limited partnerships formed to conduct oil and gas operations. All five partnerships entered into agreements with Fairfield Drilling Corporation ("Fairfield") whereby Fairfield agreed to drill, develop, and exploit any productive wells. Fairfield provided all necessary equipment and expertise. Pursuant to a "turnkey" agreement, each partnership paid cash and executed a recourse note to Fairfield. Each note was non-interestbearing and matured in fifteen years. Each was secured by virtually all of the maker-partnership's assets. The principal for each note was to be paid from net income available to each partnership if the drilling operations proved successful. Only the general partners were personally liable under the notes. Nevertheless, each partnership agreement provided that if the notes were not paid off at maturity, the limited partners would be personally obligated to make additional capital contributions to cover the deficiency when called upon to do so by the general partners.

Each partnership elected to use accrual accounting and to deduct intangible drilling costs as an expense. The partnership agreements provided that all losses were to be allocated among limited partners in proportion to their respective capital contributions. Because there was no income in the tax year in question, each limited partner deducted from taxable income a distributive share of partnership loss. The Commissioner disallowed that portion of the deduction based on the note.

The Tax Court affirmed by a 9-7 vote the Commissioner's action. The majority held that under the partnership agreements the limited partners had no persona liability on the notes for the tax year in question and therefore they were at risk under Section 465 only for the actual cash contribution made to the partnerships. [Citation omitted.] Any potential liability was "merely a contingency" since in the first year of the partnership it was not known whether income would be sufficient to pay off the note or even whether the general partners would in fact exercise their discretion to make a cash call on an unpaid balance fifteen years later.

Seven Judges dissented in three separate opinions. One judge reasoned that for federal tax purposes, "both general and limited partners are personally liable for a pro rata portion of the partnership recourse obligation to Fairfield." [Citation omitted.] Another found nothing in the agreements to indicate the general partners had unilateral discretion to waive the cash call. [Citation omitted.] A majority of the dissenting judges apparently believed, however, that the Commissioner's actions might be affirmed on the alternative ground that Section 465(b)(3)(A) provides that amounts borrowed are not at risk if the money is borrowed from someone with an interest in the activity at issue. [Citation omitted.] The majority notes this alternative ground but expressly does not adopt it.

These timely appeals followed.

DISCUSSION

In 1976 Congress added Section 465 to the Internal Revenue Code to combat abuse of tax shelters caused by nonrecourse financing.... Section 465 forbids a taxpayer from taking a loss in excess of amounts at risk in the investment. The statute provides in relevant part that:

(1)... a taxpayer shall be considered at risk for...

(A) the amount of money... contributed by the taxpayer to the activity, and

(B) amounts borrowed with respect to such activity...

(2)... a taxpayer shall be considered at risk with respect to amounts borrowed... to the extent that he --

(A) is personally liable for the repayment of such amounts...

26 U.S.C. 465(b).

The limited partners argue that the notes create at risk debt because each limited partner is personally liable. The contract provisions provide that if the notes are not paid off by the successful drilling operations, "the General Partners WILL by written notice call for additional capital contributions in an amount sufficient to pay the outstanding balance" and that "[e]ach Limited Partner SHALL be obligated to pay in cash to the Partnership" the amount called. (Emphasis added). It is clear, however, as the majority opinion notes, that the limited partners are not directly and personally liable to Fairfield. [Citation omitted.] Even assuming a third party beneficiary right, Fairfield had no recourse against the limited partners until the end of the note's fifteen year term.

Whether the Tax Court's decision is correct hinges on its characterization of taxpayer's obligation as indirect and secondary. In a decision rendered shortly after Pritchett, the Tax Court sought to distinguish between direct and indirect liability. [Citation omitted.] In that reviewed decision, the Tax Court, by a 15-1 vote, held that limited partners' pro rata shares of partnership debt that was to be repaid in whole or in part out of partnership revenues was at risk. The limited partners had a direct contractual liability to a third party seller of goods. Abramson distinguished Pritchett by noting:

In Pritchett the limited partnerships were not directly liable to the lender on the partnership obligation. Rather, the general partner was personally liable to the lender on the recourse obligation, and the limited partners were not obligated on any debt for purposes of Section 465 until the general partner called for contributions to the partnership. Consequently, in Pritchett, the limited partners had not borrowed any amount within the meaning of Section 465(b)(2). In this case, to the contrary, each partner is personally and directly liable for a pro rata part of the amount owed to the seller... . Because ach partner's liability for the partnership debt (in words of the statute, for the "amounts borrowed") ran directly to the seller and each partner's liability was personal, each partner is at risk for his proportionate share of amount owed to the seller.

We agree that Congress intended to condition Section 465's exclusion of deductions in part on whether the liability for borrowing is primary or secondary. The statute expressly requires that the taxpayer be "personally liable for the repayment." 26 U.S.C. Section 465(b)(2)(A). In debate on the Deficit Reduction Act of 1984, a House Report explained that Section 465 limits an at-risk loss to, inter alia, amounts borrowed for use in the activity with respect to which taxpayer has PERSONAL liability." [Citation omitted.] If the limited partnership agreements here create only contingent liability, we will affirm the Tax Court's decision to disallow taxpayers' deductions.

We conclude, however, that the liability of the limited partners was unavoidable and hence not contingent. In Melvin v. Commissioner, 88 T.C. 63 (1987), the Tax Court appeared to answer the question posed here by concluding that

the fact that the partnership or other partners remain in the "chain of liability" should not detract from the at-risk amount of the parties who do have the ultimate liability. The critical inquiry should be who is the obligor of last resort, and in determining who has the ultimate economic responsibility for the loan, the substance of the transaction controls.

[Citation omitted.] Applying that standard we have no reservation in concluding that taxpayers, by virtue of their contractual obligations, have ultimate responsibility for the debt. [Citation omitted.] Furthermore, we are not dissuaded by the Tax Court's reasoning that the debt is contingent because the general partners may elect to not make the cash calls. The contracts made the call mandatory and "economic reality" dictates that the partners would do so. [Citation omitted.]

The Tax Court also reasoned that the debt was contingent since it was not known in the tax year in question whether sufficient partnership revenues would satisfy the notes prior to or on maturity. We find the Tax Court's reasoning on this point faulty. If the notes required balloon payments upon maturity, the limited partners' obligation to contribute additional funds would be "certain." The acceleration of payments should not be a factor in the taxation analysis. In Abramson, like this case, early payment was tied to the success of the operation. No mention was made in Abramson that the debt was contingent. Furthermore, the fact that the obligation may not become due for several years in the future is of no significance to the allocation of a pro rata share of the taxpayers' debt in the tax year in question.

REVERSED AND REMANDED

Chapter 7

Guaranteed Payments and Other Nondistribution Transactions between Partners and the Partnership

---

Partners and partnerships often engage in transactions with each other. A partner, for example, may receive payments for the services the partner provides. Additionally, a partner may sell or lease property to the partnership. The tax consequences of such transactions differ depending upon the classification of the transaction. This chapter discusses issues relating to these partner–partnership transactions.

A. Guaranteed Payments

A partner is not considered an employee of the partnership. Thus, a partner does not receive a "salary" or "wages" from the partnership in return for services that the partner provides for the partnership. Rather, a payment to a partner for services provided is called a **guaranteed payment** if the payment is not contingent upon the profitability of the partnership.

Section 707. Transactions between partner and partnership

. . .

(c) Guaranteed payments. To the extent determined without regard to the income of the partnership, payments to a partner for services or the use of capital shall be considered as made to one who is not a member of the partnership, but only for the purposes of Section 61(a) (relating to gross income) and, subject to Section 263, for purposes of Section 162(a) (relating to trade or business expenses).

The reference to Section 61 means that a guaranteed payment is included in the gross income of the partner and the reference to Section 162 means that the guaranteed payment is deductible by the partnership (or perhaps capitalized if the services are of the nature required to be capitalized under Section 263). The partner does not directly increase or decrease the partner's outside basis when receiving a guaranteed payment. The partner's outside basis is reduced indirectly by the guaranteed payment, however, to the extent the guaranteed payment reduces the partnership's ordinary business income (or loss).

If a partnership pays a partner for the use of the partner's capital, this arrangement can also be classified as a guaranteed payment. This is similar to paying the partner interest on a loan and would generally be included in the partner's gross income and deductible to the partnership.

rzvmuR /Shutterstock.com

For a court case analyzing guaranteed payments, see *F. A. Falconer v. Commissioner*, 40 TC 1011 (1963). Excerpts of the *Falconer* case are included at the end of this chapter.

Guaranteed payments are just one type of transaction between a partner and the partnership. Another transaction between partner and partnership is a distribution from the partnership to the partner (discussed in Chapter 10). Other transactions can be arranged, such as a sale or lease of property from one to the other. We discuss these situations next.

B. Other Nondistribution Transactions between Partners and the Partnership

A partner may occasionally enter into a transaction with the partnership where the transaction is considered between unrelated parties.

Section 707. Transactions between partner and partnership

(a) Partner not acting in capacity as partner.—

(1) In general. If a partner engages in a transaction with a partnership other than in his capacity as a member of such partnership, the transaction shall, except as otherwise provided in this section, be considered as occurring between the partnership and one who is not a partner.

. . .

If a partner loans money to the partnership or if the partner leases property to the partnership it would be treated as if the transaction was between unrelated parties and the partner would have interest income (or rental income, as the case may be) and the partnership would have interest expense (or rent expense).

Example 7.1. R and J are the only members of RJ, LLC, which is treated as a partnership for federal income tax purposes. R and J agree to share profits and losses 60% to R and 40% to J. R owns a parcel of raw land that he leases to the partnership for $1,000 per month.

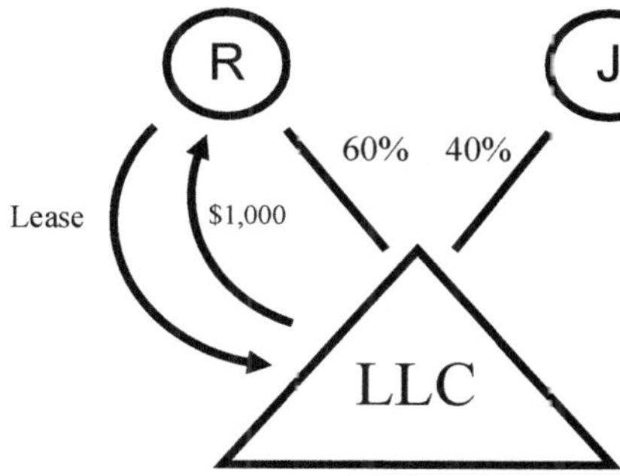

Source: Ryan H. Pace

What are the income tax consequences to R and the LLC?

Analysis:

In this situation the transaction would be considered as occurring between unrelated parties; thus, R has rental income of $1,000 and the LLC has rent expense of $1,000.

If a partner sells property to the partnership (or the partnership sells property to a partner) and realizes a loss, the loss may be disallowed.

Section 707. Transactions between partner and partnership

...

(b) Certain sales or exchanges of property with respect to controlled partnerships.—

(1) Losses disallowed. No deduction shall be allowed in respect of losses from sales or exchanges of property (other than an interest in the partnership), directly or indirectly, between—

(A) a partnership and a person owning, directly or indirectly, more than 50 percent of the capital interest, or the profits interest, in such partnership,...

Example 7.2. R and J are the only members of RJ, LLC, which is treated as a partnership for federal income tax purposes. R and J agree to share profits and losses 60% to R and 40% to J. R owns a parcel of land with a tax basis of $130 and fair market value of $100. R sells the land to the LLC for $100.

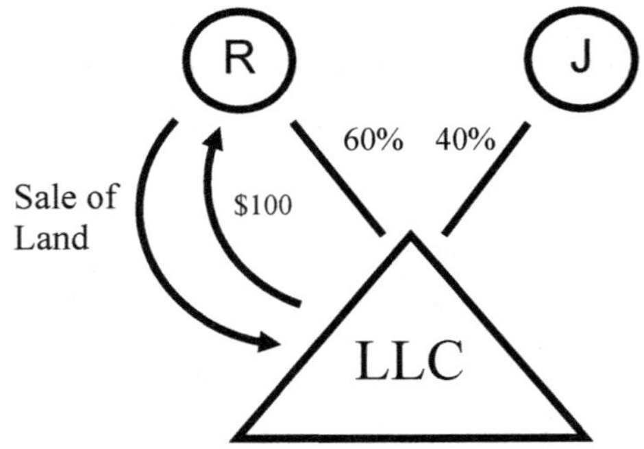

Source: Ryan H. Pace

What are the income tax consequences to R?

Analysis:

Although R realizes a $30 loss ($130 − $100), he does not recognize the loss. Section 707(b) disallows the loss because R owns more than 50% of the partnership.

Example 7.3. Assume the same facts as in Example 7.2 but the seller of the land is J. What are the income tax consequences to J?

Analysis:

Since Section 707(b) does not apply to J (because she owns less than 50% of the partnership), J recognizes a $30 loss.

Special rules also apply if a partner sells property to the partnership (or the partnership sells property to the partner) for a realized *gain*.

Section 707. Transactions between partner and partnership

...

(b) Certain sales or exchanges of property with respect to controlled partnerships.—

...

(2) Gains treated as ordinary income. In the case of a sale or exchange, directly or indirectly, of property, which in the hands of the transferee, is property other than a capital asset as defined in Section 1221—

(A) between a partnership and a person owning, directly or indirectly, more than 50 percent of the capital interest, or profits interest, in such partnership, or

(B) between two partnerships in which the same persons own, directly or indirectly, more than 50 percent of the capital interests or profits interests,

any gain recognized shall be considered ordinary income.

Example 7.4. R and J are the only members of RJ, LLC, which is treated as a partnership for federal income tax purposes. R and J agree to share profits and losses 60% to R and 40% to J. Assume that R owns an asset that is a capital asset in his hands and has a tax basis of $90 and fair market value of $100. R sells the asset to the LLC for $100. The LLC uses the asset as a Section 1231 asset.

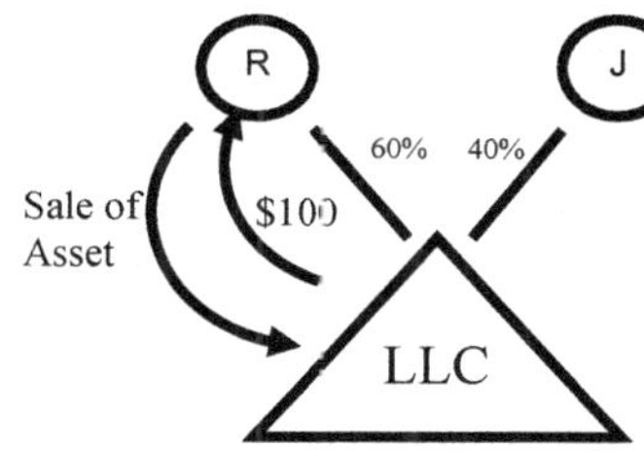

Source: Ryan H. Pace

What are the income tax consequences to R?

Analysis:

R realizes a $10 gain ($100 – $90). The character of the gain is ordinary, however, even though the asset is a capital asset in his hands. Since the LLC uses the asset in a manner other than as a capital asset, Section 707(b) requires the gain to be ordinary rather than capital.

What would be the income tax consequences to J if J were the seller instead of R?

Analysis:

J recognizes a *capital gain* of $10 because she owns less than 50% of the LLC.

CHAPTER 7 QUESTIONS FOR REVIEW

1. *Guaranteed payment.* Assume a client asks you, "What is a guaranteed payment?" Please explain what it is.

2. *Guaranteed payment.* Does a partner who receives a guaranteed payment reduce the partner's outside basis by the amount of the guaranteed payment?

3. *Guaranteed payment.* A, B, and C, all individuals, form ABC, LLC, which is treated as a partnership for federal income tax purposes. The members agree among themselves that A is entitled to a fixed annual payment of $10,000 for services without regard to the income of the LLC. They also agree that A's distributive share is 10%. After deducting the guaranteed payment, the LLC has $50,000 of ordinary business income. What are the income tax consequences to A?

4. *Guaranteed payment.* C and D, both individuals, form CD, LLC, which is treated as a partnership for federal income tax purposes. C and D agree between themselves that C is entitled to 30% of the LLC's net income, but in any event, C will not receive less than $10,000. The net income of the LLC is $60,000. Does C have a guaranteed payment in this situation? If so, how much?

5. *Guaranteed payment.* Assume the same facts as in Problem #4 except that the LLC's income is $20,000 instead of $60,000. Does C have a guaranteed payment in this situation? If so, how much?

6. *Transactions between partner and partnership.* R owns an 80% interest in the profits and capital of a partnership. R sells property to the partnership for $60,000. R's basis in the property at the time of the sale is $80,000. May R deduct the $20,000 loss? Explain your answer.

7. *Transactions between partner and partnership*. R owns an 80% interest in the profits and capital of a partnership. J owns the other 20%. R sells property to the partnership for $75,000. R's basis in the property at the time of the sale is $60,000. The property was a capital asset in R's hands, but the partnership will use the asset as a Section 1231 asset. What are the income tax consequences to R as a result of this sale? What if J was the partner who sold the property to the partnership instead of R?

F. A. Falconer v. Commissioner

United States Tax Court
40 TC 1011 (1963)

OPINION

DAWSON, *Judge*:

Respondent determined deficiencies in the petitioners' income taxes as follows:

Year	Deficiency
1957	$397.07
1958	$1,114.85

The issues for decision are:

(1) Whether amounts received by petitioner F. A. Falconer during the calendar years 1957 and 1958 from a partnership were guaranteed payments under the provisions of Section 707(c), I.R.C. 1954, and taxable income to petitioners under Section 61(a)(1).

(2) ...

(3) ...

All of the facts have been stipulated by the parties. The stipulation of facts and exhibits attached thereto are incorporated in this opinion by reference.

Petitioners are husband and wife residing in Dallas, Tex., who filed joint individual income tax returns for the years 1957 and 1958 on the calendar year basis and on the cash basis of accounting. Their 1957 income tax return was filed with the district director of internal revenue at Little Rock, Ark., and their 1958 income tax return was filed with the district director of internal revenue at Dallas, Tex.

On or about September 1, 1957, F. A. Falconer (hereinafter referred to as petitioner) entered into a partnership agreement with Stella Breazeale (sometimes hereinafter referred to as petitioner's partner) to operate an employment agency, doing business under the name of Acme Employment Service (sometimes referred to herein as the partnership. The partnership agreement, dated November 5, 1957, provided in pertinent part, as follows:

5

Each partner agrees to give all of his or her time to the business and exert his or her best efforts to the furtherance of the interests of the partnership to the end that maximum results can be obtained for their mutual benefit.

6

As compensation for services to be rendered by the partners, each is to be paid as a salary the sum of $150.00 per week, such salaries to be paid on such date of the week as may be mutually agreed. The amount of compensation for each partner so agreed to is subject to change only by the mutual agreement of the partners. The salaries so paid insofar as the partners are concerned shall be considered as a part of the operating expense of the business.

7

It is recognized by the partners that Breazeale has advanced certain sums of money to the partnership and may advance additional sums before the business has attained a sufficient volume of business and attained successful operation so as to pay the operating costs and expenses. It is agreed when the income of the business is sufficient to meet the cost of operations, any and all excess of such income shall be paid monthly to Breazeale until she has been repaid in full all of such advances.

The ownership of the partnership business shall be on the basis of 50% by Falconer and 50% by Breazeale, and after all advances referred to in the preceding paragraph have been paid to Breazeale, the share of the net profits shall be paid to Falconer as to 50% and paid to Breazeale as to 50%; the division of the net profits and the payment of the same to the respective partners shall be at such time or times as the partners may from time to time mutually agree. In the event of losses accruing to the partnership, each partner shall contribute his or her 50% portion of such loss or losses so that each partner shall bear his or her just portion of such loss and thus avoid the necessity of either partner having to suffer the entire loss. Neither partner shall draw from the business more than his or her respective portion of the net profits without the written consent of the other.

. . .

The partnership continued in business until May 12, 1958, at which time it was dissolved and was succeeded by a corporation organized under the laws of the State of Texas. ...

A partnership income tax return of petitioner and Stella Breazeale, doing business as the Acme Employment Service, was initially filed for the partnership for the period commencing September 1, 1957, and ending April 30, 1958, with the district director of internal revenue at Dallas, Tex. This return shows income in the amount of $6,434.80, operating expenses totaling $13,436.62, and a net loss of $7,001.82. It is labeled "First and Final Return."

After filing the first partnership income tax return, an unsigned partnership income tax return of petitioner and Stella Breazeale, doing business as the Acme Employment Service, for the period commencing January 1, 1958, and ending December 31, 1958, was filed with the district director of internal revenue at Dallas, Tex. A loss of $7,292.62 was shown on the return. By letter dated July 10, 1959, addressed to petitioner and Stella Breazeale, the district director advised them that the partnership income tax return had not been executed and requested them to execute a declaration which should have been signed on the return. The declaration was not executed and returned to the district director.

Subsequent to the filing of both of these partnership income tax returns, still another unsigned partnership return of petitioner and Stella Breazeale, doing business as the Acme Employment Service, covering the period commencing September 1, 1957, and ending June 30, 1958, was filed with the district director of internal revenue at Dallas, Tex. A loss of $7,292.62 was shown on this return. Attached thereto is a schedule designated "Withdrawals Made by F. A. Falconer." Such unexecuted return is identical with the return described in the preceding paragraph except that the period in the former return was interlined and another period substituted therefor. Such partnership income tax return has likewise not been executed.

During the calendar year 1957 the petitioner received weekly payments from the partnership under the terms of the partnership agreement aggregating $2,550, which sum was not reported by petitioners as income on their individual income tax return for such year or any other year.

During the period commencing September 1, 1957, and ending June 30, 1958, the petitioner received weekly payments aggregating $6,450, no part of which was reported by petitioners as income on their individual income tax return for the calendar year 1957, the calendar year 1958, or any other year.

Of such sum of $6,450, petitioner received income from the partnership under the terms of the partnership agreement in the amount of $2,850 from January 1, 1958, through May 10, 1958. From May 17, 1958, through June 28, 1958, petitioner received $1,050 from the corporation as salary, totaling $3,900 during the calendar year 1958, none of which was reported by petitioner in their income tax return for such year. The schedule attached to the last mentioned partnership return reflects the amounts paid by the partnership and the successor corporation and the dates such payments were made.

Petitioner made no contributions to the capital of the partnership. Stella Breazeale contributed all the capital of $19,775. Petitioner executed on May 12,

1958, which was the date the partnership dissolved, a demand promissory note, payable to the order of Stella Breazeale, in the principal sum of 49,862.50.

During the calendar year 1958 the petitioners claimed on their individual income tax return a loss of $3,646.31 from the operation of such partnership.

In his statutory notice of deficiency dated February 28, 1962, the respondent gave the following explanations for his adjustments:

1957

(a) It is determined that the weekly payments aggregating $2,550.00, which you received from the partnership Acme Employment Service in 1957, and which were not reported on your return, constituted taxable income under the internal revenue laws. Adjusted gross income is being increased accordingly.

1958

(a) It is determined that the weekly payments, aggregating $6,450.00, which you received from the partnership, Acme Employment Service and/or its successors, during the period September 1, 1957, through June 30, 1958, which were not reported on your returns, were taxable income to you for the calendar year 1958 under internal revenue laws. Accordingly, your 1958 income is being increased by $6,450.00

(b) It is determined that, under the internal revenue laws you are not entitled to a deduction for any part of the loss of $3,646.31 alleged to have been incurred from the operation of the partnership, Acme Employment Service, in the years 1957 and 1958.

ISSUE 1. GUARANTEED PAYMENTS

It is the petitioner's contention that the payments, totaling $5,400, which he received from the partnership in 1957 and 1958 were loaned to him by his partner, Stella Breazeale, and, therefore, created a debt to her, as evidenced by the demand promissory note executed on the date the partnership was dissolved. Respondent, on the other hand, argues that the amounts received constitute guaranteed salary payments under the provisions of Section 707(c). We agree with the respondent.

Section 707(c) has no counterpart in the Internal Revenue Code of 1939. It initially appeared in the Internal Revenue Code of 1954. Since we have been unable to locate in our research any court decisions pertaining directly to the issue here presented, we approach the problem as one of first impression. [Citation omitted.] The legislative history of Section 707(c) reveals that it was specifically intended to require ordinary income treatment to the partner receiving guaranteed salary payments and to give a deduction at the partnership level.

The touchstone for determining "guaranteed payments" is whether they are payable without regard to partnership income. And, in determining whether in a particular case an amount paid by a partnership to a partner is a "drawing" or a "guaranteed payment," the substance of the transaction, rather than its form, must govern. [Citation omitted.] These are both factual matters to be judged from all the circumstances.

We are convinced that the facts of this case clearly place the payments made to petitioner within the ambit of the term "guaranteed payments" as used in Section 707(c). Paragraph 6 of the partnership agreement provided that each partner was to receive a salary of $150 per week from the partnership as compensation for services rendered; that the amount of the *compensation* agreed to was subject to change only by mutual agreement of the partners; and that such *salaries* were to be considered a part of the operating expenses of the business. ... There is no doubt in our minds that these weekly salary payments were made "without regard to the income of the partnership." The partnership was being operated at a loss and, consequently, it was necessary to make the guaranteed salary payments out of the capital Stella Breazeale had contributed. Petitioner's mere characterization of the payments in the partnership returns as "withdrawals" is not persuasive when viewed in connection with the precise provisions of the partnership agreement. This lead us inescapably to the conclusion that the amounts received by petitioner from the partnership under the terms of the agreement are guaranteed payments without regard to the income of the partnership and, as such, are includable in his gross income.

Under the provisions of Section 706(a) such payments are characterized as ordinary income to the recipient for his taxable year within or with which ends the partnership taxable year in which the partnership deducted the payments. Hence, the taxable year of the partnership must be first determined.

In view of these rules and the facts herein, this partnership could only adopt a calendar year basis. Since the petitioner reported his income on a calendar year basis during 1957 and 1958, and was a principal partner by virtue of owning a 50-percent interest in the partnership, the partnership was precluded from adopting a fiscal year basis without the prior approval of the Secretary of the Treasury or his delegate. The record not only fails to reveal such approval, but there is no evidence that such approval was ever sought. Thus, the only recourse remaining to the partnership was the adoption of a calendar year which under the specific language of Section 1.706-1(b)(1)(ii), Income Tax Regs., does not require the prior approval of the Commissioner. [Citation omitted.] It then follows that the payments, totaling $2,550, made to petitioner during the partnership's taxable year ending December 31, 1957, were includable in his taxable income for the calendar year 1957. Since the partnership's existence terminated upon its dissolution on May 12, 1958, the partnership taxable year was closed on that date. As a result thereof the guaranteed payments of $2,850 made by the partnership during the taxable year beginning January 1, 1958, and ending May 12, 1958, were includable in petitioner's taxable income for the calendar year 1958.

Petitioner stresses that the "withdrawals by F. A. Falconer, constituted a loan to him and not income." We find no merit in this position. His attempt to cast the relationship between himself and Stella Breazeale as that of debtor and creditor is wholly inconsistent with the express terms of the partnership agreement and contrary to all outward manifestations of their intent. Nor are we swayed by the fact that the petitioner executed a demand note for $9,862.50 to Stella Breazeale on the day the partnership was terminated. We do not even know for what purpose the note was given. The petitioner, who has the burden of proof, offered no evidence regarding it. Consequently, any conclusions we might try to draw with respect to the note and the purpose for it would be purely speculative. Even if we assume, as petitioner would have us do, that the note represented the "withdrawals" by the petitioner from the partnership and "his part of the expenses" paid from the capital account, it cannot serve to convert what was paid as salaries into something else. Certainly the character of such payments cannot be changed retroactively into a loan.

....

[The Tax Court ruled in favor of the respondent.]

Chapter 8

Allocations Attributable to Built-in Gain or Loss Property

Generally, the partners agree between or among themselves how to share profits and losses from the partnership. This is usually reflected in a written partnership agreement. In some situations, the Code may override the partnership agreement. One example of such a situation is when property contributed by a partner with a pre-contribution gain or loss is later sold by the partnership.

In this chapter we will discuss the general rule applicable to profit/loss allocation and then the special rule relating to the treatment of the sale of pre-contribution gain or loss property by the partnership.

A. General Rule Relating to Allocation of Profits and Losses

Partners are wise to fashion a partnership agreement (or LLC operating agreement) to set forth details regarding partnership management, distributions, admission of new partners, etc. Of course, each partner's respective profit and loss sharing percentage is also a critical ingredient to the partnership agreement. As a general rule, the IRS respects the allocation of profits and losses agreed upon by the partners in the partnership agreement.

Section 704. Partner's distributive share

(a) Effect of partnership agreement. A partner's distributive share of income, gain, loss, deduction, or credit shall, except as otherwise provided in this chapter, be determined by the partnership agreement.

...

Section 704 overrides the partners' agreed-upon allocations in some instances, however.

Section 704. Partner's distributive share

. . .

(b) Determination of distributive share. A partner's distributive share of income, gain, loss deduction, or credit (or item thereof) shall be determined in accordance with the partner's interest in the partnership (determined by taking into account all facts and circumstances), if—

(1) the partnership agreement does not provide as to the partner's distributive share of income, gain, loss, deduction, or credit (or item thereof), or

(2) the allocation to a partner under the agreement of income, gain, loss, deduction, or credit (or item thereof) does not have substantial economic effect.

. . .

Notice that allocations will be made in accordance with a "partner's interest in the partnership" if:

- the partnership agreement does not provide for an allocation, or
- the allocation in the partnership agreement does not have "substantial economic effect."

We will discuss "substantial economic effect" in Chapter 9.

B. Regulatory Allocations Applicable to Pre-contribution Gain or Loss

You may recall from Chapter 2 that a partner does not recognize gain on the transfer of property to the partnership in return for a partnership interest,[1] and the partnership's tax basis (i.e., "inside basis") in the property contributed by the partner is the same as the partner's tax basis in the property at the time of contribution[2] unless the partnership is an "investment company"[3] or the property is encumbered by a liability.[4]

If property contributed by a partner has a **"pre-contribution" gain** or **"pre-contribution" loss** (also called "built-in" gain or "built-in" loss) and is later sold by the partnership, special rules apply as to how to allocate the gain or loss.

---

[1] Code Sec. 721.

[2] Code Sec. 723.

[3] See Chapter 2 for a discussion on investment companies.

[4] See Chapter 5 for a discussion on the impact of partnership liabilities on a partner's outside basis.

Section 704. Partner's distributive share

. . .

(c) Contributed property.—

(1) In general. Under regulations prescribed by the Secretary—

(A) income, gain, loss, and deduction with respect to property contributed to the partnership by a partner shall be shared among the partners so as to take account of the variation between the basis of the property to the partnership and its fair market value at the time of contribution,...

By requiring gain or loss to first be allocated to the partner who contributed the property with built-in gain or loss, the Code is trying to prevent the shifting of tax consequences relating to the property.

Treas. Reg. § 1.704-3. Contributed property

(a) In general.—

(1) General principles. The purpose of Section 704(c) is to prevent the shifting of tax consequences among partners with respect to precontribution gain or loss.

. . .

This provision overrides the partnership agreement with respect to the normal agreed-upon allocation of profits and losses among the partners. The Treasury Regulations provide three different ways in which allocations can be made to satisfy the requirements of Section 704(c): (1) the traditional method; (2) the traditional method with curative allocations; and (3) the remedial method. We will discuss these methods here.

1. Traditional method

Although the regulations are not an easy read when it comes to Section 704(c) methods of allocation, we will try to narrow it down to the fundamentals. Here is an excerpt from the Treasury Regulations explaining the **traditional method** of making Section 704(c) allocations.

Treas. Reg. § 1.704-3. Contributed property

...

(b) Traditional method.—

(1) In general. This paragraph (b) describes the traditional method of making Section 704(c) allocations. In general, the traditional method requires that when the partnership has income, gain, loss, or deduction attributable to Section 704(c) property, it must make appropriate allocations to the partners to avoid shifting the tax consequences of the built-in gain or loss. Under this rule, if the partnership sells Section 704(c) property and recognizes gain or loss, built-in gain or loss on the property is allocated to the contributing partner. ... However, the total income, gain, loss, or deduction allocated to the partners for a taxable year with respect to a property cannot exceed the total partnership income, gain, loss, or deduction with respect to that property for the taxable year (the ceiling rule)....

Code Section 704(c) requires that upon subsequent sale by the partnership of the contributed property, the gain or loss should first be allocated to the contributing partner up to the extent of the built-in gain or loss. Any gain or loss in excess of the built-in gain or loss can then be allocated to the partners in accordance with their gain or loss sharing ratios, as the case may be.

If the gain on the sale of the contributed property is less than the built-in gain, then all the gain is allocated to the contributing partner (this is called the **"ceiling rule"**). If the loss on the sale of the contributed property is less than the built-in loss, then all the loss is allocated to the contributing partner. Thus, under the traditional method, the noncontributing partners do not participate in the sharing of gains or losses realized on the partnership's sale of property that has a pre-contribution gain or loss unless the gain or loss exceeds the built-in gain or loss. This can be unfair to the noncontributing partners because they could, in fact, experience an economic loss as reflected in their capital accounts, but not be allocated any part of the tax loss.

2. Traditional method with curative allocations

To address distortions that can arise because of the ceiling rule in the traditional method, the Treasury Regulations allow for **"curative allocations"** to be made.

Treas. Reg. § 1.704-3. Contributed property

. . .

(c) Traditional method with curative allocations.

(1) In general. To correct distortions created by the ceiling rule, a partnership using the traditional method under paragraph (b) of this section may make reasonable curative allocations to reduce or eliminate disparities between book and tax items of noncontributing partners. A curative allocation is an allocation of income, gain, loss, or deduction for tax purposes that differs from the partnership's allocation of the corresponding book item. For example, if a noncontributing partner is allocated less tax depreciation than book depreciation with respect to an item of Section 704(c) property, the partnership may make a curative allocation to that partner of tax depreciation from another item of partnership property to make up the difference, notwithstanding that the corresponding book depreciation is allocated to the contributing partner. A partnership may limit its curative allocations to allocations of one or more particular tax items (e.g., only depreciation from a specific property or properties) even if the allocation of those available items does not offset fully the effect of the ceiling rule.

. . .

3. Remedial method

We mentioned that the traditional method may cause some distortions because of the ceiling rule (e.g., the noncontributing partners may not be allocated a tax loss even though they suffered an economic loss). The remedial method remedies that.

Treas. Reg. § 1.704-3. Contributed property

. . .

(d) Remedial allocation method.

(1) In general. A partnership may adopt the remedial allocation method described in this paragraph to eliminate distortions caused by the ceiling rule. A partnership adopting the remedial allocation method eliminates those distortions by creating remedial items and allocating those items to its partners. Under the

> remedial allocation method, the partnership first determines the amount of book items … and the partners' distributive shares of these items …. The partnership then allocates the corresponding tax items recognized by the partnership, if any, using the traditional method …. If the ceiling rule … causes the book allocation of an item to a noncontributing partner to differ from the tax allocation of the same item to the noncontributing partner, the partnership creates a remedial item of income, gain, loss, or deduction equal to the full amount of the difference and allocates it to the noncontributing partner. The partnership simultaneously creates an offsetting remedial item in an identical amount and allocates it to the contributing partner.
>
> …

Notice that the remedial method of Section 704(c) allocations allows the partnership to allocate "notional" items of tax gain or loss to the noncontributing partners to be equal to their book gain or loss. This means that an offsetting allocation of gain or loss is made to the contributing partner so that there is no net effect to the partnership.

This chapter has discussed how a partnership handles built-in gains and losses when the contributed property is later sold by the partnership. Similar concepts apply to a partnership's *depreciating* (as opposed to selling) pre-contribution gain or loss property (i.e., tax depreciation deductions will not equal book depreciation deductions if there is a built-in gain or loss).

C. Example

M contributes cash of $100 in return for a 50% interest in MN, LLC. N contributes land with a basis of $70 and a fair market value of $100 at the time of the contribution. N receives a 50% interest in the LLC in return. Suppose that sometime later the LLC sells the land to an unrelated third party for $100.

Source: Ryan H. Pace

How is the gain on the sale of land allocated between the partners?

Analysis:

The LLC recognizes a $30 gain on the sale ($100 – $70), which passes through entirely to N because of the pre-contribution gain of $30 that existed at the time N contributed the property.

Suppose the same facts except that the LLC sells the land for $120 instead of $100.

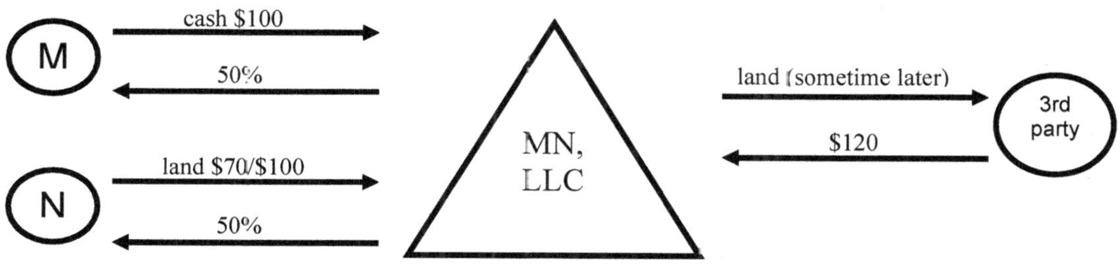

Source: Ryan H. Pace

How is the gain on the sale of the land allocated between the partners?

Analysis:

The LLC recognizes a gain of $50 ($120 – $70). The first $30 of the gain passes through solely to N and the remaining $20 of the gain is split $10 to each member according to their profit sharing ratios. Thus, N recognizes a $40 gain and M recognizes a $10 gain.

Suppose the same facts except that the LLC sells the land for $80 instead of $100.

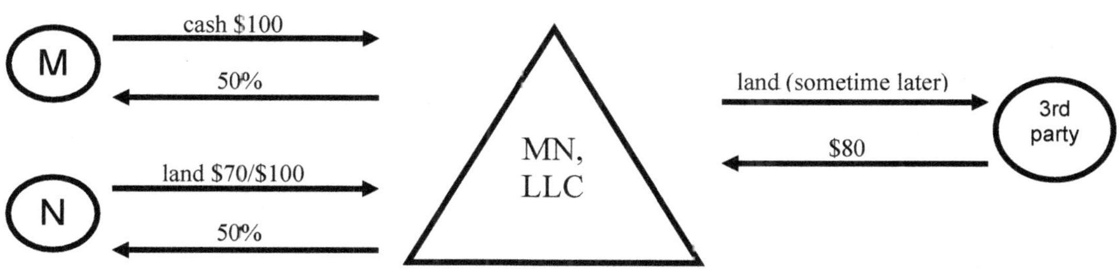

Source: Ryan H. Pace

How is the gain on the sale of the land allocated between the partners?

Analysis:

The partnership recognizes a tax gain of $10, but a book loss of $20. Under the *traditional method*, the entire $10 gain is allocated to N since N was the partner that contributed the property with the pre-contribution gain. This may be viewed as unfair to M because in reality M suffered a $10 economic loss (i.e., the property went down in value by $20 after N contributed it and M's share of that loss is 50%). Under the *remedial method*, M would be allocated a tax loss of $10 to equal his book loss. This would require an offsetting $10 gain to be allocated to N, thus causing N to recognize a $20 gain instead of a $10 gain. If the LLC used the *traditional method with curative allocations*, the LLC would find a loss on another asset (assuming it has such a loss on the sale of another asset) and allocate the loss in such a manner so as to give M a $10 tax loss to equal his $10 book loss on the sale of the land.

CHAPTER 8 QUESTIONS FOR REVIEW

1. *Pre-contribution gain/loss.* R and J form a limited liability company, which is treated as a partnership for federal income tax purposes. R contributes $100 cash in return for a 50% interest in the LLC. J contributes property (a capital asset to J) with a basis of $60 and fair market value of $100 in return for a 50% interest in the LLC. J has held the property for five years at the time of the contribution. What does the LLC's balance sheet look like on the date of formation (from both a tax basis standpoint and a book standpoint)?

   Now assume that during the year nothing happens except that the LLC sells the property contributed by J for $100.

   a. How much gain (or loss) is recognized by the LLC for book purposes?

   b. How much gain (or loss) is recognized by the LLC for tax purposes?
   c. How much book gain (or loss) is allocated to each member?
   d. How much of the tax gain (or loss) should be allocated to each member?

   Now assume that the LLC sells the property for $130 instead of $100.

   e. How much gain (or loss) is recognized by the LLC for book purposes?
   f. How much gain (or loss) is recognized by the LLC for tax purposes?
   g. How much book gain (or loss) is allocated to each member?
   h. How much of the tax gain (or loss) is allocated to each member?

   Now assume that the LLC sells the property for $70 instead of $100.

   i. How much gain (or loss) is recognized by the LLC for book purposes?
   j. How much gain (or loss) is recognized by the LLC for tax purposes?
   k. How much book gain (or loss) is allocated to each member?
   l. How much of the tax gain (or loss) is allocated to each member if the LLC adopts the traditional method of making Section 704(c) allocations?

m. How much of the tax gain (or loss) is allocated to each member if the LLC adopts the remedial method of making Section 704(c) allocations?

2. *Section 704(c) allocations.* What is the purpose of Section 704(c)?

Chapter 9

Special Allocations, Substantial Economic Effect, and Nonrecourse Deductions

---

This chapter discusses the limitation on the partners' ability to allocate items of income, loss, gain, etc., in a manner that does not have "substantial economic effect."

A. General Rule Relating to Allocation of Profits and Losses

As a general rule, the IRS respects the allocation of profits and losses made among the partners in the partnership agreement.

> **Section 704. Partner's distributive share**
>
> **(a) Effect of partnership agreement**. A partner's distributive share of income, gain, loss, deduction, or credit shall, except as otherwise provided in this chapter, be determined by the partnership agreement.
>
> . . .

Section 704 limits the partners' flexibility in allocating profits and losses in some instances.

> **Section 704. Partner's distributive share**
>
> . . .
>
> **(b) Determination of distributive share**. A partner's distributive share of income, gain, loss, deduction, or credit (or item thereof) shall be determined in accordance with the partner's interest in the partnership (determined by taking into account all facts and circumstances), if—

(1) the partnership agreement does not provide as to the partner's distributive share of income, gain, loss, deduction, or credit (or item thereof), or

(2) the allocation to a partner under the agreement of income, gain, loss, deduction, or credit (or item thereof) does not have substantial economic effect.

. . .

Notice that allocations will be made in accordance with the "partner's interest in the partnership" if:

- the partnership agreement does not provide for an allocation, or
- the allocation in the partnership agreement does not have "substantial economic effect."

B. Substantial Economic Effect

Special allocations of income, expense, gain, loss, etc., among the partners must have substantial economic effect for the allocation to be respected by the IRS. The substantial economic effect test is comprised of two separate tests: (1) the *economic effect* test and (2) the *substantiality* test.

1. Economic effect test

A partnership meets the economic effect prong of the substantial economic effect requirement by meeting any one of three tests: (1) the general test; (2) the alternate test; and (3) economic effect equivalence test.

a. Economic effect: the general test

The Treasury Regulations provide how a partnership can meet the general test for economic effect.

Treas. Reg. § 1.704-1. Partner's distributive share

. . .

(b) Determination of partner's distributive share.

. . .

(2) Substantial economic effect.

(i) Two-part analysis. The determination of whether an allocation of income, gain, loss, or deduction (or item thereof) to a partner has substantial economic effect involves a two-part analysis that is made as of the end of the partnership taxable year to which the allocation relates. First, the allocation must have economic effect .... Second, the economic effect of the allocation must be substantial ... .

(ii) Economic effect.

(a) Fundamental principles. In order for an allocation to have economic effect, it must be consistent with the underlying economic arrangement of the partners. This means that in the event there is an economic benefit or economic burden that corresponds to an allocation, the partner to whom the allocation is made must receive such economic benefit or bear such economic burden.

(b) Three requirements. Based on the principles contained in paragraph (b)(2)(ii)(a) of this section, and except as otherwise provided in this paragraph, an allocation of income, gain, loss, or deduction (or item thereof) to a partner will have economic effect if, and only if, throughout the full term of the partnership, the partnership agreement provides—

(1) For the determination and maintenance of the partners' capital accounts in accordance with the rules of paragraph (b)(2)(iv) of this section.

(2) Upon liquidation of the partnership (or any partner's interest in the partnership), liquidating distributions are required in all cases to be made in accordance with the positive capital account balances of the partners, as determined after taking into account all capital account adjustments for the partnership taxable year during which such liquidation occurs ..., and

(3) If such partner has a deficit balance in his capital account following the liquidation of his interest in the partnership, as determined after taking into account all capital account adjustments for the partnership taxable year during which such liquidation occurs ..., he is unconditionally obligated to restore the amount of such deficit balance to the partnership by the end of such taxable year ..., which amount shall, upon liquidation of the partnership, be paid to creditors of the partnership or distributed to other partners in accordance with their positive capital account balances ... .

In summary, a partnership allocation has economic effect under the general test if:

- The partnership agreement provides for the maintenance of the partners' capital accounts in accordance with the regulations;

- Upon liquidation of the partnership, the liquidating distributions are made in accordance with the positive capital account balances of the partners; and
- If a partner has a deficit balance in his capital account following the liquidation, he is unconditionally obligated to restore the amount of the deficit balance to the partnership.

The first two elements of the general test are usually not problematic. The third test, however, is not ideal. After all, if the business is organized as an LLC, isn't a primary purpose of operating via an LLC to provide protection to the members from the debts of the LLC? Why would a member of an LLC agree to restore a deficit capital account? Because of this third requirement of the general test for economic effect, many partnerships adopt the alternate test for economic effect.

b. Economic effect: the alternate test

The alternate test for meeting the economic effect requirement adopts the first two elements of the general test (relating to maintenance of capital accounts and liquidating according to capital account balances), but provides for an alternate third element:

Treas. Reg. § 1.704-1. Partner's distributive share

. . .

(b)(2)(ii)(d) Alternate test for economic effect. If—

(1) Requirements (1) and (2) of paragraph (b)(2)(ii)(b) of this section are satisfied, and

(2) The partner to whom an allocation is made is not obligated to restore the deficit balance in his capital account to the partnership ..., or is obligated to restore only a limited dollar amount of such deficit balance, and

(3) The partnership agreement contains a "qualified income offset," such allocation will be considered to have economic effect under this paragraph ... to the extent such allocation does not cause or increase a deficit balance in such partner's capital account ... as of the end of the partnership taxable year to which such allocation relates.

. . .

The partnership agreement contains a "qualified income offset" if, and only if, it provides that a partner who unexpectedly receives an adjustment, allocation, or distribution ..., will be allocated items of income and gain ... in an amount and manner sufficient to eliminate such deficit balance as quickly as possible.

...

Notice that if the partnership agreement provides for a **qualified income offset** (QIO), then the partnership agreement does not need a provision that obligates a partner to restore a negative capital account balance upon the liquidation of the partnership. Rather, according to a QIO provision, items of income are allocated to the partner with a negative capital account as quickly as possible until the capital account is brought back to zero.

c. Economic effect: economic effect equivalence

A third test available to meet the economic effect requirement is the "economic effect equivalence" test.

Treas. Reg. § 1.704-1. Partner's distributive share

...

(b)(2)(ii)(i) Economic effect equivalence. Allocations made to a partner that do not otherwise have economic effect under this paragraph (b)(2)(ii) shall nevertheless be deemed to have economic effect, provided that as of the end of each partnership taxable year a liquidation of the partnership at the end of such year or at the end of any future year would produce the same economic results to the partners as would occur if requirements ... of this section had been satisfied ... .

Thus, even though the partnership agreement may not specifically comply with the general test or alternate test, allocations to partners may still be respected if the end result is the same as if the partnership agreement did meet either one of those two tests.

2. Substantiality test

Even if an allocation to a partner has economic effect, the allocation must still be **substantial.**

Treas. Reg. § 1.704-1. Partner's distributive share

. . .

(b)(2)(iii) Substantiality.

(a) General rules. Except as otherwise provided in this paragraph (b)(2)(iii), the economic effect of an allocation (or allocations) is substantial if there is a reasonable possibility that the allocation (or allocations) will affect substantially the dollar amounts to be received by the partners from the partnership, independent of tax consequences. Notwithstanding the preceding sentence, the economic effect of an allocation (or allocations) is not substantial if, at the time the allocation becomes part of the partnership agreement, (1) the after-tax economic consequences of at least one partner may, in present value terms, be enhanced compared to such consequences if the allocation (or allocations) were not contained in the partnership agreement, and (2) there is a strong likelihood that the after-tax economic consequences of no partner will, in present value terms, be substantially diminished compared to such consequences if the allocation (or allocations) were not contained in the partnership agreement. ...

A partnership allocation fails the substantiality prong of the substantial economic effect requirement if the allocations (1) have shifting tax consequences or (2) are transitory allocations.

a. Shifting tax consequences

An allocation is not substantial if the allocation has **shifting tax consequences.** The Treasury Regulations provide guidance in this area.

Treas. Reg. § 1.704-1. Partner's distributive share

. . .

(b)(2)(iii)(b) Shifting tax consequences. The economic effect of an allocation (or allocations) in a partnership taxable year is not substantial if, at the time the allocation (or allocations) becomes part of the partnership agreement, there is a strong likelihood that—

(1) The net increases and decreases that will be recorded in the partners' respective capital accounts for such taxable year will not differ substantially from the net increases and decreases that would be recorded in such partners' respective capital accounts for such year if the allocations were not contained in the partnership agreement, and

(2) The total tax liability of the partners (for their respective taxable years in which the allocations will be taken into account) will be less than if the allocations were not contained in the partnership agreement (taking into account tax consequences that result from the interaction of the allocation (or allocations) with partner tax attributes that are unrelated to the partnership).

. . .

If a partnership allocates all long-term capital gains to one partner and an equal amount of ordinary income to another partner, could that decrease the total tax paid by the two partners without affecting their capital accounts compared to a situation where the items had been allocated equally to each partner instead? The answer is "yes" depending upon the tax rates involved. Thus, if partners' total tax liability is decreased, but the partners' capital accounts are not substantially affected, then the allocation is likely not substantial and the IRS will not respect the allocation. Rather, the IRS will allocate the items in accordance with each partner's interest in the partnership.

b. Transitory allocations

Allocations are not substantial if they are **transitory allocations.** The Treasury Regulations provide guidance in this area.

Treas. Reg. § 1.704-1. Partner's distributive share

(b)(2)(iii)(c) Transitory allocations. If a partnership agreement provides for the possibility that one or more allocations (the "original allocation(s)") will be largely offset by one or more other allocations (the "offsetting allocation(s)"), and, at the time the allocations become part of the partnership agreement, there is a strong likelihood that—

(1) The net increases and decreases that will be recorded in the partners' respective capital accounts for the taxable years to which the allocations relate will not differ substantially from the net increases and decreases that would be recorded in such partners' respective capital accounts for such years if the original allocation(s) and offsetting allocation(s) were not contained in the partnership agreement, and

(2) The total tax liability of the partners (for their respective taxable years in which the allocations will be taken into account) will be less than if the allocations were not contained in the partnership agreement (taking into account tax consequences that result from the interaction of the allocation (or allocations)

with partner tax attributes that are unrelated to the partnership) the economic effect of the original allocation(s) and offsetting allocations(s) will not be substantial. ...

Transitory allocations are similar to shifting tax consequences, but transitory allocations occur over multiple years rather than in just one tax year. Thus, for example, what if in Year 1, a partner (assume the partner is a corporation) has an expiring capital loss carryover so the partnership allocates that partner all capital gains (presumably, this would lower the tax liability of the partner because the partner could offset the capital losses that would otherwise expire). In Year 2, the partnership allocates the other partner all capital gains to make up for the fact that the partner received no allocation of capital gains in Year 1. This could constitute transitory allocations if the overall tax liability of the partners is reduced and, over time, the capital accounts of the partners are not substantially different than they would have been without the special allocations.

In summary, the "substantiality" prong of the substantial economic effect requirement attempts to prevent manipulation of the *timing* of the allocations among the partners or the *character* of the allocations in order to reduce the overall tax liability of the partners without substantially affecting the partners economically.

rzvmuR /Shutterstock.com

For a court case related to the concept of substantial economic effect, see *Orrisch v. Commissioner*, 55 TC 395 (1970). Excerpts of the *Orrisch* case are included at the end of this chapter.

C. Evolution of "Targeted" Allocations

Notwithstanding the regulatory requirements applicable to the economic effect test, drafters of partnership agreements have developed a different way to represent the partners' agreement. Rather than requiring partners' capital accounts to be adjusted strictly in accordance with the regulations, the partnership agreement states that the partners will receive an amount of cash upon liquidation that represents the economic deal negotiated between the partners. This basically forces allocations to be made among the partners consistent with the distributions each partner is entitled to in order to "hit" the contemplated economic target. For example, a targeted allocation provision might provide as follows:

> Upon liquidation of the partnership, cash available for distribution shall be distributed in the following manner: first, to Partner M equal to the aggregate capital contributions M has made to the partnership; second, to N equal to the

aggregate capital contributions N has made to the partnership; finally, to M and N in an equal amount.

Notice that the liquidation provision is not based upon the positive capital accounts of the partners (as is required in the general and alternate test for economic effect). Rather, there is a distribution "waterfall" that goes to the partners in a particular order in accordance with their economic agreement. The IRS has yet to issue guidance specifically with respect to targeted allocations. Consequently, taxpayers and tax advisors would need to be able to argue that such allocations are consistent with the "partners' interest in the partnership" to be recognized by the IRS.

D. Nonrecourse Deductions

The overall concept of substantial economic effect is that items of income, gain, loss, deduction, etc., allocated to the partners for income tax purposes follow the economics of their agreement. For example, a deduction allocated to a partner for income tax purposes should also decrease the partner's capital account so that upon liquidation of the partnership, the partner receives less.

You may also recall our discussion in Chapter 5 relating to determining a partner's share of a partnership's nonrecourse liabilities. Remember that the partners' shares of nonrecourse liabilities are determined according to a partner's share of (1) the partnership's minimum gain; (2) the partner's share of 704(c)-type gain; and (3) the partner's share of the partnership's excess nonrecourse liabilities. We now address some unique issues related to deductions attributable to nonrecourse liabilities (e.g., depreciation deductions on a building that was acquired through nonrecourse financing).

The Treasury Regulations point out that since no partner bears the economic risk of loss with respect to a nonrecourse liability, deductions generated from nonrecourse liabilities cannot have economic effect. In other words, no partner is economically at risk to have to repay the liability, but the partner may still benefit from tax deductions generated by property acquired by the liability. Thus, special rules are needed to deal with these types of deductions, which are called **nonrecourse deductions**.

Treas. Reg. § 1.704-2. Allocations attributable to nonrecourse liabilities

...

(b) General principles and definitions.

(1) Definition of and allocations of nonrecourse deductions. Allocations of losses, deductions, or Section 705(a)(2)(B) expenditures attributable to

partnership nonrecourse liabilities ("nonrecourse deductions") cannot have economic effect because the creditor alone bears any economic burden that corresponds to those allocations. Thus, nonrecourse deductions must be allocated in accordance with the partners' interest in the partnership. Paragraph (e) of this section provides a test that deems allocations of nonrecourse deductions to be in accordance with the partners' interests in the partnership. If that test is not satisfied, the partners' distributive shares of nonrecourse deductions are determined under §1.704-1(b)(3), according to the partners' overall economic interests in the partnership. ...

(2) Definition of and allocations pursuant to a minimum gain chargeback. To the extent a nonrecourse liability exceeds the adjusted tax basis of the partnership property it encumbers, a disposition of that property will generate gain that at least equals that excess ("partnership minimum gain"). An increase in partnership minimum gain is created by a decrease in the adjusted tax basis of property encumbered by a nonrecourse liability below the amount of that liability and by a partnership nonrecourse borrowing that exceeds the adjusted tax basis of the property encumbered by the borrowing. Partnership minimum gain decreases as reductions occur in the amount by which the nonrecourse liability exceeds the adjusted tax basis of the property encumbered by the liability. Allocations of gain attributable to a decrease in partnership minimum gain (a "minimum gain chargeback," as required under paragraph (f) of this section) cannot have economic effect because the gain merely offsets nonrecourse deductions previously claimed by the partnership. Thus, to avoid impairing the economic effect of other allocations, allocations pursuant to a minimum gain chargeback must be made to the partners that either were allocated nonrecourse deductions or received distributions of proceeds attributable to a nonrecourse borrowing. Paragraph (e) of this section provides a test that, if met, deems allocations of partnership income pursuant to a minimum gain chargeback to be in accordance with the partners' interests in the partnership. If property encumbered by a nonrecourse liability is reflected on the partnership's books at a value that differs from its adjusted tax basis, paragraph (d)(3) of this section provides that minimum gain is determined with reference to the property's book basis. ...

Notice the opportunity here to misunderstand the definition of partnership minimum gain. Although the regulation starts out stating that partnership minimum gain is the extent to which the nonrecourse liability exceeds the *tax basis* of the property that is encumbered by the liability, later in the regulation, however, it states that if the tax basis and book value of a property are different, then partnership minimum gain is the extent to which the nonrecourse liability exceeds the *book value* of the property that is encumbered by the liability. Thus, the safest approach is just to think of partnership minimum gain as the extent to which the liability exceeds book value of the property that the liability encumbers. This point is reinforced by the following regulation provision.

Treas. Reg. § 1.704-2. Allocations attributable to nonrecourse liabilities

...

(d) Partnership minimum gain.—

...

(3) Partnership minimum gain if there is a book/tax disparity. If partnership property subject to one or more nonrecourse liabilities is ... reflected on the partnership's books at a value that differs from its adjusted tax basis, the determinations under this section are made with reference to the property's book value. ...

If partnership minimum gain exists in the partnership, then each partner has a "share" of that minimum gain. To the extent a partner is allocated deductions attributable to his or her share of partnership minimum gain, then when partnership minimum gain *decreases*, the partner must be allocated items of income to the extent of his or her share of the decrease. Partnership minimum gain may decrease, for example, when the partnership pays down some of the nonrecourse liability or when there is a permitted revaluation of the book value of the property encumbered by the nonrecourse liability.

Treas. Reg. § 1.704-2. Allocations attributable to nonrecourse liabilities

...

(e) Requirements to be satisfied. Allocations of nonrecourse deductions are deemed to be in accordance with the partners' interests in the partnership only if—

(1) Throughout the full term of the partnership requirements (1) and (2) of §1.704-1(b)(2)(ii)(b) are satisfied (i.e., capital accounts are maintained in accordance with §1.704-1(b)(2)(iv) and liquidating distributions are required to be made in accordance with positive capital account balances), and requirement (3) of either §1.704-1(b)(2)(ii)(b) or §1.704-1(b)(2)(ii)(d) is satisfied (i.e., partners with deficit capital accounts have an unconditional deficit restoration obligation or agree to a qualified income offset);

(2) Beginning in the first taxable year of the partnership in which there are nonrecourse deductions and thereafter throughout the full term of the partnership, the partnership agreement provides for allocations of nonrecourse deductions in a manner that is reasonably consistent with allocations that have substantial economic effect of some other significant partnership item attributable to the property securing the nonrecourse liabilities;

(3) Beginning in the first taxable year of the partnership that it has nonrecourse deductions or makes a distribution of proceeds of a nonrecourse liability that are allocable to an increase in partnership minimum gain, and thereafter throughout the full term of the partnership, the partnership agreement contains a provision that complies with the minimum gain chargeback requirement of paragraph (f) of this section; … .

(f) Minimum gain chargeback requirement.

(1) In general. If there is a net decrease in partnership minimum gain for a partnership taxable year, the minimum gain chargeback requirement applies and each partner must be allocated items of partnership income and gain for that year equal to that partner's share of the net decrease in partnership minimum gain …

CHAPTER 9 QUESTIONS FOR REVIEW

1. *Substantial economic effect.* For an allocation to be respected by the IRS, it must have substantial economic effect. Explain what this means.

2. *Economic effect.* For an allocation to have economic effect, it must meet at least one of the three tests for economic effect. What are they?

3. *Economic effect.* Under the general test for economic effect, what three requirements must be met? Why is the third test often viewed as problematic for partners?

4. *Economic effect.* How does the alternate test for economic effect differ from the general test?

5. *Economic effect.* What does a QIO provision cause the partnership to do?

6. *Economic effect.* R and J form an LLC by contributing $50,000 each. They agree to share all profits and losses equally except that R will be allocated 100% of the depreciation deductions. During Year 1, the LLC had $100,000 of ordinary income (exclusive of depreciation deductions) and $40,000 in depreciation deductions. Thus, R is allocated $50,000 of ordinary income (one-half of the $100,000) and $40,000 in depreciation deductions. J is allocated the other $50,000 of ordinary income. The operating agreement states that capital accounts will be maintained according to the regulations, distributions upon liquidation will be made in accordance with their overall profit sharing ratios (i.e., 50%/50%), and the partners have an unconditional obligation to restore their respective deficit capital accounts, if any. Does this agreement have economic effect? Why or why not?

7. *Substantiality.* What are the two specific ways mentioned in the regulations that would cause an allocation to not be "substantial?"

8. *Substantiality*. R and J form a partnership by contributing $50,000 each. Assume that R has a net capital loss carryover resulting from an activity unrelated to the partnership. Assume further that the partnership agreement states that "all items of income, loss, deduction, etc., shall be allocated equally to R and J except that if either partner has a net capital loss carryover, the partnership will allocate 100% of all capital gains to that partner up to the amount of that partner's capital loss carryover. Is the allocation of the capital gains 'substantial?'" Why or why not?

9. *Orrisch v. Commissioner*. Summarize the facts in the *Orrisch v. Commissioner* case. Discuss the issues, analysis, and holding of the case.

10. *Partnership minimum gain*. What is partnership minimum gain?

11. *Nonrecourse deductions*. What are nonrecourse deductions?

12. *Minimum gain chargeback*. What is a minimum gain chargeback?

Orrisch v. Commissioner

United States Tax Court
55 TC 395 (1970)

Featherston, *Judge*:

Respondent determined deficiencies in petitioners' income tax for 1966 and 1967 in the respective amounts of $2,814.19 and $3,018.11. The only issue for decision is whether an amendment to a partnership agreement allocating to petitioners the entire amount of depreciation deduction allowable on two buildings owned by the partnership was made for the principal purpose of avoidance of tax within the meaning of Section 704(b). [Footnotes omitted throughout.]

FINDINGS OF FACT

Stanley C. Orrisch (hereinafter sometimes referred to as Orrisch) and Gerta E. Orrisch were husband and wife until a judgment of divorce was entered by the Superior Court of San Mateo County, Calif., on May 22, 1969. They filed joint Federal income tax returns for 1966 and 1967 with the district director of internal revenue, San Francisco, Calif. At the time they filed their petition, they were legal residents of Burlingame, Calif.

In May of 1963, Domonick J. and Elaine J. Crisafi (hereinafter the Crisafis) and petitioners formed a partnership to purchase and operate two apartment houses, one located at 1255 Taylor Street, San Francisco, and the other at 600 Ansel Road, Burlingame, Calif. The cost of the Taylor Street property was $229,011.08, and of the Ansel Road property was $155,974.90. The purchase of each property was financed principally by a secured loan. Petitioners and the Crisafis initially contributed to the partnership cash in the amounts of $26,500 and $12,500, respectively. During 1964 and 1965 petitioners and the Crisafis each contributed additional cash in the amounts of $8,800. Under the partnership agreement, which was not in writing, they agreed to share equally the profits and losses from the venture.

During each of the years 1963, 1964, and 1965, the partnership suffered losses, attributable in part to the acceleration of depreciation—the deduction was computed on the basis of 150 percent of straight-line depreciation. ...

Petitioners and the Crisafis respectively reported in their individual income tax returns for these years the partnership losses allocated to them.

Petitioners enjoyed substantial amounts of income from several sources, the principal one being a nautical equipment sales and repair business. ...

Early in 1966, petitioners and the Crisafis orally agreed that, for 1966 and subsequent years, the entire amount of the partnership's depreciation deductions would be specially allocated to petitioners, and that the gain or loss from the partnership's business, computed without regard to any deduction for depreciation, would be divided equally. They further agreed that, in the event the partnership property was sold at a gain, the specially allocated depreciation would be "charged back" to petitioner's capital account and petitioners would pay the tax on the gain attributable thereto.

. . .

The partnership returns for these years [1966 and 1967] show that, taking into account the special arrangement as to depreciation, losses, in the amounts of $18,904 and $16,870.76 were allocated to petitioners for 1966 and 1967, respectively, and petitioners claimed these amounts as deductions in their joint income tax returns for those years. ...

. . .

In May of 1968, before petitioners Stanley C. Orrisch and Greta E. Orrisch were divorced, they entered into a marital property settlement agreement which, as part of paragraph 8, contained the following:

(c) The parties recognize that each of said parcels of real property is encumbered by loans and requires certain maintenance, upkeep and repair and certain other expenses for the operation thereof. The parties further understand that at the present time neither of said parcels of real property produces sufficient cash flow to meet loan payments and the other expenses above referred to. For this reason, husband agrees that from the date of this agreement forward, so long as they shall own or hold either or both of said parcels of real property, he (as between the parties hereto) shall be responsible for providing from time to time any money required to meet said loan payments or expenses. Husband further agrees to hold wife free and harmless of and from any losses or claims in connection with either or both of said parcels of real property. Upon the sale or disposition of either or both of said parcels of real property, the parties hereto will equally divide the profits or proceeds of such sale or disposition, provided that from such profits or proceeds husband shall be first reimbursed for such moneys as he may have advanced for the parties' joint benefit for either or both of said parcels of real property as hereinabove provided.

(d) In consideration of the foregoing, wife agrees that she will not deduct on her Federal and State income tax returns any depreciation allowable by reason of the ownership of the said 2 parcels of real property. Wife makes no representation or warranty as to the propriety of husband's taking on his income tax returns the depreciation that would be otherwise allowable to her. Husband is informed and advised that this would be proper by reason of the burdens of the ownership assumed by him under this paragraph. Upon the sale or other disposition of either or both of said parcels of real property, each party hereto shall be responsible for reporting on his or her respective income tax returns one-half of the capital gain or loss, if any, realized from such sale or disposition.

By an agreement dated May 12, 1969, the foregoing provisions were modified as follows:

(c) The parties recognize that each of said parcels of rea property is encumbered by loans and requires certain maintenance, upkeep and repair and certain other expenses for the operation thereof. The parties further understand that at the present time neither of said parcels of real property produces sufficient cash flow to meet loan payments and the other expenses above referred to. Commencing with the calendar year 1969, the parties hereto shall contribute equally to their collective share of the money required to meet said loan payments or expenses. Except as otherwise provided herein, the parties shall each report on their federal and state income tax returns one-half of their collective share of the income and one-half of their collective share of the deductions, including (but not limited to) depreciation, arising from or related to said property. Upon the sale or other disposition of either or both of said parcels of real property, each party shall be responsible for reporting on his or her respective income tax returns his or her share of the gain or loss, if any, realized from such sale or disposition, and for purposes of computing the same, all depreciation taken by Husband with respect to said property in the calendar year 1968 shall only reduce the basis of Husband in said property and not the basis of Wife.

In the notice of deficiency, respondent determined that the special allocation of the depreciation deduction provided by the amendment to the partnership agreement "was made with the principal purpose of avoidance of income taxes" and should, therefore, be disregarded. Partnership losses for 1966 and 1967, adjusted to reflect a correction of the amount of depreciation allowable, were allocated equally between the partners.

ULTIMATE FINDING OF FACT

The principal purpose of the special allocation to petitioners of all of the deductions for depreciation taken by the Orrisch-Crisafi partnership for 1966 and 1967 was the avoidance of income tax.

OPINION

The only issue presented for decision is whether tax effect can be given the agreement between petitioners and the Crisafis that, beginning with 1966, all the partnership's depreciation deductions were to be allocated to petitioners for their use in computing their individual income tax liabilities. In our view, the answer must be in the negative, and the amounts of each of the partners' deductions for the depreciation of partnership property must be determined in accordance with the ratio used generally in computing their distributive shares of the partnership's profits and losses.

Among the important innovations of the 1954 Code are limited provisions for flexibility in arrangements for the sharing of income, losses, and deductions arising from business activities conducted through partnerships. The authority for special allocations of such items appears in Section 704(a), which provides that a partner's share of any item of income, gain, loss deduction, or credit shall be determined by the partnership agreement. That rule is coupled with a limitation in Section 704(b), however, which states that a special allocation of an item will be disregarded if its "principal purpose" is the avoidance or evasion of Federal income tax. [Citation omitted.] In case a special allocation is disregarded, the partner's share of the item is to be determined in accordance with the ratio by which the partners divide the general profits or losses of the partnership. [Citation omitted.]

The report of the Senate Committee on Finance accompanying the bill finally enacted as the 1954 Code ... explained the tax-avoidance restriction prescribed by Section 704(b) as follows:

Subsection (b)

***

Provides that if the principal purpose of any provision in the partnership agreement dealing with a partner's distributive share of a particular item is to avoid or evade the Federal income tax, the partner's distributive share of that item shall be redetermined in accordance with his distributive share of partnership income or loss described in Section 702(a)(9) [i.e., the ratio used by the partners for dividing general profits or losses].

***

Where, however, a provision in a partnership agreement for a special allocation of certain items has substantial economic effect and is not merely a device for reducing the taxes of certain partners without actually affecting their shares of partnership income, then such a provision will be recognized for tax purposes.

***

This reference to "substantial economic effect" did not appear in the House Ways and Means Committee report ... discussing Section 704(b), and was apparently added in the Senate Finance Committee to allay fears that special allocations of income or deductions would be denied effect in every case where the allocation resulted in a reduction in the income tax liabilities of one or more of the partners. The statement is an affirmation that special allocations are ordinarily to be recognized if they have business validity apart from their tax consequences. [Citation omitted.]

In resolving the question whether the principal purpose of a provision in a partnership agreement is the avoidance or evasion of Federal income tax, all the facts and circumstances in relation to the provision must be taken into account. Section 1.704-1(b)(2), Income Tax Regs., lists the following as relevant circumstances to be considered:

Whether the partnership or a partner individually has a business purpose for the allocation; whether the allocation has "substantial economic effect", that is, whether the allocation may actually affect the dollar amount of the partners' shares of the total partnership income or loss independently of tax consequences; whether related items of income, gain, loss, deduction, or credit from the same source are subject to the same allocation; whether the allocation was made without recognition of normal business factors and only after the amount of the specially allocated item could reasonably be estimated; the duration of the allocation; and the overall tax consequences of the allocation.

***

Applying these standards, we do not think the special allocation of depreciation in the present case can be given effect.

The evidence is persuasive that the special allocation of depreciation was adopted for a tax-avoidance rather than a business purpose. Depreciation was the only item which was adjusted by the parties; both the income from the buildings and the expenses incurred in their operation, maintenance, and repair were allocated to the partners equally. Since the deduction for depreciation does not vary from year to year with the fortunes of the business, the parties obviously knew what the tax effect of the special allocation would be at the time they adopted it. Furthermore, as shown by our Findings, petitioners had large amounts of income which would be offset by the additional deduction for depreciation; the Crisafis, in contrast, had no taxable income from which to subtract the partnership depreciation deductions, and, due to depreciation deductions which they were obtaining with respect to other housing projects, could expect to have no taxable income in the near future. On the other hand, the insulation of the Crisafis from at least part of the potential capital gains tax was an obvious tax advantage. The inference is unmistakably clear that the agreement did not reflect normal business considerations but was designed primarily to minimize the overall tax liabilities of the partners.

Petitioners urge that the special allocation of the depreciation deduction was adopted in order to equalize the capital accounts of the partners, correcting a disparity ($14,000) in the amounts initially contributed to the partnership by them ($26,500) and the Crisafis ($12,500). But the evidence does not support this contention. Under the special allocation agreement, petitioners were to be entitled, in computing their individual income tax liabilities, to deduct the full amount of the depreciation realized on the partnership property. For 1966, as an example, petitioners were allocated a sum ($18,904) equal to the depreciation on the partnership property ($18,412) plus one-half of the net loss computed without regard to depreciation ($492). The other one-half of the net loss was, of course, allocated to the Crisafis. Petitioners' allocation ($18,904) was then applied to reduce their capital account. The depreciation specially allocated to petitioners ($18,412) in 1966 alone exceeded the amount of the disparity in the contributions. Indeed, at the end of 1967, petitioners' capital account showed a deficit of $25,187.11 compared with a positive balance of $405.65 in the Crisafis' account. By the time the partnership's properties are fully depreciated, the amount of the reduction in petitioners' capital account will approximate the remaining basis for the buildings as of the end of 1967. The Crisafis' capital account will be adjusted only for contributions, withdrawals, gain or loss, without regard to depreciation, and similar adjustments for these factors will also be made in petitioners' capital account. Thus, rather than correcting an imbalance in the capital accounts of the partners, the special allocation of depreciation will create a vastly greater imbalance than existed at the end of 1966. In the light of these facts, we find it incredible that equalization of the capital accounts was the objective of the special allocation.

Petitioners rely primarily on the argument that the allocation has "substantial economic effect" in that it is reflected in the capital accounts of the partners. Referring to the material quoted above from the report of the Senate Committee on finance, they contend that this alone is sufficient to show that the special allocation served a business rather than a tax-avoidance purpose.

According to the regulations, an allocation has economic effect if it "may actually affect the dollar amount of the partners' shares of the total partnership income or loss independently of tax consequences." The agreement in this case provided not only for the allocation of depreciation to petitioners but also for gain on the sale of the partnership property to be "charged back" to them. The charge back would cause the gain, for tax purposes, to be allocated on the books entirely to petitioners to the extent of the special allocation of depreciation, and their capital account would be correspondingly increased. The remainder of the gain, if any, would be shared equally by the partners. If the gain on the sale were to equal or exceed the depreciation specially allocated to petitioners, the increase in their capital account caused by the charge back would exactly equal the depreciation deductions previously allowed to them and the proceeds of the sale of the property would be divided equally. In such circumstances, the only effect of the allocation would be a trade of tax consequences, i.e., the Crisafis would relinquish a current depreciation deduction in exchange for exoneration from all or part of the capital gains tax when the property is sold, and petitioners would enjoy a larger current depreciation deduction but would assume a larger ultimate capital gains tax liability. Quite clearly, if the property is sold at a gain, the special allocation will affect only the tax liabilities of the partners and will have no other economic effect.

To find any economic effect of the special allocation agreement aside from its tax consequences, we must, therefore, look to see who is to bear the economic burden of the depreciation if the buildings should be sold for a sum less than their original cost. There is not one syllable of evidence bearing directly on this crucial point. We have noted, however, that when the buildings are fully depreciated, petitioners' capital account will have a deficit, or there will be a disparity in the capital accounts, approximately equal to the undepreciated basis of the buildings as of the beginning of 1966. Under normal accounting procedures, if the building were sold at a gain less than the amount of such disparity petitioners would either be required to contribute to the partnership a sum equal to the remaining deficit in their capital account after the gain on the sale had been added back or would be entitled to receive a proportionately smaller share of the partnership assets on liquidation. Based on the record as a whole, we do not think the partners ever agreed to such an arrangement. On dissolution, we think the partners contemplated an equal division of the partnership assets which would be adjusted only for disparities in cash contributions or withdrawals. Certainly there is no evidence to show otherwise. That being true, the special allocation does not "actually affect the dollar amount of the partners' share of the total partnership income or loss independently of tax consequences" within the meaning of the regulation referred to above.

Our interpretation of the partnership agreement is supported by an analysis of a somewhat similar agreement, quoted in material part in our Findings, which petitioners made as part of a marital property settlement agreement in 1968. Under this agreement, Orrisch was entitled to deduct all the depreciation for 1968 in computing his income tax liability, and his wife was to deduct none; but on the sale of the property they were to first reimburse Orrisch for "such moneys as he may have advanced," and then divide the balance of the "profits or proceeds" of the sale equally, each party to report one-half of the capital gain or loss on his income tax return. In the 1969 amendment to this agreement the unequal allocation of the depreciation deduction was discontinued, and a provision similar to the partnership "charge back" was added, i.e., while the proceeds of the sale were to be divided equally, only Orrisch's basis was to be reduced by the depreciation allowed for 1968 so that he would pay taxes on a larger portion of the gain realized on the sale. Significantly, in both this agreement and the partnership agreement, as we interpret it, each party's share of the sales proceeds was determined independently from his share of the depreciation deduction.

In the light of all the evidence we have found as an ultimate fact that the "principal purpose" of the special allocation agreement was tax avoidance within the meaning of Section 704(b). Accordingly, the deduction for depreciation for 1966 and 1967 must be allocated between the parties in the same manner as other deductions.

Decision will be entered for the respondent.

Part III

Distributions from a Partnership to a Partner

Chapter 10

Nonliquidating and Liquidating Distributions

A. Nonliquidating Distributions
B. Liquidating Distributions
C. Death or Retirement of a Partner

A partnership often makes distributions of money and sometimes other property to the partners. The tax consequences of these distributions can differ depending upon whether the distributions are nonliquidating distributions or liquidating distributions. In this chapter we discuss nonliquidating (also called "current") distributions and liquidating distributions in general and in Chapter 13 we cover unique distribution issues.

A. Nonliquidating Distributions

Nonliquidating distributions are distributions where the partner continues to be a partner after the distribution is made. The partner often wonders to what extent a distribution is included in the partner's gross income. We provide that analysis here.

1. Reduction in partner's outside basis

Nonliquidating distributions occur when a partner receives a distribution of money and/or other property and the partner still continues to be a partner in the partnership after the distribution. A distribution to the partner decreases the partner's outside basis.

Section 733. Basis of distributee partner's interest

In case of a distribution by a partnership to a partner other than in liquidation of a partner's interest, the adjusted basis to such partner of his interest in the partnership shall be reduced (but not below zero) by—

(1) the amount of any money distributed to such partner, and

(2) the amount of the basis to such partner of distributed property other than money as determined under Section 732.

2. Gain or loss recognition

The Code allows for the distribution to a partner without the recognition of a gain or loss if the distribution meets certain requirements. The partner recognizes no gain unless the distribution of *money* is more than the adjusted basis of the partner's interest in the partnership before the distribution. A partner recognizes no loss on a nonliquidating distribution. The partnership recognizes no gain or loss on a nonliquidating distribution to a partner. Section 731 provides the law in this regard. (Note: There are some unique situations where gains and losses could be recognized if "disproportionate" distributions are made by the partnership. We will discuss that in Chapter 11. Distributions that are considered a part of a "disguised sale" transaction could also trigger gain or loss recognition. Disguised sales are also discussed in Chapter 11.)

Section 731. Extent of recognition of gain or loss on distribution

(a) Partners. In the case of a distribution by a partnership to a partner—

(1) gain shall not be recognized to such partner, except to the extent that any money distributed exceeds the adjusted basis of such partner's interest in the partnership immediately before the distribution,

(2) loss shall not be recognized... except... upon a distribution in liquidation of a partner's interest in a partnership.

(b) Partnership. No gain or loss shall be recognized to a partnership on a distribution to a partner of property, including money.

...

If money and other assets are distributed as part of the same distribution, the distribution must be analyzed in the following order: (a) money, (b) inventory and unrealized receivables, and then (c) all other assets. The partner's outside basis will first be reduced by cash, then the basis of the inventory and/or unrealized receivables, and, finally, the adjusted basis of all other assets.

3. Partner's tax basis in the property distributed

Generally, the tax basis to the partner of the property distributed by the partnership will be the property's adjusted basis to the partnership before the distribution. If the property has an adjusted basis greater than the outside basis of the partner receiving the distribution, however, then the partner's outside basis will be reduced to zero and the property will take on a tax basis equal to that of the partner's outside basis prior to the distribution.

Section 732. Basis of distributed property other than money

(a) Distributions other than in liquidation of a partner's interest.—

(1) General rule. The basis of property (other than money) distributed by a partnership to a partner other than in liquidation of the partner's interest shall, except as provided in paragraph (2), be its adjusted basis to the partnership immediately before such distribution.

(2) Limitation. The basis to the distributee partner of property to which paragraph (1) is applicable shall not exceed the adjusted basis of such partner's interest in the partnership reduced by any money distributed in the same transaction.

...

4. A partner's subsequent disposition of distributed property

If a distributee partner subsequently disposes of an asset received in a distribution by the partnership, the partner must determine the character of the gain or loss. Code Section 735 provides the law in this regard.

Section 735. Character of gain or loss on disposition of distributed property

(a) Sale or exchange of certain distributed property.—

(1) Unrealized receivables. Gain or loss on the disposition by a distributee partner of unrealized receivables (as defined in Section 751(c)) distributed by a partnership, shall be considered as ordinary income or as ordinary loss, as the case may be.

(2) Inventory items. Gain or loss on the sale or exchange by a distributee partner of inventory items (as defined in Section 751(d)) distributed by a partnership shall, if sold or exchanged within 5 years from the date of the distribution, be considered as ordinary income or as ordinary loss, as the case may be.

(b) Holding period for distributed property. In determining the period for which a partner has held property received in a distribution from a partnership (other than for purposes of subsection (a)(2)), there shall be included the holding period of the partnership, as determined under Section 1223, with respect to such property.

. . .

B. Liquidating Distributions

If a partner is no longer a partner after receiving a distribution, then that distribution is a **liquidating distribution**. We analyze the tax impact of those distributions here.

1. Reduction in partner's outside basis

Just as with nonliquidating distributions, a partner reduces the partner's outside basis by the amount of money received in the distribution plus the adjusted basis of any other property received. Unlike in a nonliquidating distribution, however, the partner's outside basis is, of necessity, equal to zero following a liquidating distribution.

2. Gain or loss recognition

Also similar to nonliquidating distributions, a partner recognizes no gain unless the money distributed is more than the adjusted basis of the partner's interest in the partnership before the distribution. A loss can be recognized on a liquidating distribution, however, when cash, inventory, or accounts receivable are the only assets distributed, and after the distribution, the partner still has an outside basis more than zero. If the distribution by the partnership includes any assets other than cash, unrealized receivables, or inventory, then the partner will not recognize a loss. The partnership does not recognize a gain or loss on a liquidating distribution to a partner.

Section 731. Extent of recognition of gain or loss on distribution

(a) Partners. In the case of a distribution by a partnership to a partner—

(1) gain shall not be recognized to such partner, except to the extent that any money distributed exceeds the adjusted basis of such partner's interest in the partnership immediately before the distribution,

(2) loss shall not be recognized to such partner, except that upon a distribution in liquidation of a partner's interest in a partnership where no property other than that described in subparagraph (A) or (B) is distributed to such partner, loss shall be recognized to the extent of the excess of the adjusted basis of such partner's interest in the partnership over the sum of—

(A) any money distributed, and

(B) the basis to the distributee, as determined under Section 732, of any unrealized receivables (as defined in Section 751(c)) and inventory (as defined in Section 751(d)).

Any gain or loss recognized under this subsection shall be considered as gain or loss from the sale or exchange of the partnership interest of the distributee partner.

(b) Partnerships. No gain or loss shall be recognized to a partnership on a distribution to a partner of property, including money.

. . .

3. Partner's tax basis in the property distributed

In addition to determining gain or loss, the partner must also determine the partner's tax basis in each of the assets distributed to the partner.

Section 732. Basis of distributed property other than money

(a) Distributions other than in liquidation of a partner's interest.—

(1) General rule. The basis of property (other than money) distributed by a partnership to a partner other than in liquidation of the partner's interest shall, except as provided in paragraph (2) be its adjusted basis to the partnership immediately before such distribution.

(2) Limitation. The basis to the distributee partner of property to which paragraph (1) is applicable shall not exceed the adjusted basis of such partner's interest in the partnership reduced by any money distributed in the same transaction.

(b) Distributions in liquidation. The basis of property (other than money) distributed by a partnership to a partner in liquidation of the partner's interest shall be an amount equal to the adjusted basis of such partner's interest in the partnership reduced by any money distributed in the same transaction.

(c) Allocation of basis.—

(1) In general. The basis of distributed properties to which subsection (a)(2) or (b) is applicable shall be allocated—

(A)

(i) first to any unrealized receivables (as defined in Section 751(c)) and inventory items (as defined in Section 751(d)) in an amount equal to the adjusted basis of each such property to the partnership, and

(ii) if the basis to be allocated is less than the sum of the adjusted bases of such properties to the partnership, then, to the extent any decrease is required in order to have the adjusted bases of such properties equal the basis to be allocated, in the manner provided in paragraph (3), and

(B) to the extent of any basis remaining after the allocation under subparagraph (A), to other distributed properties—

(i) first by assigning to each such other property such other property's adjusted basis to the partnership, and

(ii) then, to the extent any increase or decrease in basis is required in order to have the adjusted bases of such other distributed properties equal such remaining basis, in the manner provided in paragraph (2) or (3), whichever is appropriate.

(2) Methods of allocating increase.—Any increase required under paragraph (1)(B) shall be allocated among the properties—

(A) first to properties with unrealized appreciation in proportion to their respective amounts of unrealized appreciation before such increase (but only to the extent of each property's unrealized appreciation), and

(B) then, to the extent such increase is not allocated under subparagraph(A), in proportion to their respective fair market values.

(3) Method of allocating decrease. Any decrease required under paragraph (1)(A) or (1)(B) shall be allocated—

(A) first to properties with unrealized depreciation in proportion to their respective amounts of unrealized depreciation before such decrease (but only to the extent of each property's unrealized depreciation), and

(B) then, to the extent such decrease is not allocated under subparagraph (A), in proportion to their respective adjusted bases (as adjusted under subparagraph (A)).

...

In short, if the property has an adjusted basis *greater* than the outside basis of the partner receiving the distribution, then the partner's outside basis will be reduced to zero and the property will take on a basis equal to that of the partner's outside basis prior to the distribution. If the property being distributed (other than inventory and/or unrealized receivables) has a tax basis *less* than the outside basis of the partner receiving the distribution, then the partner's outside basis will be reduced to zero and the property will take on a tax basis equal to that of the partner's outside basis immediately before the distribution.

4. Impact of partnership liabilities on liquidating distributions

If a partnership has liabilities, a withdrawing partner must account for the resulting decrease in his or her share of the partnership's liabilities as if it were a distribution of money (see Section 752). This deemed distribution of money could cause the partner to recognize gain if the combination of money distributed and the decrease in the partner's share of partnership liabilities exceeds the partner's outside basis.

Section 752. Treatment of certain liabilities

(a) Increase in partner's liabilities. Any increase in a partner's share of the liabilities of a partnership, or any increase in a partner's individual liabilities by reason of the assumption by such partner of partnership liabilities, shall be considered as a contribution of money by such partner to the partnership.

(b) Decrease in partner's liabilities. Any decrease in a partner's share of the liabilities of a partnership, or any decrease in a partner's individual liabilities by reason of the assumption by the partnership of such individual liabilities, shall be considered as a distribution of money to the partner by the partnership.

(c) Liability to which property is subject. For purposes of this section, a liability to which property is subject shall, to the extent of the fair market value of such property, be considered as a liability of the owner of the property. ...

C. Death or Retirement of a Partner

Special issues come into play on the death or retirement of a partner. The character of payments to the partner (or the partner's estate in the case of a deceased partner) can be quite different depending upon the underlying reason for the payments. Section 736 addresses this issue.

Section 736. Payments to a retiring partner or a deceased partner's successor in interest

(a) Payments considered as distributive share or guaranteed payment. Payments made in liquidation of the interest of a retiring partner or a deceased partner shall, except as provided in subsection (b), be considered—

(1) as a distributive share to the recipient of partnership income if the amount thereof is determined with regard to the income of the partnership, or

(2) as a guaranteed payment described in Section 707(c) if the amount thereof is determined without regard to the income of the partnership.

(b) Payments for interest in partnership.—

(1) General rule. Payments made in liquidation of the interest of a retiring partner or a deceased partner shall, to the extent such payments (other than payments described in paragraph (2)) are determined, under regulations prescribed by the Secretary, to be made in exchange for the interest of such partner in partnership property, be considered as a distribution by the partnership and not as a distributive share or guaranteed payment under subsection (a).

(2) Special rules. For purposes of this subsection, payments in exchange for an interest in partnership property shall not include amounts paid for—

(A) unrealized receivables of the partnership, (as defined in Section 751(c)), or

(B) good will of the partnership, except to the extent that the partnership agreement provides for a payment with respect to good will.

(3) Limitation on application of paragraph (2). Paragraph (2) shall apply only if—

(A) capital is not a material income-producing factor for the partnership, and

(B) the retiring or deceased partner was a general partner in the partnership.

Notice that the payment to a deceased or retiring partner can be classified generally in one of three ways: (1) a payment representing the profits of the partnership; (2) a guaranteed payment; and (3) a payment for the partner's share of partnership assets.

As a general rule, payments are first considered as payments for the partner's share of partnership property. Payments in excess of this represent either the partner's share of the partnership's profits or a guaranteed payment. Of course, the distinction is important because if it is a guaranteed payment, the payment is ordinary income to the partner and deductible to the partnership. If it represents a payment of the partner's share of partnership profits, then the amount is not deductible to the partnership and would be a return of capital (reduction in outside basis) to the partner since the partner would recognize his or her share of the partnership profits into income.

Note that there are special rules to general partners that retire. If capital is not a material income-producing factor (in other words, the partnership is a service partnership), then payments to the partner representing the partnership's accounts receivable and goodwill will not be treated as Section 736(b) payments. Rather, the payments will be classified as guaranteed payments (if the payments are fixed) or the partner's share of the partnership's profits (if the payments are not fixed) under Section 736(a).

A "retiring" partner means that the partner is withdrawing from the partnership (not necessarily that the partner is going to retire permanently from all work because the partner is getting older). A partner technically remains a partner for income tax purposes (e.g., partner receives a Schedule K-1) as long as the partner is receiving a share of partnership profits even though the partner may have retired and is no longer involved in the partnership from a nontax standpoint.

CHAPTER 10 QUESTIONS FOR REVIEW

1. *Nonliquidating distributions*. R and J are equal members of an LLC, which is treated as a partnership for income tax purposes. R's outside basis is $50. J's outside basis is $10. The LLC distributes $30 cash to each member in a nonliquidating distribution.

   a. What is R's gain recognized?
   b. What is J's gain recognized?
   c. What is R's outside basis after the distribution?
   d. What is J's outside basis after the distribution?

2. *Nonliquidating distributions*. R and J are equal members of an LLC, which is treated as a partnership for income tax purposes. R's outside basis is $50. J's outside basis is $10. The LLC distributes property with a basis of $30 and FMV of $50 to each member in a nonliquidating distribution.

   a. What is R's gain recognized?
   b. What is J's gain recognized?
   c. What is R's basis in the property distributed?
   d. What is J's basis in the property distributed?
   e. What is R's outside basis after the distribution?
   f. What is J's outside basis after the distribution?

3. *Nonliquidating distributions*. R and J are equal members of an LLC, which is treated as a partnership for income tax purposes. R's outside basis is $50. J's outside basis is $10. The LLC distributes to both R and J in a nonliquidating distribution the following assets: $30 cash, inventory (basis $30, FMV $40) and land (basis $40, FMV $50).

   a. What is R's gain recognized?
   b. What is J's gain recognized?
   c. What is R's basis in the inventory and the land?
   d. What is J's basis in the inventory and the land?
   e. What is R's outside basis after the distribution?
   f. What is J's outside basis after the distribution?
   g. Suppose that after the distribution R uses the inventory as a capital asset in his hands. Then, four years later R sells the asset for $100. What are the income tax consequences to R upon the sale of the asset?

4. *Liquidating distributions*. J, R, and M are partners in a partnership. As part of a liquidating distribution, J's entire partnership interest is terminated by the following distribution: $100 cash, inventory (basis $100, FMV $125), and land (basis $275, FMV $300). The partnership has no liabilities.

   a. What is J's basis in each of the distributed assets if her outside basis immediately before the distribution is $800? Does J recognize any gain or loss?
   b. What is J's basis in each of the distributed assets if J receives only the cash and inventory and her basis immediately before the distribution is $800? Does J recognize any gain or loss?
   c. What is J's basis in each of the distributed assets if J receives all three assets and J's outside basis immediately before the distribution is $450? Does J recognize any gain or loss?
   d. What is J's basis in each of the distributed assets if J receives all three assets and J's outside basis immediately before the distribution is $300? Does J recognize any gain or loss?
   e. What is J's basis in the distributed property if J's outside basis immediately before the distribution is $50? Does J recognize any gain or loss?

5. *Payments to a retiring partner*. What are the three ways a payment from a partnership to a retiring partner can be classified?

6. *Payments to a retiring partner*. If payments to a retiring partner are not based upon the partner's share of partnership property and not on the profits of the partnership, how are the payments classified?

7. *Esler v. Commissioner*. Summarize the facts in the *Esler v. Commissioner* case. What was the issue? Summarize the court's analysis and conclusion.

Esler, et al., v. Commissioner

United States Tax Court
T.C. Memo 1988-417

MEMORANDUM FINDINGS OF FACT AND OPINION

FEATHERSON, *Judge*: Respondent determined the following deficiencies in petitioners' Federal income tax:

		Year	
Petitioners	1979	1980	1981
Michael J. Esler and Marcia E. Lorenzen, formerly Marcia E. Esler	$ -0-	$11,190	$1,349
Eric R. Haessler and Alice A Haessler	$1,838	$4,694	$1,933
Robert P. Johnson and Janice P. Johnson	$ -0-	$ -0-	$1,762
Roger G. Tilbury and Margaret M. Tilbury	$1,662	$6,630	$ -0-
Jack R. Platten and Estate of Carol E. Platten, Deceased, Jack R. Platten, Personal Representative	$1,092	$3,268	$ -0-
Jack R. Platten	$ -0-	$ -0-	$1,730

This issue for decision is whether certain payments received by petitioner Michael A. Esler during 1979, 1980 and 1981 on his withdrawal from a law firm constituted payments for his interest in partnership property, taxable to him as capital gain under Section 736(b), or "guaranteed payments" which constituted a liquidation of his interest in the partnership, taxable to him as ordinary income under Section 736(a)(2) and deductible by the firm in computing its ordinary income.

FINDINGS OF FACT

All petitioners in these consolidated proceedings were legal residents of Oregon when the petitions were filed.

For several years prior to 1976, Howard Stamer (Stamer) was "of counsel" and petitioner Eric R. Haessler (Haessler) was a partner in the law firm of Keane, Haessler, Harper, Perlman & Copeland in Portland, Oregon. Petitioner Michael J. Esler (Esler) was an associate in the firm. Haessler and Stamer decided to withdraw and form a firm of their own. At about the same time, Esler had also decided to withdraw. Stamer learned of Esler's plan to withdraw and approached him in regard to joining the new firm. Esler and Stamer worked out an arrangement for Esler to become a member of the new firm.

On or about February 1, 1976, Esler, Haessler, and Stamer entered into an oral agreement to form a partnership known as Haessler, Stamer, and Esler (Partnership I) to engage in the practice of law in Portland, Oregon. No written partnership agreement was prepared to govern any of the rights and obligations of the parties. Haessler's and Stamer's interests in the partnership were fixed at 42.5 percent each and Esler's interest at 15 percent.

On September 30, 1978, petitioner Roger Tilbury (Tilbury) and Jack Rosen (Rosen) entered Partnership I and the name of the firm was changed to Haessler, Stamer, Tilbury, and Esler (Partnership II). Drafts of a written partnership agreement were prepared for Partnership II but no written agreement was executed. Upon the formation of Partnership II, Esler's partnership interest increased from 15 to 19 percent and Haessler and Stamer's partnership interests decreased from 42.5 to 22 percent. Subsequently, petitioner Jack R. Platten (Platten), who started working for the firm in the latter part of 1976, became a partner in the firm. In February of 1977 Alan Schneider (Schneider) joined the firm as an associate.

In addition to practicing law, Haessler and Stamer during the life of Partnerships I and II engaged in entrepreneurial and business investment activities outside of the law practice. Haessler was involved with Northwest Hardwoods, Inc., Omega Securities, Inc., and Webster Ford. He was chairman of the board of Northwest Hardwoods, and he and his family members had been the largest shareholders of Northwest Hardwoods for years. Northwest Hardwoods was the largest hardwood lumber company in the United States. Haessler received compensation of $48,000 per annum from Northwest which he paid over to the alw[sic] firm. The firm also received fees from Webster Ford. Stamer was involved in such ventures as Downtown Athletic Club; Nancy Lee, Inc.; Love-it Ice Cream Company; and Agoil, Inc., among others. Haessler and Stamer's business relationships directly and indirectly produced a large part of the law firm's business.

Stamer developed Agoil, Inc., during 1977 and 1978, while Haessler, Esler, and Stamer were partners. Agoil was organized as an oil exploration operation in Victoria, Texas; it was expanded to include a conglomeration of corporations and a vehicle for the syndication of about 15 limited partnerships. On September 30, 1979, the approximate date of the settlement agreement between petitioner and the other partners, its book value was in excess of $600,000. The firm did not bill Agoil for the time Stamer spent developing Agoil but billed Agoil and other similar enterprises for the services performed by other attorneys in the firm.

In about November or December 1978, Esler decided that he wanted to withdraw from the Haessler, Stamer & Esler partnership. While both Esler and Haessler were in New York on business, they discussed Esler's withdrawal. Esler originally demanded $125,000 for his interest in the partnership. Haessler said that $75,000 was more reasonable. No settlement was reached at this meeting.

In March 1979 Esler submitted his notice of intent to withdraw from this partnership. Thereafter, Esler and other attorneys physically set up new offices. Esler transferred his client files and work in progress to the new offices. The partnership did not pay Esler any money upon withdrawal.

Effective May 15, 1979, the parties formally dissolved the law partnership. As of that date, Haessler, Stamer, Tilbury, Rosen and Platten (sometimes hereafter the Haessler group) continued the practice of law under the firm name of Haessler, Stamer & Tilbury in the offices of the former partnership. Esler joined with Alan L. Schneider, who previously had worked in the firm, in the practice of law under the firm name of Esler & Schneider at a different location.

The Haessler, Stamer, Tilbury and Esler law firm's balance sheet as of March 31, 1979, when Esler submitted his notice of withdrawal, shows the following:

Assets	
Cash Accounts	$11,601
Accounts Receivable	68,807
Advanced Costs	11,307
Office Equipment, Furniture, library and leasehold improvements less accumulated depreciation	49,559
Investments	9,100
Total Assets	$150,374
Liabilities	
Payroll taxes	$ 4,540
Notes payable	99,402
Investment contract liabilities	1,199
Total Liabilities	$105,141
Net Equity	
Total Assets Less Total Liabilities	$ 45,223

Notes to this balance sheet show that, as to accounts receivable, "Net amount is the gross amount less all receivables of clients with a balance that is greater than 90 days old" and that the item for investments "Does not include disputed claims to various Stamer & Haessler business ventures."

In June 1979 Esler filed a complaint against Haessler, Tilbury, Platten, Stamer, and Rosen in the Circuit Court of the State of Oregon for Multnomah County; in August 1979 Esler filed an amended complaint. Esler's amended complaint alleged, among other things, that Stamer and Haessler had converted certain property and assets of the partnership, and requested an accounting.

To resolve the lawsuit, a settlement agreement was entered on October 30, 1979. The agreement recites that it was made by and between Esler, Schneider, Haessler, Stamer, Tilbury, Rosen and Platten. It states that the parties "desire to resolve the dissolution of the partnership of Haessler, Stamer, Tilbury & Esler and other predecessor firms, to settle all claims between themselves with regard to the Firm and the predecessor firms and to compromise their differences." The agreement states that as of May 15, 1979, Haessler, Stamer, Tilbury, Rosen and Platten continued the practice of law under the firm name of Haessler, Stamer & Tilbury which is referred to in the agreement as the "Firm." The agreement provides:

1. DISTRIBUTION OF ASSETS

Firm shall pay to Esler the sum of $67,000 which shall be paid as follows: $10,000 shall be paid out of the first proceeds collected for the Firm pursuant to Exhibit A, attached hereto and incorporated herein by reference. The remaining $57,000 shall be paid in equal monthly installments without interest, the first installment of $2,777.72 to be due October 30, 1979, and a like installment of $2,777.78 on the fifteenth day of each month thereafter until such balance is paid in full.

The agreement authorizes the Firm to bill certain clients for services performed prior to May 15, 1979, and Esler to bill such clients for services performed after that date. Exhibit A, referred to in the above-quoted paragraph, set forth the manner in which the fees collected from those clients were to be divided. The Firm agreed to hold Esler harmless and indemnify and protect him from any and all notes, accounts payable and other obligations of the Firm.

The partnership returns of Haessler, Stamer and Tilbury for 1979, of Haessler, Tilbury and Platten for 1980 and Haessler, Platten and Johnson for 1981 show "guaranteed payments" to Esler as follows:

1979	$15,570
1980	33,333
1981	12,557

These payments were made in installments by checks drawn on the firm's account. The amounts of the payments were subtracted from the income shown on the returns in computing the ordinary income of the partnership. Neither the returns for 1979, 1980 and 1981 nor the returns for 1976, 1977 and 1978 contain any references to any business activity other than the practice of law.

Esler's individual income tax returns for 1979, 1980 and 1981 reported 96.69 percent of the foregoing payments received from the law firm as capital gain. His income tax return for 1981 contains the following explanation:

Installment Sales Computation

Sale of 19% interest in Haessler, Stamer & Tilbury partnership. Acquired 2/76 and sold 5/15/79.

Gross sales price	$67,000
Total cost/Adj. Basis	2,219
Adjusted cost	$64,781
Gross profit percentage 64,781 divided by 67,000	.9669

Taxable Year Ended	Total Payments	Ratio Profit	Taxable Portion
12/31/79	$ 5,333	.9669	$ 5,187
12/31/80	$42,262	.9669	$40,863
12/31/81	$12,556	.9669	$12,140

In the notice of deficiency issued to Esler, respondent determined that the payments made to him by the law firm were made in connection with a liquidation rather than a sale of a partnership interest and, therefore, the amount received is ordinary income rather than capital gain. To protect the revenue, the notices of deficiency issued to the other petitioners in these proceedings made the inconsistent determination that deductions by the law partnership for guaranteed payments to Esler were not allowable because the amounts of the payments were made in connection with a sale rather than a liquidation of his partnership interest.

OPINION

Esler and the Haessler group have taken inconsistent positions as to tax treatment of the $67,000 paid Esler following his withdrawal from the law firm. Esler now concedes that, upon his withdrawal from the firm, he did not sell his partnership interest as such within the meaning of Section 741. [Citation omitted.] He contends, however, that the $67,000 was paid in exchange for his interest in partnership property under Section 736(b) and was, therefore, taxable to him as long-term capital gain rather than ordinary income. The Haessler group maintains that the payments to Esler were guaranteed payments under Section 736(a)(2), and not payments under Section 736(b). They thus contend the partnership properly deducted the $67,000 as a business expense. As stakeholder, respondent argues only that Esler and the Haessler group should treat the liquidation payments consistently.

Section 736 and the regulations thereunder prescribe specific rules on the treatment of liquidation payments by a partnership to a withdrawing partner. In applying these rules, liquidation payments must be classified as either: (1) Section 736(b) payments or (2) Section 736(a) payments.

Section 736(b) payments generally are liquidation payments made by the partnership to purchase the withdrawing partner's interest in the partnership's property. Under Section 736(b)(2), however, Section 736(b) payments do not include amounts paid for the partnership's "unrealized receivables" or amounts paid for the partnership's goodwill in excess of its partnership basis, unless the partnership agreement provides for a reasonable payment for goodwill.... Because the oral partnership agreement in this case did not deal with goodwill, any payments attributable to goodwill on dissolution of the partnership would fall within Section 736(b)(2) and would not be Section 736(b) payments.

Section 736(b) payments are considered a distribution by the partnership. Thus, except to the extent the partnership had substantially appreciated inventory so that Section 751(b) is applicable, the withdrawing partner's gain or loss from the sale of his interest in partnership property is determined under Section 731.... Because any such gain or loss recognized under Section 731 is considered as a gain or loss from the sale or exchange of the withdrawing partner's partnership interest, it is a capital gain or a capital loss.... Correspondingly, no deduction is allowed to the partnership or the remaining partners for the Section 736(b) payments because such payments represent either a distribution or a purchase by the partnership of the withdrawing partner's capital interest....

Those liquidation payments which are not Section 736(b) payments are Section 736(a) payments. Section 736(a) payments are treated: (1) as a distributive share of partnership income where determined with regard to the partnership'[s income or (2) as "guaranteed payments," defined in Section 707(c) to include payments "determined without regard to the income of the partnership... to a partner for services or the use of capital." Section 736(a) payments which are considered a distributive share of partnership income are taken into account under Section 702 in the income of the withdrawing partner, thereby reducing the partnership income to be reported by the remaining partners. Section 736(a) payments which are guaranteed payments are deductible by the partnership as a business expense and are taxable as ordinary income to the withdrawing partner....

Esler contends that Haessler, Stamer, and he agreed that the partnership they created on February 1, 1976, would engage in two businesses, the practice of law and the development of business ventures. Haessler and Stamer were each to have 42.5-percent ownership interests and Esler was to have a 15-percent interest. Esler maintains that the $67,000 he received on withdrawing from the partnership was his compensation for his 15-percent interest in certain property and assets accumulated by the partnership, mainly for his interest in the stock of Agoil, which he describes in his brief as "a successful business venture developed primarily by Stamer while he was in partnersh p with Haessler and Petitioner [Esler].

The Haessler group maintains that the partnership covered only the practice of law. Stamer and, to a lesser extent, Haessler engaged in a variety of business activities which produced legal work for the firm but they argue that Esler had no capital interest in those businesses. Accordingly, they contend, none of the $67,000 constituted compensation to Esler for any business assets.

Although the oral testimony is conflicting, we think its most reasonable interpretation favors the Haessler group. As we view the evidence, Esler decided to withdraw from the firm because he felt that he performed a disproportionate part of the firm's income-producing legal work while Stamer and Haessler devoted much of their time to private business endeavors. The $67,000 payment was designed to compensate Esler for income, accounts receivable and work in progress retained by the firm and for the firm's goodwill or going concern value that Esler had help build through his past services.

Under the settlement agreement, $10,000 of the $67,000 was expressly related to the first amounts collected "for the Firm" on specifically described accounts receivable. In fact, the record shows that Esler received direct payments of $7,958.92 and $2,041.08, a total of $10,000, from named clients; this $10,000 was taxable to him as his "distributive share" of partnership income.... Also included in the $67,000 was a Keogh account adjustment; the firm failed to make a timely $7,000 contribution to the plan and, as part of the settlement, included this amount in the installment payments. The installment payments made to discharge the $57,000 over and above the named accounts receivable were, in our view, "guaranteed payments" determined without regard to the income of the partnership within the meaning of Section 736(a)(2).

A number of circumstances, as well as the testimony of Haessler, Platten and Tilbury, support our factual conclusions with respect to the $57,000 the firm paid Esler in installments. The settlement agreement states that the parties, who included Haessler, Stamer, Tilbury, Platten, Esler, and Esler's new partner, Schneider, had engaged "in the practice of law in Portland, Oregon, as a partnership." The agreement makes no reference to any business activities other than the law practice in which Haessler or Stamer were involved. If the $57,000 had constituted payments for Esler's interest in businesses standing in Stamer's name, it seems only reasonable that the agreement would have identified those business interests. Because it did not do so, the inference is that the agreement related only to the law practice.

Moreover, the settlement agreement obligated the law firm, described therein as consisting of Haessler, Stamer, Tilbury, Rosen, and Platten, rather than only Haessler and Stamer, to make the payments to Esler. [Citation omitted.] Consistent with that obligation, the 1979, 1980, and 1981 partnership returns of the law firm show "guaranteed payments' to Esler of $15,570 (plus ordinary income of $3,985) for 1979, $33,333 for 1980, and $12,557 for 1981. The record also shows that checks covering the payments to Esler were drawn on the firm's account. Esler's own testimony states that Tilbury and Rosen entered the law firm in late 1978, several months before he withdrew from the firm, and that they received no interest in any businesses developed by Haessler and Stamer. Yet, according to the partnership returns, Tilbury's and Rosen's proportionate shares of the firm's earnings were reduced by the payments to Esler. It seems hardly reasonable that Tilbury and Rosen would pay Esler part of the value of property retained by Stamer or Haessler.

Furthermore, there are no clues in the partnership returns introduced in evidence indicating that the partnership engaged in any other business than the practice of law or owned any business property unrelated to the law practice. Although the law firm's 1976, 1977 and 1978 returns were not offered in evidence, the testimony indicated that they did not contain entries regarding the various business activities in which Esler argues the partnership engaged. If businesses organized by Stamer and Haessler were, in fact, partnership endeavors, the income, losses, sales and other transactions with respect to those businesses would, in the ordinary case, have been reflected in the returns. Bearing in mind this partnership was composed of lawyers, it seems only reasonable that they would have known that the partnership returns should have reflected the gains or losses derived from any business activities in which the firm engaged.

In fact, in the latter part of 1977, as detailed in our findings, Esler and Stamer took over a business which was in bankruptcy and established an organization known as Portland Workout Committee. Haessler did not participate in this venture. Esler and Stamer ultimately sold the business in early 1978 for a profit. Esler admitted that the gain on this venture was treated as individual capital gain and was not reported on the partnership return. The record contains no convincing explanation why this business venture was not owned by the partnership if Agoil, for example, was a partnership venture.

Other circumstances support our conclusion. The paragraph of the settlement agreement quoted in our findings expressly states that no interest was to be paid on the installments payable to Esler. Ordinarily, deferred payments for the purchase of property bear interest. Further, when the settlement agreement was negotiated, Platten and other partners, as well as Stamer and Haessler, participated in the negotiations. Unless the interests of the remaining partners were affected by the amount of the payment, there would have been no real reason for their participation in the negotiations. Haessler's investments in Northwest Hardwoods, moreover, were made by him and his family years before he formed the firm with Esler. He lent his personal credit to some of the other ventures. Haessler's compensation from Northwest Hardwoods was turned over to the firm but he expressly denied any transfer of his investment in that company or any other company to the firm. There is no evidence to the contrary.

Esler contends that none of the payments can be attributed to goodwill. He maintains that, when he left the firm, he took with him essentially the entire litigation department. In effect, he argues, he took his goodwill and the firm kept its goodwill. "Goodwill has been defined as the probability that 'old customers will resort to the old place' without contractual compulsion." [Citation omitted.] Significantly, when Esler left the firm, the only change made in its name was to drop Esler's name. The firm retained the same offices and continued as a going concern. We think that some of the firm's clients for whom Esler had performed services would first contact the firm's offices and that the quality of Esler's past performance would be of at least an initial advantage to the firm in obtaining new clients and retaining old ones. In other words, the $57,000 paid in installments in part compensated Esler for the firm's going concern value and goodwill which he relinquished.

We recognize that bona fide misunderstandings often arise with respect to the terms of oral partnership agreements. Also, where some of the partners in a law firm engage in business ventures as well as the practice of law, disputes may arise, particularly where, as in this case, the firm performs legal services related to those business ventures. As we view the evidence before us, however, it does not support Esler's contention that the $67,000 was payment for partnership property within the meaning of Section 736(b). Accordingly, the $67,000 is taxable to Esler as ordinary income and the disallowed guaranteed payments are deductible by the surviving law firm.

. . .

Chapter 11

Disproportionate Distributions, Disguised Sales, and Other Distribution Issues

---

Chapter 10 discussed the general rules relating to nonliquidating and liquidating distributions from a partnership to a partner. This chapter discusses special situations involving distributions.

A. Disproportionate Distributions

Individual taxpayers tend to favor long-term capital gains over ordinary income because of the preferential tax rates that apply to long-term capital gains. Thus, some partners may have an incentive to have the partnership distribute to them capital assets rather than ordinary assets in a manner that is not proportionate to all partners. When the partner then later sells the assets received in the distribution, the partner could recognize capital gain rather than ordinary income. Congress has enacted Section 751 to prevent partners from not recognizing their share of ordinary income. Distributions where capital assets and ordinary assets are distributed to the partners in a disproportionate manner are referred to as **disproportionate distributions**.

Section 751. Unrealized receivables and inventory items

...

(b) Certain distributions treated as sales or exchanges.—

(1) General rule. To the extent a partner receives in a distribution—

(A) partnership property which is—

(i) unrealized receivables, or

(ii) inventory items which have appreciated substantially in value, in exchange for all or a part of his interest in other partnership property (including money), or

(B) partnership property (including money) other than property described in subparagraph (A)(i) or (ii) in exchange for all or a part of his interest in partnership property described in subparagraph (A)(i) or (ii),

such transactions shall, under regulations prescribed by the Secretary, be considered as a sale or exchange of such property between the distributee and the partnership (as constituted after the distribution).

(2) Exceptions. Paragraph (1) shall not apply to—

(A) a distribution of property which the distributee contributed to the partnership, or

(B) payments, described in section 736(a), to a retiring partner or successor in interest of a deceased partner.

(3) Substantial appreciation. For purposes of paragraph (1)—

(A) In general. Inventory items of the partnership shall be considered to have appreciated substantially in value if their fair market value exceeds 120 percent of the adjusted basis to the partnership of such property.

(B) Certain property excluded. For purposes of subparagraph (A), there shall be excluded any inventory property if a principal purpose for acquiring such property was to avoid the provisions of this subsection relating to inventory items.

. . .

In short, if a partner receives in a distribution more than the partner's proportionate share of capital assets and less than the partner's share of ordinary income assets, the partner will be <u>deemed</u> to have received his proportionate share of ordinary income assets and then sold those assets back to the partnership (thus, generating ordinary income). Notice that the ordinary assets (or "hot" assets as they are sometimes called) consist of unrealized receivables and inventory. A definition of those terms is in order here.

Section 751. Unrealized receivables and inventory items

...

(c) Unrealized receivables. For purposes of this subchapter, the term "unrealized receivables" includes, to the extent not previously includible in income under the method of accounting used by the partnership, any rights (contractual or otherwise) to payment for—

(1) goods delivered, or to be delivered, to the extent the proceeds therefrom would be treated as amounts received from the sale or exchange of property other than a capital asset, or

(2) services rendered, or to be rendered.

For purposes of this section and, sections 731, 732, and 741 (but not for purposes of section 736), such term also includes mining property..., stock in a DISC..., section 1245 property..., stock in certain foreign corporations..., section 1250 property..., farm land..., franchises, trademarks, or trade names..., and an oil, gas, or geothermal property ...but only to the extent of the amount which would be treated as gain to which section 617(d)(1), 995(c), 1245(a), 1248(a), 1250(a), 1252(a), 1253(a) or 1254(a) would apply if (at the time of the transaction described in this section or section 731, 732, or 741, as the case may be) such property had been sold by the partnership at its fair market value. ...

(d) Inventory items. For purposes of this subchapter, the term "inventory items" means—

(1) property of the partnership of the kind described in section 1221(a)(1),

(2) any other property of the partnership which, on sale or exchange by the partnership, would be considered property other than a capital asset and other than property described in section 1231, and

(3) any other property held by the partnership which, if held by the selling or distribute partner, would be considered property of the type described in paragraph (1) or (2).

...

Notice how broad the definition of "unrealized receivables" is. It is much broader than simply "accounts receivable." In summary, the disproportionate distribution rules prevent partners from "trading" capital gain property for ordinary income property by receiving distributions that are not proportionate to their share of the respective partnership assets.

B. Disguised Sales

Suppose a partner contributes some land to a partnership. Another partner contributes cash. Suppose within a short time period the partnership then distributes the cash to the partner that contributed the land. This could be treated as a sale of the land by the contributing partner since a short time after contributing the land the partner receives cash from the partnership. Thus, Congress has put in place a few rules to address this situation.

Section 707. Transactions between partner and partnership

(a) Partner not acting in capacity as partner.—

(1) In general. If a partner engages in a transaction with a partnership other than in his capacity as a member of such partnership, the transaction shall, except as otherwise provided in this section, be considered as occurring between the partnership and one who is not a partner.

(2) Treatment of payments to partners for property or services.—

...

(B) Treatment of certain property transfers. If—

(i) there is a direct or indirect transfer of money or other property by a partner to a partnership,

(ii) there is a related direct or indirect transfer of money or other property by the partnership to such partner (or another partner), and

(iii) the transfers described in clauses (i) and (ii), when viewed together, are properly characterized as a sale or exchange of property,

such transfers shall be treated either as a transaction described in paragraph (1) or as a transaction between 2 or more partners acting other than in their capacity as members of the partnership.

...

Notice that when a contribution of property by a partner and a distribution of property (or, most likely, cash) by the partnership to the partner are related, the transaction can be recharacterized as a sale. In these cases, the term of art is “disguised” sale. The Treasury Regulations provide more guidance.

Treas. Reg. § 1.707-3. Disguised sales of property to partnership; general rules

. . .

(b) Transfers treated as a sale.—

(1) In general. A transfer of property ...by a partner to a partnership and a transfer of money or other consideration (including the assumption of or the taking subject to a liability) by the partnership to the partner constitute a sale of property, in whole or in part, by the partner to the partnership only if based on all the facts and circumstances—

(i) the transfer of money or other consideration would not have been made but for the transfer of property; and

(ii) in cases in which the transfers are not made simultaneously, the subsequent transfer is not dependent on the entrepreneurial risks of partnership operations.

. . .

(c) Transfers made within two years presumed to be a sale.—

(1) In general. For purposes of this section, if within a two-year period a partner transfers property to a partnership and the partnership transfers money or other consideration to the partner (without regard to the order of the transfers), the transfers are presumed to be a sale of the property to the partnership unless the facts and circumstances clearly establish that the transfers do not constitute a sale.

. . .

Thus, there is a two-year presumption of a disguised sale if money is distributed to a partner and the money distributed to the partner wasn't dependent on the entrepreneurial risks of partnership operations (in other words, the distribution wasn't a regular distribution of profits).

rzvmuR /Shutterstock.com

For a court case analyzing the disguised sale issue, see *Virginia Historic Tax Credit Fund 2001, LP v. Commissioner*, 639 F.3d 129 (4th Cir. 2011). Excerpts of this case are included at the end of this chapter.

C. Distributions of Contributed Property

Special rules apply if a partner contributes property and then either (1) that property is distributed to another partner within seven years or (2) the contributing partner receives a distribution of other property. This part of the chapter discusses these two scenarios.

1. Contributed property being distributed to another partner

Section 704. Partner's distributive share

...

(c) Contributed property.—

(1) In general. Under regulations prescribed by the Secretary—

(A) income gain, loss, and deduction with respect to property contributed to the partnership by a partner shall be shared among the partners so as to take account of the variation between the basis of the property to the partnership and its fair market value at the time of contribution,

(B) if any property so contributed is distributed (directly or indirectly) by the partnership (other than to the contributing partner) within 7 years of being contributed—

(i) the contributing partner shall be treated as recognizing gain or loss (as the case may be) from the sale of such property in an amount equal to the gain or loss which would have been allocated to such partner under subparagraph (A) by reason of the variation described in subparagraph (A) if the property had been sold at its fair market value at the time of the distribution,

(ii) the character of such gain or loss shall be determined by reference to the character of the gain or loss which would have resulted if such property had been sold by the partnership to the distributee, and

(iii) appropriate adjustments shall be made to the adjusted basis of the contributing partner's interest in the partnership and to the adjusted basis of the property distributed to reflect any gain or loss recognized under this subparagraph,...

Notice that if property contributed by a partner is distributed to another partner, then the contributing partner must recognize any built-in gain or loss as if the property were sold.

2. Other property being distributed to the contributing partner

Section 737. Recognition of precontribution gain in case of certain distributions to contributing partner

(a) General rule. In the case of any distribution by a partnership to a partner, such partner shall be treated as recognizing gain in an amount equal to the lesser of—

(1) the excess (if any) of (A) the fair market value of property (other than money) received in the distribution over (B) the adjusted basis of such partner's interest in the partnership immediately before the distribution reduced (but not below zero) by the amount of money received in the distribution, or

(2) the net precontribution gain of the partner.

Gain recognized under the preceding sentence shall be in addition to any gain recognized under section 731. The character of such gain shall be determined by reference to the proportionate character of the net precontribution gain.

(b) Net precontribution gain. For purposes of this section, the term "net precontribution gain" means the net gain (if any) which would have been recognized by the distributee partner under section 704(c)(1)(B) if all property which—

(1) had been contributed to the partnership by the distributee partner within 7 years of the distribution, and

(2) is held by such partnership immediately before the distribution,

had been distributed by such partnership to another partner.

(c) Basis rules.—

(1) Partner's interest. The adjusted basis of a partner's interest in a partnership shall be increased by the amount of any gain recognized by such partner under subsection (a). For purposes of determining the basis of the distributed property (other than money) such increase shall be treated as occurring immediately before the distribution.

(2) Partnership's basis in contributed property. Appropriate adjustments shall be made to the adjusted basis of the partnership in the contributed property referred to in subsection (b) to reflect gain recognized under subsection (a).

. . .

Thus, pre-contribution gain to a contributing partner is recognized if the partner receives property other than the property contributed within seven years of the contribution. (If the partner receives in a distribution the same property that the partner contributed, this rule is not triggered.)

D. Optional Basis Adjustments to Partnership Assets (Section 754 Election)

The Code allows the partnership to make adjustments to the tax basis of its assets in certain situations when a partner recognizes gain or loss on a distribution from the partnership. Section 734 addresses this issue.

Section 734. Adjustment to basis of undistributed partnership property where section 754 election or substantial basis reduction

(a) General rule. The basis of partnership property shall not be adjusted as the result of a distribution of property to a partner unless the election, provided in Section 754 (relating to optional adjustment to basis of partnership property), is in effect with respect to such partnership or unless there is a substantial basis reduction with respect to such distribution.

(b) Method of adjustment. In the case of a distribution of property to a partner by a partnership with respect to which the election provided in Section 754 is in effect or with respect to which there is a substantial basis reduction, the partnership shall—

(1) increase the adjusted basis of partnership property by—

(A) the amount of any gain recognized to the distributee partner with respect to such distribution under Section 731(a)(1), and

(B) in the case of distributed property to which Section 732(a)(2) or (b) applies, the excess of the adjusted basis of the distributed property to the partnership immediately before the distribution (as adjusted by Section 732(d)) over the basis of the distributed property to the distributee, as determined under Section 732, or

(2) decrease the adjusted basis of partnership property by—

(A) the amount of any loss recognized to the distributee partner with respect to such distribution under Section 731(a)(2), and

(B) in the case of distributed property to which Section 732(b) applies, the excess of the basis of the distributed property to the distributee, as determined under Section 732, over the adjusted basis of the distributed property to the partnership immediately before such distribution (as adjusted by Section 732(d)).

. . .

(c) Allocation of basis. The allocation of basis among partnership properties where subsection (b) is applicable shall be made in accordance with the rules provided in Section 755.

. . .

Notice that the general rule is that a partnership *does not* adjust the tax basis of its property as a consequence of making a distribution to a partner. Section 734 does, however, allow an adjustment if a Section 754 election is in effect.

Section 754. Manner of electing optional adjustment to basis of partnership property

If a partnership files an election, in accordance with regulations prescribed by the Secretary, the basis of partnership property shall be adjusted, in the case of a distribution of property, in the manner provided in Section 734 and, in the case of a transfer of a partnership interest, in the manner provided in Section 743. Such an election shall apply with respect to all distributions of property by the partnership and to all transfers of interests in the partnership during the taxable year with respect to which such election was filed and all subsequent taxable years. Such election may be revoked by the partnership, subject to such limitations as may be provided by regulations prescribed by the Secretary.

Once made, the Section 754 election is in effect for the current year and all subsequent years and cannot be revoked without IRS consent. If a Section 754 election is in effect for the partnership, Section 734(b) allows adjustments to the tax basis of partnership assets as a result of a partner recognizing gain or loss on a distribution.[1] A partnership may also adjust the tax basis of its assets if the partnership distributed assets other than cash to the partner and the distributed assets did not end up with a carryover basis in the hands of the partner due to the rules provided in Section 732.[2]

Calculating the amount of basis adjustments can be quite a task. Section 755 explains how to do this.

---

[1] Section 754 elections can also be made to reflect gains/losses recognized as a result of a partner's selling the partner's partnership interest. This topic is addressed in Chapter 12.

[2] These rules were discussed in Chapter 10.

Section 755. Rules for allocation of basis

(a) General rule. Any increase or decrease in the adjusted basis of partnership property under Section 734(b) (relating to the optional adjustment to the basis of undistributed partnership property) ...shall, except as provided in subsection (b), be allocated—

(1) in a manner which has the effect of reducing the difference between the fair market value and the adjusted basis of partnership properties, or

(2) in any other manner permitted by regulations prescribed by the Secretary.

(b) Special rule. In applying the allocation rules provided in subsection (a), increases or decreases in the adjusted basis of partnership property arising from a distribution of, or a transfer of an interest attributable to, property consisting of—

(1) capital assets and property described in Section 1231(b), or

(2) any other property of the partnership,

shall be allocated to a partnership property of a like character except that the basis of any such partnership property shall not be reduced below zero. If, in the case of a distribution, the adjustment to basis of property described in paragraph (1) or (2) is prevented by the absence of such property or by insufficient adjusted basis for such property, such adjustment shall be applied to subsequently acquired property of a like character in accordance with regulations prescribed by the Secretary.

...

The Treasury regulations under Section 755 provide the minutia relating to allocating the basis adjustments among the partnership's assets. The details of these regulations will not be discussed here.

CHAPTER 11 QUESTIONS FOR REVIEW

1. *Disproportionate distribution*. Assume an LLC has the following assets immediately before a *liquidating* distribution:

	Basis	FMV
Cash	$3,000	$3,000
A/R	$0	$3,000

   Assume also that the partnership has no liabilities. Members A and B are equal members of the LLC. There is no Section 704(c) built-in gain associated with the accounts receivable. In the distribution, A receives $3,000 cash and B receives the accounts receivable. What are the tax consequences to A and B (ignoring the impact on A's and B's respective outside bases)?

2. *Disguised sale*. Luís transfers property to a partnership in exchange for a partnership interest. At the time of the transfer of the property Luís has a tax basis of $3,200,000 and a fair market value of $4,000,000. Immediately after the transfer, the partnership transfers $2,000,000 in cash to Luís. What are the income tax consequences to Luís?

3. *Disguised sale*. What if in Question #2, the transfer of cash from the partnership to Luís was one year after Luís contributed the property?

4. *Virginia Historic Tax Credit Fund LP v. Commissioner*. Summarize the facts in the Virginia Historic Tax Credit Fund LP case. Discuss the issues, analysis, and holding of the court.

5. *Distribution of contributed property*. Pre-contribution gain of property contributed by a partner is recognized if the contributed property is distributed to another partner within ________ years.

6. *Contributing partner receiving other property*. What happens if a partner contributes property that has a pre-contribution gain and within seven years the partner then receives a distribution from the partnership consisting of property other than the contributed property?

7. *Section 754 election*. R, J, and M are all equal one-third partners in Partnership RJM. R decides to withdraw from the partnership. The partners agree that the partnership will distribute $10,000 in cash to R in a liquidating distribution. R's outside basis at the time of the distribution is $9,000. The partnership has two assets—$20,000 cash and land (tax basis $7,000 and fair market value of $10,000). If the partnership does not have a Section 754 election in place, what is the adjusted basis of the land after the transaction? What if the partnership does have a Section 754 election in place?

8. *Section 754 election*. R, J, and M are all equal one-third partners in Partnership RJM. M decides to withdraw from the partnership. At the time of M's withdrawal, the partnership has the following assets:

Asset	Partnership's Tax Basis	Fair Market Value
Cash	$30,000	$30,000
Greenacre	$24,000	$30,000
Redacre	$24,000	$30,000

The partnership has no liabilities and each partner's capital account is $30,000. Also, assume that the properties are capital assets and none were contributed by a partner. All appreciation in the properties occurred while the properties were owned by the partnership. Assume that the partners agree to distribute Redacre to M as a liquidating distribution to M. M's outside basis in the partnership at the time of distribution is $26,000.

a. How much gain or loss does M recognize as a result of the distribution?
b. What is M's tax basis in Redacre after the distribution?
c. If the partnership does not have a Section 754 election in place, what is the partnership's tax basis in Greenacre after the distribution?
d. What if the partnership does have a Section 754 election in place, what is the partnership's tax basis in Greenacre after the distribution?

Virginia Historic Tax Credit Fund 2001, LP v. Commissioner

United States Court of Appeals, Fourth Circuit
639 F.3d 129 (2011)

OPINION

Judge: DUNCAN, Circuit Judge:

Reversed and remanded by published opinion. Judge Duncan wrote the opinion, in which Judge Niemeyer and Judge Keenan joined.

This appeal presents the question of whether certain transactions between a partnership and its partners amounted to "sales" for purposes of federal tax law. During an audit, the Commissioner of Internal Revenue (the "Commissioner") challenged the way that Virginia Historic Tax Credit Fund 2001, LLC ("2001 LLC"), as the tax matters partner of Virginia Historic Tax Credit Fund 2001 LP ("2001 LP"), Virginia Historic Tax Credit Fund 2001 SCP, LLC ("SCP LLC") and Virginia Historic Tax Credit Fund 2001, SCP, LP ("SCP LP") (collectively, "the Funds"), reported a series of transactions with investor partners in the Funds' 2001 and 2002 federal tax returns. The United States Tax Court found that the Funds had properly characterized these transactions, and the Commissioner appealed. For the reasons set forth below, we reverse the Tax Court and find that the Commissioner properly treated the challenged transactions as "sales" under I.R.C. § 707.

I.

The facts in this case are not in dispute. Our recitation is drawn primarily from the Tax Court's findings of fact and the parties' stipulations. By way of background, we begin by describing Virginia's Historic Rehabilitation Credit Program (the "Virginia Program"), in which the Funds were designed to participate. We then turn to the details of the Funds and the challenged transactions before summarizing the findings of the Tax Court.

A.

Because the cost of renovating historic property often exceeds the property's market value, many states have enacted legislation designed to encourage investment in this area.

Virginia has chosen to provide an incentive to historic developers in the form of tax credits. Under the rules of the Virginia Program, any person rehabilitating a historic property can seek state approval and certification of the project by the Virginia Department of Historic Resources ("DHR"). Once the property is certified, its developer is entitled to receive tax credits of up to twenty-five percent of eligible expenses incurred in renovating the property. [Citation omitted.] These state tax credits can be applied dollar-for-dollar against Virginia income tax liability.

At times, the amount of historic tax credits issued to a historic property developer exceeds the developer's income tax liability. Unlike some other states, Virginia does not allow tax credits to be sold or transferred in this event. Virginia does, however, have a partnership allocation provision that permits state tax credits allocated to a partnership to be divided among the partners "as the partners or shareholders mutually agree." This provision is often used by developers to "allocate a disproportionate share of [their] State tax credits to limited partners whose [monetary] contributions then fill the credit gap." [Citation omitted.]

Although the scheme described above reflects the rules of the Virginia Program both as originally enacted in 1996 and as currently in force, a brief change that occurred in these rules is relevant to the instant appeal. Before Virginia finalized its Program rules, some historic renovation projects began under the assumption that the Program would permit the sale or transfer of credits. To protect projects that had begun under this assumption, Virginia temporarily amended its program in 1999 to allow for a one-time transfer (i.e., sale) of credits for projects that received certification prior to the publication of the Program's final regulations. Such transfers had to be approved by the director of DHR.

B.

In 2001, Daniel Gecker ("Gecker"), Robert Miller ("Miller"), and George Brower ("Brower") came together to set up the Funds in question. All three had previously been consultants in the design and implementation of the Virginia Program and were familiar with its workings and limitations. One such limitation was that smaller historic renovation projects were still having difficulty obtaining funding. To address this issue, they structured the Funds as partnerships that investors could join by contributing capital. The Funds would use that capital to partner with historic property developers renovating smaller projects, in exchange for state tax credits.

Gecker, Miller, and Brower became principals of the Funds and designated four linked partnership entities as Fund partners. They named 2001 LLC as the Funds' general partner and tax matters partner, and 2001 LP as the "source partnership" that would partner with historic developers. Gecker and Miller each held a 35% interest in the general partner, 2001 LLC, with Miller's interest held through his wholly owned entity BKM, LLC. Brower held the remaining 30% interest. 2001 LLC became, in turn, the 97% owner of 2001 LP. 2001 LLC also became the 99% owner of two pass-through partners, SCP LLC, and SCP LP, which were lower-tier partnerships. SCP LLC and SCP LP were each 1% owners in 2001 LP; the remaining 1% interest in 2001 LP was reserved for sale to investors, as was a 1% interest in SCP LLC and SCP LP.

The Funds began soliciting investors willing to contribute capital to the partnership in exchange for the allocation of state tax credits in late 2001. The precise rates of return offered to investors differed slightly depending on the partnership through which they invested—2001 LP, SCP LLC, or SCP LP—but otherwise the arrangements were the same. Each investor was promised a certain amount of tax credits and a limited partnership interest in the Funds in exchange for a capital contribution to the Funds. The lower-tier partnerships passed their capital contributions on to 2001 LP.

Investors received a confidential offering memorandum (the "offering memo") and partnership agreements that set forth their arrangement with the Funds in detail. For every $.74 - $.80 contributed by an investor, the Fund would provide the investor with $1 in tax credits. If such credits could not be obtained, the partnership agreement promised a refund of capital to the investor, "net of expenses."

The partnership agreement also explained that each investor (or, in the agreement, "Limited Partner") would be given "a percentage participation in the Partnership equal to one percent (1%) multiplied by a fraction the number [sic] of which is the number of units owned by the Limited Partner and denominator of which is the total number of units outstanding." In practice, however, this complex formula appears not to have been applied: the subscription agreements signed by the investors indicate that most were simply given a .01% interest in the Funds, irrespective of their capital contributions, although some subscription agreements for SCP LP state that a 1% interest was acquired. These slight discrepancies were of limited importance, however, as the offering memo explained that investors should expect to receive no material amounts of partnership income or loss.

The partnership agreement and offering memo also addressed the Funds' plan for partnering with developers. The Funds would become a .01% limited partner in selected historic property development partnerships (termed "Operating Partnerships" in the partnership agreement), and would provide capital contributions in exchange for tax credits. However, the Funds promised not to "make a capital contribution in excess of $100 to an Operating Partnership until the General Partner has received certification from the [DHR] that the rehabilitation constitutes a qualified rehabilitation and the amount of qualified rehabilitation expenditures paid or incurred by the Operating Partnership." In other words, the partnership agreement stated that the Funds would invest only in completed projects, thereby eliminating a significant area of risk. In addition, the Funds' agreements with their Operating Partners provided that the Operating Partners would reimburse the Funds in the event that any of their credits could not be delivered or were later revoked by the state. At least some of these agreements were further backed by guarantors.

The offering memo also explained how the Funds would pay their operating expenses. The Operating Partnerships would "make available to the General Partner a total of $20,000 to pay for the cost of the Partnership's annual accounting expenses and other Partnership operating expenses." Should annual expenses be higher than this, the General Partner promised to fund them, explaining that "[a]lthough the General Partner does not have any significant amount of assets, it is not anticipated that the annual operating expenses of the Partnership will be high."

Between November 2001 and April 2002, 282 investors signed partnership agreements, subscriptions agreements, and options agreements with the Funds. The source partnership, 2001 LP, obtained 181 investors, while SCP LLC obtained 93 investors and SCP LP obtained eight investors. The subscription agreements specified the dollar amount contributed by each investor, and stated that this amount was paid in exchange for the allocation of a corresponding number of tax credits "*simultaneously* with Investor's admission." The options agreements gave the Funds the sole option to purchase each partner's interest for fair market value during 2002, and assigned to Gecker a limited power of attorney to execute all documents necessary to effectuate these purchases.

In total, the Funds collected \$6.99 million from investors between November 2001 and April 2002. During this same time period, the Fund paid a total of fifteen developers 5.13 million, at a price of \$.55/\$1 tax credit, to obtain \$9.2 million in historic rehabilitation tax credits. Approximately one-third of these tax credits were purchased from developers under Virginia's one-time transfer provision; the rest were obtained in exchange for capital contributions to Operating Partnerships with which the Fund partnered. In April 2002, the Funds distributed to investors "Schedules K-1" designating to each investor his promised amount of tax credits and attaching the DHR Certificates of Rehabilitation from the Funds' Operating Partnerships. However, "[s]pecific credits were not designated as being allocated to any one particular investor ...; instead the investors were informed of the amount allocated to them from the pool of credits." The Funds then exercised their option to buy out all investors in May 2002, paying them each .001 times their contribution for a total buyout cost of approximately \$7,000.

C.

The instant dispute arose from the way the Funds reported this series of transactions in their federal tax filings. In both their 2001 and 2002 Forms 1065, U.S. Return of Partnership Income, the Funds reported the money paid to Operating Partnerships in exchange for tax credits as partnership expenses and reported the investors' contributions to the Funds as nontaxable contributions to capital. The Funds' returns therefore reflected that the Funds sustained a total of \$3.28 million in losses for 2001 and 2002.

The Internal Revenue Service ("IRS") audited the Funds and challenged their characterization of investors' funding as "contributions to capital." Instead, the Commissioner concluded that the investors were not actual partners of the Funds, and that "these investors' capital contributions to the partnership and receipt of the state income tax credits in return was a sale of income tax credits to the investors." Accordingly, the Commissioner believed that the Funds should have reported the money they received from investors as income.

The IRS issued to the Funds six Final Partnership Administrative Adjustments ("FPAAs"), which reflected its contention that investors' contributions should have been reported as income on the Funds' 2001 and 2002 returns. Based on the numbers provided by the Funds in their tax returns, the Commissioner originally calculated that the Funds should have recognized income in the amount of $4.02 million. The parties have since stipulated that if the Commissioner is correct, the Funds should have reported income of $1.53 million as a result of investor contributions. The parties have also stipulated that although the Commissioner originally challenged both the Funds' 2001 and 2002 returns, if the Commissioner prevails, the gains realized by the Funds will be treated as having occurred in 2002.

D.

The Funds disputed the Commissioner's characterization of their partnership arrangement and timely filed petitions for readjustment of partnership items with the Tax Court pursuant to I.R.C. § 6226(a). At trial, the Commissioner presented two bases for his assertion that the FPAAs were correct: (1) under the substance-over-form doctrine, the investors were not "bona fide" partners in the Funds for federal tax purposes, but instead were mere purchasers; and (2) the transactions between the investors and the partnerships were "disguised sales" under I.R.C. § 707. The Commissioner only needed to establish one basis to prevail.

After trial, the Tax Court issued an opinion rejecting both of the Commissioner's assertions. It first found that the investors were in fact partners for federal tax purposes under the partnership test announced by the Supreme Court in Commissioner v. Culbertson, [citation omitted]. The Tax Court reasoned that the partnership agreements, the parties' conduct in their execution, the parties' statements, the testimony of disinterested persons, the relationship of the parties, and the control of income and purposes for which it was used all pointed to a conclusion that the investors and the Funds fully intended to enter into a partnership arrangement.

The Tax Court further found that the substance-over-form doctrine did not dictate that the partnership arrangement between the investors and the Funds was not bona fide. It found that investors' contributions did not reflect merely the purchase price of credits; instead, "the contributions were pooled to facilitate investment in the developer partnerships, to purchase additional credits under the one-time transfer provision..., to cover the expenses of the partnerships, to insure against the risks of the partnerships, and to provide capital for successor entities ...." [Citation omitted.] The Tax Court also found that investors bore sufficient risk to make them partners, including the risks that developers might not provide the promised tax credits or that the credits might be revoked. The Tax Court acknowledged that "investors received assurance that their contributions would be refunded" if the tax credits were not received or were revoked, but found this assurance counteracted by the lack of a guarantee "that the resources would remain available in the source partnership to do so."

The Tax Court also rejected the Commissioner's argument that the transactions between the investors and the Funds were "disguised sales" under I.R.C. § 707. Section 707(a)(2)(B) allows the Commissioner to treat a transaction that occurs between a partner and his partnership as though it occurred "between the partnership and one who is not a partner" if the partner transfers money to the partnership in exchange for "a related direct or indirect transfer of money or other property by the partnership to such partner," such that the transaction is "properly characterized as a sale or exchange." The Tax Court found that although such transactions are "presumed sales" when they occur within two years of one another, the transactions here were not disguised sales because the transactions were "not simultaneous" and the investors faced "entrepreneurial risks' in the partnership. [Citation omitted.] This appeal followed.

II.

On appeal, the Commissioner makes the same two arguments he made before the Tax Court: that the investors were not bona fide partners of the Funds, and that even if they were, the transactions between the investors and the Funds should nevertheless be classified as sales for federal tax purposes under the relevant Code provisions and regulations. Assuming, without deciding, that a "bona fide" partnership existed, we nevertheless find that the Commissioner properly recharacterized the transactions at issue as "sales" under I.R.C. § 707.

In the sections that follow, we first set forth the rules and regulations governing the question of when a purported partnership transfer should be reclassified as a sale. Normally, we would then proceed to consider our standard of review and whether the transactions at issue should be reclassified under these rules. However, the Funds make a preliminary argument that their transactions should not be analyzed under these rules because no transfer of "property" occurred between the Funds and their investors. Accordingly, we address this argument before turning to the appropriate standard of review and consideration of the relevant criteria to determine whether a "disguised sale" occurred here.

A.

A partnership is not itself liable for the payment of income taxes; instead, partnerships operate as "pass-through" entities and each partner must pay taxes on his or her allocated share of the partnership's income or loss. [Citations omitted.] "However, each year a partnership must file an information return (IRS Form 1065) reporting items of gross income and allowable deductions." [Citation omitted.] Items that must be reported include "gains and losses from sales or exchanges of capital assets." I.R.C. § 702. But I.R.C. § 721 provides that "[n]o gain or loss shall be recognized to a partnership or to any of its partners in the case of a contribution of property to the partnership in exchange for an interest in the partnership." Similarly, "[n]o gain or loss shall be recognized to a partnership on a distribution to a partner of property, including money." In other words, whereas a partnership must report any proceeds received from the sale of its assets as taxable income, partners' contributions to capital and a partnership's distributions to partners are tax-free.

These rules have been recognized as susceptible to manipulation by persons wishing to shield transactions that are more accurately characterized as sales from their proper tax consequences. [Citations omitted.] To guard against this problem, the Tax Code "recognizes that in some cases partners do not deal with a partnership in their capacity as partners." [Citation omitted.] Specifically, I.R.C. § 707 "prevents use of the partnership provisions to render nontaxable what would in substance have been a taxable exchange if it had not been 'run through' the partnership."

Section 707, as strengthened by Congress in 1984, provides that "[i]f a partner engages in a transaction with a partnership other than in his capacity as a member of such partnership, the transaction shall, except as otherwise provided in this section, be considered as occurring between the partnership and one who is not a partner." I.R.C. § 707(a)(1). Non-partnership-capacity transactions include the situation where:

(i) there is a direct or indirect transfer of money or other property by a partner to a partnership,
(ii) there is a related direct or indirect transfer of money or other property by the partnership to such partner (or another partner), and
(iii) the transfers described in clauses (i) and (ii), when viewed together, are properly characterized as a sale or exchange of property[.]

§ 707(a)(2)(B). Such a transaction, in which a "partner contributes property to a partnership and soon thereafter receives a distribution of money or other consideration from the partnership," is often referred to as a "disguised sale." [Citations omitted.]

Treasury Regulations clarify which partnership transfers should be "properly characterized as a sale or exchange of property" under § 707(a)(2). [Citation omitted.] Section 1.707-3 applies, by its terms, to transfers of property *to* a partnership in exchange for money *from* the partnership—in other words, the reverse of what occurred here. However, § 1.707-6 specifies:

> Rules similar to those provided in § 1.707-3 apply in determining whether a transfer of property by a partnership to a partner and one or more transfers of money or other consideration by that partner to the partnership are treated as a sale of property, in whole or in part, to the partner.

§ 1.707-6(a). Accordingly, we look to § 1.707-3 to determine whether the transfers disputed here have the characteristics of a sale.

Section 1.707-3 calls for an evaluation of "all the facts and circumstances" surrounding the transaction to determine whether

(i) The transfer of money or other consideration would not have been made *but for* the transfer of property; and

(ii) In cases in which the transfers are not made simultaneously, the subsequent transfer is not dependent on the entrepreneurial risks of partnership operations.

§ 1.707-3(b)(1) (emphasis added). It goes on to list ten factors, five of which are of particular relevance here, to be taken into consideration:

(i) That the timing and amount of a subsequent transfer are determinable with reasonable certainty at the time of an earlier transfer;

(ii) That the transferor has a legally enforceable right to the subsequent transfer;
(iii) That the partner's right to receive the transfer of money or other consideration is secured in any manner, taking into account the period during which it is secured;

. . .

(ix) That the transfer of money or other consideration by the partnership to the partner is disproportionately large in relationship to the partner's general and continuing interest in partnership profits; and (x) That the partner has no obligation to return or repay the money or other consideration to the partnership, or has such an obligation but it is likely to become due at such a distant point in the future that the present value of that obligation is small in relation to the amount of money or other consideration transferred by the partnership to the partner.

§ 1.707-3(b)(2).

Significantly here, § 1.707-3 also sets forth a presumption that all transfers "made within two years" of each other are sales, "unless the facts and circumstances clearly establish that the transfers do not constitute a sale." § 1.707-3(c). This presumption places a high burden on the partnership to establish the validity of any suspect partnership transfers.

B.

The Funds argue that § 707 cannot be applied to recharacterize their transactions with investors because these transactions did not involve an exchange of money for "property." Specifically, they argue that Virginia's historic rehabilitation tax credits are not "property" because they are non-transferable and non-heritable under state law. There was thus, they argue, no "transfer of money or other property" from the Funds to the investors. Because of its reliance on a finding of entrepreneurial risk, the Tax Court found it unnecessary to reach this issue. [Citation omitted.] Finding it necessary to our § 707 analysis, however, we consider it for the first time on appeal.

The Internal Revenue Code does not define "property" as the term is used in § 707, and so we must go beyond the bounds of the statute to determine whether Virginia tax credits count as such. This determination is a hybrid federal and state law question. [Citation omitted.] [The Supreme Court] has succinctly explained the dual roles of state and federal law in determining whether a particular item or arrangement constitutes property for purposes of federal tax law:

A common idiom describes property as a "bundle of sticks"—a collection of individual rights which, in certain combinations, constitute property. State law determines only which sticks are in a person's bundle. Whether those sticks qualify as "property" for purposes of the federal tax lien statute is a question of federal law. [Citation omitted.] Although [the Supreme Court] examined the characterization of property for purposes of the federal tax lien statute, I.R.C. § 6321, we believe the same basic analysis adheres in determining whether a particular "bundle of sticks" constitutes property for purposes of I.R.C. § 707.

Accordingly, to determine whether Virginia's historic rehabilitation tax credits are "property" for federal tax purposes, we ask whether they embody "some of the most essential property rights." [Citation omitted.] In particular, the Supreme Court ... identified the "right to use the property, to receive income produced by it, and to exclude others from it," as fundamental property rights. Similarly, ...the Supreme Court placed primary emphasis on the "breadth of the control the taxpayer could exercise over the property" and whether the right in question was "valuable." [Citation omitted.] [The Supreme Court] noted that transferability, although not essential, is also a relevant factor. [Citation omitted.]

Applying these factors to the instant case, we find that the transfer of tax credits from the Funds to investors under the circumstances presented here constituted a transfer of "property." It is clear on these facts that the Funds' tax credits were both "valuable" and imbued with "some of the most essential property rights." [Citations omitted.] That the Funds' tax credits had pecuniary value is evidenced by the fact that the Funds used the credits to induce investors to contribute money. Additionally the Funds exercised proprietary control over the tax credits: once the historic developers allocated to the Funds the rights to use or distribute these credits, the Funds could exclude others from utilizing the credits and were free to keep or pass along the credits to partners as they saw fit.

As for the tax credits' transferability, although Virginia law prohibits historic tax credits from being bought and sold directly, this is a nominal prohibition. As the facts here illustrate, it is a relatively simple matter in Virginia to effectuate a third-party transfer by forming a partnership with an interested buyer who is then "allocated" the credits in exchange for a contribution to the partnership. To hold that these tax credits, which the Funds undeniably gave to investors in exchange for money, are not property simply because they could not be directly bought and sold would elevate form over substance in precisely the manner we are advised to guard against. [Citation omitted.]

Furthermore, including the exchange of tax credits for dollars within the scope of § 707 "property" comports with Congress's intent to widen the provision's reach in 1984. Congress strengthened § 707 specifically because of concern "that taxpayers ha[d] deferred or avoided tax on sales of property" and that courts were allowing "tax-free treatment in cases which were economically indistinguishable from sales ...." [Citations omitted.] To combat this problem, the Department of the Treasury was instructed to promulgate new regulations, which allow for a flexible evaluation of "all the facts and circumstances" in determining whether any particular transaction should be treated as a sale. [Citation omitted.] This Congressional and regulatory treatment strengthens our conclusion that a transfer of tax credits in exchange for money qualifies as a transfer of "property" on the facts before us.

C.

(i)

Having found that the Funds' exchange of tax credits for investor contributions included the transfer of "property" from the Funds to investors for purposes of § 707(a)(2)(B), we turn to the question of whether these transfers should be properly recharacterized as "sales" under that provision and the factors enumerated in Treasury Regulation § 1.707-3. However, before addressing the particulars of the transactions at issue, we must determine the level of deference we owe to the Tax Court's holding that these transactions did not meet the disguised sale criteria of I.R.C. § 707 or Treas. Reg. § 1.707-3.

The Tax Court's holding relied largely on its factual findings, which we review for clear error. [Citation omitted.] However, the ultimate issue of whether a transaction is properly characterized as a "sale" is legal in nature. [Citations omitted.] Accordingly, we will review the Tax Court's factual findings for clear error, but will review de novo its legal conclusion that the transfers here did not constitute a "sale."

(ii)

We begin, as Treasury Regulation § 1.707-3 requires, with a presumption that the Funds' exchange of tax credits for investor contributions was a sale because the transfers undisputedly occurred well within two years of one another. See Treas. Reg. § 1.707-3(c). This presumption can be overcome only if we determine that the facts as found by the Tax Court "clearly establish[ed] that the transfers do not constitute a sale." We consider those facts in light of the factors enumerated in § 1.707-3(b).

Treasury Regulation § 1.707-3(b)(2) first instructs us to consider whether "the timing and amount of a subsequent transfer [were] determinable with reasonable certainty at the time of an earlier transfer." § 1.707-3(b)(2)(i). In this case, they were. When investors signed partnership and subscriptions agreements and made their contributions to the Funds, the Funds promised them a precise number of tax credits in exchange, so that each investor knew with specificity the size of the subsequent transfer he or she could expect. The Funds further promised to deliver these credits for use in investors' 2001 tax calculations, making the timing of these transfers reasonably certain as well.

We next examine whether the investors had "a legally enforceable right" to the later transfer of credits. § 1.707-3(b)(2)(ii). This factor also weighs in favor of finding a sale.

The partnership and subscriptions agreements between the Funds and their investors explicitly promised delivery of tax credits to investors in exchange for capital contributions. Had the Funds acquired tax credits that they then refused to allocate to investors, the investors could have pursued a breach of contract claim against them.

The third relevant factor is whether "the partner's right to receive the transfer of money or other consideration is secured in any manner." § 1.707-3(b)(2)(iii). The investors' contributions were secured in several ways. First, the Funds promised that investor capital would be refunded if sufficient credits could not be obtained or were revoked. Second, the Funds protected investors' contributions by requiring their Operating Partnerships to agree to refund the Funds' contributions in the event that promised credits were not delivered.

Moreover, investors' receipt of tax credits was further secured by the Funds' promise to give investor money only to Operating Partnerships that had "received certification from the [DHR] that the rehabilitation constitutes a qualified rehabilitation and the amount of qualified rehabilitation expenditures ...." The Funds' promise not to make any significant investment until rehabilitations were already guaranteed to meet state approval meant that there was little risk of funding being given to Operating Partnerships who could not deliver credits in return.

The Treasury Regulation's ninth factor—whether "the transfer of money or other consideration by the partnership to the partner is disproportionately large in relationship to the partner's general and continuing interest in partnership profits"—strongly counsels in favor of finding a disguised sale. Treas. Reg. § 1.707-3(b)(2)(ix). The investors had essentially no interest in partnership profits under their arrangement with the Funds. According to their subscription agreements, most investors owned a .01% partnership interest in one of the Funds, even though the partnership agreements reflect that a more complicated apportionment mechanism had been contemplated. In any event, investors were likely unconcerned about the precise amount of their partnership interest because the offering memo told them to expect no material amounts of partnership profits. Thus, the transfer of tax credits to each investor by the partnership had no correlation to each investor's interest in partnership profits whatsoever. To the contrary, the size of each transfer was tied exclusively to the amount of money the investor contributed to the Funds.

Finally, the Treasury Regulation's tenth factor, whether partners had any "obligation to return or repay the money or other consideration to the partnership," § 1.707-3(b)(2)(x), also points toward finding a sale. After receiving the tax credits, the investors had no further obligations or relationship with the partnership. Instead, they were free to use the credits for their own benefit.

Particularly in light of the presumption that a sale occurred unless clearly demonstrated otherwise, the foregoing factors strongly counsel for a finding that these transactions were sales. We note as well that the partnership status of the investors to the Funds was transitory in nature. Investors joined at the end of 2001 or beginning of 2002 and were all bought out for the proverbial pittance, through the power of attorney given to Gecker at the time they entered the partnership, in May 2002, soon after tax filings were due. Although this factor is not included in the Department of the Treasury's regulations, the Joint Committee deems it relevant, explaining that "[t]ransitory partner status (which limits the duration of a purported joint undertaking for profit) suggests that a payment is a fee or is in return for property." [Citation omitted.]

Instead of examining the enumerated § 1.707-3(b)(2) factors, the Tax Court conducted its own evaluation of the investors' level of "entrepreneurial risk," which it is certainly free to do. Section 1.707-3(b)(2) simply reflects those characteristics the Department of the Treasury, given its experience and expertise, thinks significant. [Citation omitted.] Thus, although we would have found the Tax Court's analysis of the factors helpful, we cannot say that a court in every instance is required to tick through them mechanically. Even if the Tax Court's independent assessment of entrepreneurial risk was appropriate, however, we believe its conclusions in that regard miss the mark.

Again, § 1.707-3(b)(1) explains that a transaction should be reclassified as a sale if: (1) the transfer of money "would not have been made but for" the transfer of property in exchange; and (2) the later transfer "is not dependent on the entrepreneurial risks of partnership operations." There is no dispute that the "but for" test is satisfied here. The Tax Court instead relied on its conclusion that the Funds' investors, after giving their money but before receiving tax credits in exchange, faced the "entrepreneurial risks" involved in the Funds' partnership operations. It clarified as follows:

> [T]he partners faced the risk that developers would not complete their projects on time because of construction, zoning, or management issues. They also faced the risk that the DHR would not be satisfied with the rehabilitation and the developers would not receive the credits. Finally, they faced the risk that the DHR would revoke the credits and recapture them in later years. Accordingly, the partners risked their anticipated net economic benefit.
>
> ...
>
> The investors also faced risks from the partnerships' ownership interests in the developer partnerships. These risks ranged from liability for improper construction to the risk of mismanagement or fraud at the developer partnership level.... Further, the investors faced the risks of fraud by another investor, retroactive changes in the law, and litigation in general.

[Citation omitted.]

Upon closer examination, however, these risks appear both speculative and circumscribed. As the Tax Court acknowledged, "[t]he investors received assurance that their contributions would be refunded if ...the anticipated credits could not be had or were revoked." [Citation omitted.] It is true, as the court recognized, that there was indeed no guarantee that resources would remain available in the source partnership to make the promised refunds. But it is also true that the Funds were structured in such a way as to render the possibility of insolvency remote.

Several facts point to the conclusion that there was no true entrepreneurial risk faced by investors here. First, investors were promised what was, in essence, a fixed rate of return on investment rather than any share in partnership profits tied to their partnership interests. The Funds explained the fixed arrangement that they would have with investors in precise terms in their offering memorandum: "An Investor will make a capital contribution to the Partnership in an amount equal to $.74 for each $1.00 of Virginia Historic Credit available for use by the Investor in calendar year 2001 ...." [Citation omitted.] Second, the Funds assigned each investor an approximate .01% partnership interest and explicitly told investors to expect no allocations of "material amounts of ... partnership items of income, gain, loss or deduction." [Citation omitted.] Third, investors were secured against losing their contributions by the promise of a refund from the Funds if tax credits could not be delivered or were revoked. And fourth, the Funds hedged against the possibility of insolvency by promising investors that contributions would be made only to completed projects and by requiring the Operating Partnerships to promise refunds, in some cases backed by guarantors, if promised credits could not be delivered.

We find persuasive the Commissioner's contention that the only risk here was that faced by any advance purchaser who pays for an item with a promise of later delivery. It is not the risk of the entrepreneur who puts money into a venture with the hope that it might grow in amount but with the knowledge that it may well shrink. [Citation omitted.] For these reasons, we disagree with the Tax Court's conclusion that the Funds "clearly established" that their investors faced entrepreneurial risks sufficient to overcome the regulatory presumption that these transactions were sales. We therefore agree with the Commissioner that the Funds should have included the money received from investors as income in their tax returns, and uphold the adjustments in the FPAAs issued to the Funds in 2002.

III.

The decision of the Tax Court is hereby reversed and remanded for further proceedings consistent with this opinion.

REVERSED AND REMANDED

Part IV

Sale of a Partnership Interest and Partnership Terminations

Chapter 12

Sale of a Partnership Interest

A. Gain or Loss Recognition
B. Exception for "Hot" Assets
C. Buyer's Initial Outside Basis
D. Optional Basis Adjustment to Partnership Assets (Section 754 Election)

A. Gain or Loss Recognition

When a partner sells his or her partnership interest, the partner recognizes gain to the extent by which the amount realized exceeds the partner's outside basis; the partner recognizes loss to the extent by which the partner's outside basis exceeds the amount realized on the sale transaction.[1] An important concept to remember in determining the "amount realized" when a partner sells his or her partnership interest is that, in addition to the cash or other property received as a result of the sale, the partner must also include the partnership's liabilities of which the partner no longer has a share.

Code Section 741 sets forth the treatment of the sale of a partnership interest.

Section 741. Recognition and character of gain or loss on sale or exchange

In the case of a sale or exchange of an interest in a partnership, gain or loss shall be recognized to the transferor partner. Such gain or loss shall be considered as gain or loss from the sale or exchange of a capital asset, except as otherwise provided in section 751 (relating to unrealized receivables and inventory items).

Thus, the general rule is that the sale of a partnership interest generates a *capital* gain or loss to the selling partner.

rzymuR /Shutterstock.com

For a court case analyzing the character of gain on the sale of a partnership interest, see *Pollack v. Commissioner*, 69 TC 142 (1977). Excerpts of the *Pollack* case are included at the end of this chapter.

[1] Section 1001(a).

B. Exception for "Hot" Assets

Notice that there is an important exception provided in Code Section 741 relating to the character of the gain or loss recognized by the selling partner. We cannot ignore the exception contained in Section 751.

Section 751. Unrealized receivables and inventory items

(a) Sale or exchange of interest in partnership. The amount of any money, or the fair market value of any property, received by a transferor partner in exchange for all or a part of his interest in the partnership attributable to—

(1) unrealized receivables of the partnership, or

(2) inventory items of the partnership,

shall be considered as an amount realized from the sale or exchange of property other than a capital asset.

...

Thus, the sale of a partnership interest generates a capital gain or loss except to the extent the partnership has unrealized receivables or inventory on its balance sheet. The partner's share of the income or loss if the partnership were to hypothetically sell its unrealized receivables and/or inventory causes the partner to recognize *ordinary* income or loss instead of entirely a capital gain or loss. Since "unrealized receivables" and "inventory" on the partnership's balance sheet can cause a selling partner to recognize some ordinary income instead of solely capital gain, these assets are commonly referred to as "hot" assets.

As also presented in Chapter 11 (with respect to disproportionate distributions), Code Section 751 defines unrealized receivables and inventory as follows:

Section 751. Unrealized receivables and inventory items

...

(c) Unrealized receivables. For purposes of this subchapter, the term "unrealized receivables" includes, to the extent not previously includible in income under the method of accounting used by the partnership, any rights (contractual or otherwise) to payment for—

(1) goods delivered, or to be delivered, to the extent the proceeds therefrom would be treated as amounts received from the sale or exchange of property other than a capital asset, or

(2) services rendered, or to be rendered.

For purposes of this section and, sections 731, 732, and 741 (but not for purposes of section 736), such term also includes mining property..., stock in a DISC..., section 1245 property..., stock in certain foreign corporations..., section 1250 property..., farm land..., franchises, trademarks, or trade names..., and an oil, gas, or geothermal property... but only to the extent of the amount which would be treated as gain to which section 617(d)(1), 995(c), 1245(a), 1248(a), 1250(a), 1252(a), 1253(a) or 1254(a) would apply if (at the time of the transaction described in this section or section 731, 732, or 741, as the case may be) such property had been sold by the partnership at its fair market value....

(d) Inventory items. For purposes of this subchapter, the term "inventory items" means—

(1) property of the partnership of the kind described in section 1221(a)(1),

(2) any other property of the partnership which, on sale or exchange by the partnership, would be considered property other than a capital asset and other than property described in section 1231, and

(3) any other property held by the partnership which, if held by the selling or distribute partner, would be considered property of the type described in paragraph (1) or (2).

...

C. Buyer's Initial Outside Basis

Section 742 provides how an incoming partner determines his initial outside basis.

Section 742. Basis of transferee partner's interest

The basis of an interest in a partnership acquired other than by contribution shall be determined under part II of subchapter O (sec. 1011 and following).

The general rules applicable to determining tax basis apply in this situation depending upon whether the new partner acquired the partnership interest by gift, inheritance, purchase, etc. Remember that a new partner will include in the partner's initial outside basis the partner's share of the partnership's liabilities. Consequently, in sale transactions, the buyer's initial outside basis will be a cost basis plus the partner's share of partnership liabilities.

D. Optional Basis Adjustment to Partnership Assets (Section 754 Election)

You may recall our discussion of a Section 754 election that is available to partnerships as a result of distributions made to a partner.[2] The same election is available to partnerships when a partner sells a partnership interest. Section 743 explains the availability of this election.

Section 743. Special rules where Section 754 election or substantial built-in loss

(a) General rule. The basis of partnership property shall not be adjusted as the result of a transfer of an interest in a partnership by sale or exchange or on the death of a partner unless the election provided by Section 754 (relating to optional adjustment to basis of partnership property) is in effect with respect to such partnership or unless the partnership has a substantial built-in loss immediately after such transfer.

(b) Adjustment to basis of partnership property. In the case of a transfer of an interest in a partnership by sale or exchange or upon the death of a partner, a partnership with respect to which the election provided in Section 754 is in effect or which has a substantial built-in loss immediately after such transfer shall—

(1) increase the adjusted basis of the partnership property by the excess of the basis to the transferee partner of his interest in the partnership over his proportionate share of the adjusted basis of the partnership property, or

(2) decrease the adjusted basis of the partnership property by the excess of the transferee partner's proportionate share of the adjusted basis of the partnership property over the basis of his interest in the partnership.

Under regulations prescribed by the Secretary, such increase or decrease shall constitute an adjustment to the basis of partnership property with respect to the transferee partner only. ...

(c) Allocation of basis. The allocation of basis among partnership properties where subsection (b) is applicable shall be made in accordance with the rules provided in Section 755. ...

The partnership's election to adjust the basis of its assets is provided by Code Section 754.

[2] See the discussion of Section 734(b) and the Section 754 election in Chapter 11.

Section 754. Manner of electing optional adjustment to basis of partnership property

If a partnership files an election, in accordance with regulations prescribed by the Secretary, the basis of partnership property shall be adjusted, in the case of a distribution of property, in the manner provided in Section 734 and, in the case of a transfer of a partnership interest, in the manner provided in Section 743. Such an election shall apply with respect to all distributions of property by the partnership and to all transfers of interests in the partnership during the taxable year with respect to which such election was filed and all subsequent taxable years. Such elections may be revoked by the partnership, subject to such limitations as may be provided by regulations prescribed by the Secretary.

Notice that Section 743 indicates that the basis adjustments to the partnership's assets are accomplished in a manner as set forth in Section 755.

Section 755. Rules for allocation of basis

(a) General rule. Any increase or decrease in the adjusted basis of partnership property under Section 734(b) (relating to the optional adjustment to the basis of undistributed partnership property) or Section 743(b)(relating to the optional adjustment to the basis of partnership property in the case of a transfer of an interest in a partnership) shall, except as provided in subsection (b), be allocated—

(1) in a manner which has the effect of reducing the difference between the fair market value and the adjusted basis of partnership properties, or

(2) in any other manner permitted by regulations prescribed by the Secretary.

(b) Special rule. In applying the allocation rules provided in subsection (a), increases or decreases in the adjusted basis of partnership property arising from a distribution of, or a transfer of an interest attributable to, property consisting of—

(1) capital assets and property described in Section 1231(b), or

(2) any other property of the partnership,

shall be allocated to partnership property of a like character except that the basis of any such partnership property shall not be reduced below zero. If, in the case of a distribution, the adjustment to basis of property described in paragraph (1) or (2) is prevented by the absence of such property or by insufficient adjusted basis for such property, such adjustment shall be applied to subsequently acquired property of a like character in accordance with regulations prescribed by the Secretary.

. . .

In short, Section 755 requires that assets be grouped together so that ordinary income/loss recognized by the partner upon the sale of his partnership interest is reflected in the basis adjustments to the ordinary income assets. Capital gain/loss or Section 1231 gain/loss recognized by the partner upon the sale of his or her partnership interest is reflected in the basis adjustments to the capital assets and Section 1231 assets. The Treasury Regulations go into considerable detail as to how this is to be done, but we won't go into those here.

CHAPTER 12 QUESTIONS FOR REVIEW

1. *Sale of a partnership interest.* R is a 40% partner and J is a 60% partner in a partnership that owns only one asset, a parcel of land. The land has a tax basis of $600 and a value of $800 to the partnership. R and J formed the partnership six years ago. The land was not contributed by either partner, but acquired by the partnership after formation. The land is encumbered by a $100 nonrecourse liability. R's outside basis is $80. R then sells his entire interest to M for $280.

   a. What is R's amount realized?
   b. What is R's gain or loss realized?
   c. What is R's gain or loss recognized?
   d. What is the character of R's gain?
   e. What is M's initial outside basis?

2. *Sale of a partnership interest.* R and J are equal partners. The partnership owns land (basis $90, FMV $100) and inventory (basis $70, FMV $100). The partnership has no liabilities. R sells his partnership interest to M for $100. R's outside basis at the time of the sale is $80.

   a. What is R's amount realized?
   b. What is R's gain or loss realized?
   c. What is R's gain or loss recognized?
   d. What is the character of R's gain or loss recognized?
   e. What is M's initial outside basis?

3. *Sale of a partnership interest.* R and J are equal partners. The partnership owns land (basis $110, FMV $100) and inventory (basis $70, FMV $100). The partnership has no liabilities. R sells his partnership interest to M for $100. R's outside basis at the time of the sale is $90.

   a. What is R's amount realized?
   b. What is R's gain or loss realized?
   c. What is R's gain or loss recognized?
   d. What is the character of R's gain or loss recognized?
   e. What is M's initial outside basis?

4. *Pollack v. Commissioner.* Summarize the facts of the *Pollack v. Commissioner* case. Discuss the issue, analysis, and conclusion of the court.

5. *Sale of a partnership interest*. R and J are equal partners. The partnership owns land (basis $90, FMV $100) and inventory (basis $70, FMV $100). The partnership has no liabilities. R sells his partnership interest to M for $100. R's outside basis at the time of the sale is $80.

   a. What is R's amount realized?
   b. What is R's gain or loss realized?
   c. What is R's gain or loss recognized?
   d. What is the character of R's gain or loss recognized?
   e. What is M's initial outside basis?
   f. Suppose after M purchases the partnership interest from R the partnership sells the inventory for $100. How much gain/income does M recognize? How much gain/income does J recognize?
   g. How would your answers change if the partnership had a Section 754 election in effect?

6. *Sale of a partnership interest*. R and J are equal partners. The partnership owns land (basis $110, FMV $100) and inventory (basis $70, FMV $100). The partnership has no liabilities. R sells his partnership interest to M for $100. R's outside basis at the time of the sale is $90.

   a. What is R's amount realized?
   b. What is R's gain or loss realized?
   c. What is R's gain or loss recognized?
   d. What is the character of R's gain or loss recognized?
   e. What is M's initial outside basis?
   f. Suppose after M purchases the partnership interest from R the partnership sells the inventory for $100. How much gain/income does M recognize? How much gain/income does J recognize?
   g. How would your answers change if the partnership had a Section 754 election in effect?

7. *Section 754 election*. A colleague of yours asks you what a Section 754 election is. Provide an explanation to your colleague.

8. *Section 754 election*. What Code Section (and subsection) allows an adjustment to the partnership's basis in its assets upon the sale of a partnership interest by a partner?

Pollack v. Commissioner

United States Tax Court
69 TC 142 (1977)

FAY, *Judge*:

Respondent determined deficiencies in petitioners' Federal income tax as follows:

Year	Deficiency
1966............ .	$ 2,545.03
1967............ .	$ 1,433.98

The deficiency for 1966 resulted from a disallowance by respondent of a claimed net operating loss carryback from 1969. We are to decide whether petitioner H. Clinton Pollack, Jr., is entitled to an ordinary loss treatment on the disposition of his interest in a limited partnership during 1969.

FINDINGS OF FACT

Certain facts have been stipulated by the parties.

Petitioners H. Clinton Pollack, Jr., and Wendy Pollack are husband and wife who resided in Greenwich, Conn., at the time they filed their petition with this Court. They filed joint Federal income tax returns for the years in issue with the North Atlantic Service Center, Andover, Mass.

Petitioner H. Clinton Pollack, Jr. (hereinafter referred to solely as petitioner) is a management consultant who was, during the years in question, associated full time with a large New York City consulting firm. Petitioner's duties consisted primarily of rendering services pursuant to contracts entered into by his employer. Such services included providing advice in the areas of marketing, business communications, and the structuring or restructuring of businesses. Although he was employed full time, petitioner sought and apparently accepted outside consulting work unassociated with his employer's business. Such is not an unusual case. Performing outside work is an accepted practice in the consulting field so long as no conflict of interest arises between the employer's work and the outside work.

In 1968 petitioner became acquainted with Leonard Turk, the designated general partner of a soon to be formed limited partnership named Millworth Associates. The purpose of the limited partnership was to invest in fledgling and troubled business concerns with the idea of developing such businesses into successful enterprises. As a result of his discussions with Turk, it was petitioner's understanding that the businesses to be acquired by Millworth would require services of various professionals such as management consultants, accountants, and attorneys. It was petitioner's further understanding that it would be the policy of the limited partnership to offer, if possible, any such professional assignments to the limited partners of Millworth who practiced these professions. In this regard, petitioner was aware of several such professionals among the subscribing partners in Millworth, including attorneys and accountants. It was petitioner's understanding that if he were to become a limited partner in Millworth, Turk, as general partner, would supply him with a considerable amount of consulting work. In August 1968 in anticipation of receiving a significant number of profitable consulting assignments, petitioner borrowed $50,000 and became a limited partner in Millworth.

The scheme of the partnership, as originally conceived—to provide its limited partners with professional assignments—did not eventuate. Millworth's emphasis, as petitioner viewed it, was changing to that of an investment club or company. Petitioner, however, was not interested in a passive investment posture in any way, having entered the partnership solely for the reason of securing a new source of potential consulting business.

In December 1969 petitioner therefore decided to withdraw from Millworth, since it failed to serve his purposes. As a result of the liquidation of his interest, petitioner incurred a loss of $27,069.

On his Federal income tax return for 1969 petitioner claimed this amount as an ordinary business loss. Additionally, he filed an application for a tentative refund from the carryback of a net operating loss for the year 1969 of $15,743. Both deductions were subsequently disallowed by respondent.

OPINION

At issue is the character of loss, whether capital or ordinary, incurred by petitioner on the disposition of his interest in a limited partnership. [Citations and footnotes omitted throughout.]

Generally, the treatment accorded gain or loss from an isolated transaction constituting the sale or exchange of a partnership interest is covered by Section 741 which specifically provides that "Such gain or loss shall be considered as gain or loss from the sale or exchange of a capital asset, except as otherwise provided in Section 751." Similarly, the regulations provide that "The sale or exchange of an interest in a partnership shall be treated as the sale or exchange of a capital asset."

The focus of the present controversy is whether Section 741, if applicable, or Section 1221 is dispositive of the treatment accorded the gain or loss realized by a partner on the sale or exchange of a partnership interest.

Petitioner maintains that the interest involved failed to qualify as a capital asset under Section 1221 and that, despite the language of Section 741, the interest constituted an ordinary asset in his hands. Consequently, he concludes, the loss he suffered on its disposition entitles him to either an ordinary and necessary business expense deduction under Section 162(a) or an ordinary business loss deduction under Section 165(a).

Respondent, on the other hand, contends that except for specific exceptions not relevant herein, Section 741 mandates the loss be characterized as a capital loss. We agree with respondent that both the legislative history of Section 741 and its language indicate that Congress intended it to operate independently of Section 1221 so as to be dispositive of the character of petitioner's loss.

Section 741 was enacted by Congress as part of subchapter K of the Internal Revenue Code of 1954. Subchapter K was enacted to resolve the chaos which permeated the partnership area under the 1939 Code. While it would serve no useful purpose here to attempt to articulate each and every difficulty which led to the enactment of subchapter K, the general situation can be aptly summarized by the following observation contained in its legislative history:

> The existing tax treatment of partners and partnerships is among the most confused in the entire income tax field. The present statutory provisions are wholly inadequate. The published regulations, rulings, and court decisions are incomplete and frequently contradictory. As a result partners today cannot form, operate, or dissolve a partnership with any assurance as to tax consequences.
>
> . . .
>
> Because of the vital need for clarification, your committee has undertaken the first comprehensive statutory treatment of partners and partnerships in the history of the income tax laws. In establishing a broad pattern applicable to partnerships generally, the principal objectives have been simplicity, flexibility, and equity as between the partners.

A prime example of such confusion under the 1939 Code was the treatment of gain or loss from the sale or exchange of a partnership interest. Prior to 1950 the Government took the position, under the so-called aggregate theory of partnership, that the selling partner actually sold his undivided interest in each of the partnership's assets, and the character and amounts resulting from the disposition of those assets should be considered individually.

This position, however, found no acceptance in the courts, which consistently held a partnership interest to be a capital asset in its entirely regardless of the nature of the underlying partnership assets. ... In response, the Government in 1950 reversed its position in G.C.M. 26379 stating that

> the sale of a partnership interest should be treated as the sale of a capital asset under the provisions of Section 117 of the Internal Revenue Code [of 1939].

The result of the Government's concession, however, was to engender the use of the "collapsible partnership" device, by which a partner was able to convert his share of what would otherwise be ordinary income to capital gain by means of the sale of his partnership interest.

Faced with this situation, Congress, in the 1954 Code, sought to eliminate the confusion on this point by codifying the Government's concession in G.C.M. 26379 and, at the same time, reduce the availability of the collapsible partnership as a tax avoidance device....Congress accomplished its dual purpose by enactment of Section 741, which treated the sale of a partnership interest as the sale of a capital asset, and Section 741, which specifically excluded from capital gain or loss treatment that portion of the partnership interest representing income from unrealized receivables and substantially appreciated inventory items.

In view of the foregoing legislative record and the plain language of the statute itself, we conclude that Congress intended Section 741, if applicable, to provide capital gain or loss treatment on the sale or exchange of a partnership interest by a partner without regard to Section 1221. Indeed, congressional use of the phrase "shall be considered as" in Section 741 is unambiguous and mandatory on its face. Furthermore, the singular meaning of such phrase is demonstrated by its consistent interpretation in sections 731, 735, 736, and 751. In fact, where Congress has intended Section 1221 to apply despite similar statutory specificity, it has generally either expressly or impliedly said so.

Accordingly, we hold that petitioner realized a capital loss on the disposition of his limited partnership interest in Millworth Associates, irrespective of his motive in acquiring such interest.

Decision will be entered for the respondent.

Chapter 13

Partnership Terminations, Mergers, and Divisions

A. Partnership Terminations in General
B. Partnership Mergers
C. Partnership Divisions

This chapter discusses issues related to partnership technical terminations as well as the regulations governing partnership mergers and divisions

A. Partnership Terminations in General

According to Code Section 708, a partnership can terminate for federal income tax purposes in two ways.

> **Section 708. Continuation of partnership**
>
> **(a) General rule**. For purposes of this subchapter, an existing partnership shall be considered as continuing if it is not terminated.
>
> **(b) Termination**.—
>
> (1) General rule. For purposes of subsection (a), a partnership shall be considered as terminated only if—
>
> (A) no part of any business, financial operation, or venture of the partnership continues to be carried on by any of its partners in a partnership, or
>
> (B) within a 12-month period there is a sale or exchange of 50 percent or more of the total interest in partnership capital and profits.
>
> . . .

We'll discuss each of the two ways a partnership can terminate for federal income tax purposes.

1. No business being carried on by partnership or partners

A partnership terminates when the partners no longer carry on the business of the partnership. In these situations, the partners will typically plan to cease doing business, wind up the affairs of the partnership, and then liquidate the partnership. The partnership, of course, would file a final return for the year in which the liquidation occurs. Importantly, it is federal tax law that governs whether a partnership terminates for federal income tax purposes rather than the termination of a partnership under state law. Thus, it is possible that a Form 1065 would be necessary and Schedules K-1 be provided to partners even after the partnership terminated for state law purposes.

rzymuR /Shutterstock.com

For a court case analyzing the termination of a partnership for federal income tax purposes, see *Fensel v. United States*, 617 F.Supp 22 (1985). Excerpts of the *Fensel* case are included at the end of this chapter.

2. Technical termination of a partnership

A partnership "technically" terminates if 50% or more of the partnership's capital and profits is sold or exchanged during any 12-month consecutive period. The consequences of a technical termination are that for income tax purposes the old partnership is deemed to end and a new partnership is deemed to immediately form.[1] Thus, the partnership will need to make new determinations and elections as to method of accounting, taxable year, optional basis adjustments, etc., as well as file a short-year return for both the old partnership and the new partnership. Importantly, a partnership does not terminate under state law as a result of a technical termination for federal income tax purposes and vice versa.

Notice in the language in Section 708 that a technical termination occurs if the total capital and profits in a partnership is *sold or exchanged* within a 12-month period. This means that a *gift* or *inheritance* of a partnership interest, for example, is not included in the determination of how much capital and profits have been sold or exchanged. Moreover, if the same interest is sold or exchanged more than once during a 12-month period, the transfer is counted only once toward the 50% threshold.[2]

B. Partnership Mergers

Section 708 provides special rules for mergers and divisions of partnerships and the impact of such mergers and divisions on the termination of a partnership.

[1] Treas. Reg. 1.708-1(b)(4).

[2] Treas. Reg. 1.708-1(b)(2).

Section 708. Continuation of partnership

. . .

(b) Termination.—

. . .

(2) Special rules.—

(A) Merger or consolidation. In the case of the merger or consolidation of two or more partnerships, the resulting partnership shall, for purposes of this section, be considered the continuation of any merging or consolidating partnership whose members own an interest of more than 50 percent in the capital and profits of the resulting partnership.

. . .

The Treasury Regulations provide more detail with respect to accomplishing a partnership merger.

Treas. Reg. § 1.708-1. Continuation of partnership

(a) General rule. For purposes of subchapter K, chapter 1 of the Code, an existing partnership shall be considered as continuing if it is not terminated.

(b) Termination.—

. . .

(2) Special rules.—

(i) Merger or consolidation. If two or more partnerships merge or consolidate into one partnership, the resulting partnership shall be considered a continuation of the merging or consolidating partnership the members of which own an interest of more than 50 percent in the capital and profits of the resulting partnership. If the resulting partnership can, under the preceding sentence, be considered a continuation of more than one of the merging or consolidating partnerships, it shall, unless the Commissioner permits otherwise, be considered the continuation of that partnership which is credited with the contribution of the greatest dollar value of assets to the resulting partnership. Any other merging or consolidating partnerships shall be considered as terminated. If the members of none of the merging or consolidating partnerships have an interest of more than 50 percent in the capital and profits of the resulting partnership, all of the merged or consolidated partnerships are terminated, and a new partnership results. ...

The provisions of this subdivision may be illustrated by the following example:

Example. Partnership AB, in whose capital and profits A and B each own a 50-percent interest, and partnership CD, in whose capital and profits C and D each own a 50-percent interest, merge on September 30, 1955, and form partnership ABCD. Partners A, B, C, and D are on a calendar year; partnership AB is also on a calendar year; and partnership CD is on a fiscal year ending June 30th. After the merger, the partners have capital and profits interests as follows: A, 30 percent; B, 30 percent; C, 20 percent; and D, 20 percent. Since A and B together own an interest of more than 50 percent in the capital and profits of partnership ABCD, such partnership shall be considered a continuation of partnership AB and shall continue to file returns on a calendar year basis. Since C and D own an interest of less than 50 percent in the capital and profits of partnership ABCD, the taxable year of partnership CD closes as of September 30, 1955, the date of the merger, and CD partnership is terminated as of that date. Partnership ABCD is required to file a return for the taxable year January 1 to December 31, 1955, indicating thereon that, until September 30, 1955, it was partnership AB, Partnership CD is required to file a return for its final taxable year, July 1 through September 30, 1955.

The Treasury Regulations continue to provide further details regarding the termination of a partnership because of a merger with another partnership. According to the regulations, a partnership can choose to accomplish a merger with another partnership in one of two ways: (1) the assets-over form and (2) the assets-up form.

1. Assets-over form

Treasury Regulation § 1.708-1. Continuation of partnership

...

(c) Merger or consolidation.—

...

(3) Form of a merger or consolidation.—

(i) Assets-over form. When two or more partnerships merge or consolidate into one partnership under the applicable jurisdictional law without undertaking a form for the merger or consolidation, or undertake a form for the merger or consolidation that is not described in paragraph (c)(3)(ii) of this section, any merged or consolidated partnership that is considered terminated under paragraph (c)(1) of this section is treated as undertaking the assets-over form for Federal income tax purposes. Under the assets-over form, the merged or consolidated partnership that is considered terminated under paragraph (c)(1) of this section contributes all of its assets and liabilities to the resulting partnership in exchange for an interest in the resulting partnership, and immediately thereafter, the terminated partnership distributes interests in the resulting partnership to its partners in liquidation of the terminated partnership.

...

2. Assets-up form

Treasury Regulation 1.708-1. Continuation of partnership

...

(c) Merger or consolidation.

...

(3) Form of a merger or consolidation.

...

(ii) Assets-up form. Despite the partners' transitory ownership of the terminated partnership's assets, the form of a partnership merger or consolidation will be respected for Federal income tax purposes if the merged or consolidated partnership that is considered terminated under paragraph (c)(1) of this section distributes all of its assets to its partners (in a manner that causes the partners to be treated, under the laws of the applicable jurisdiction, as the owners of such assets) in liquidation of the partners' interests in the terminated partnership, and immediately thereafter, the partners in the terminated partnership contribute the distributed assets to the resulting partnership in exchange for interests in the resulting partnership.

...

C. Partnership Divisions

Occasionally the partners in a partnership will desire to separate a single partnership into two or more partnerships. Section 708 addresses this issue as well.

Section 708. Continuation of partnership

...

(b) Termination.—

...

(2) Special rules.—

...

(B) Division of partnership. In the case of a division of a partnership into two or more partnerships, the resulting partnerships (other than any resulting partnership the members of which had an interest of 50 percent or less in the capital and profits of the prior partnership) shall, for purposes of this section, be considered a continuation of the prior partnership.

As with partnership mergers, the Treasury Regulations provide examples of partnership divisions and the impact upon the termination of a partnership.

Treas. Reg. § 1.708-1. Continuation of partnership

(a) General rule. For purposes of subchapter K, chapter 1 of the Code, an existing partnership shall be considered as continuing if it is not terminated.

(b) Termination.

...

(2) Special rules.—

...

(ii) Division of a partnership. Under the division of a partnership into two or more partnerships, any resulting partnership or partnerships shall be considered a continuation of the prior partnership if its members had an interest of more than 50 percent in the capital and profits of the prior partnership. Any other resulting partnership will not be considered a continuation of the prior partnership but will be considered a new partnership. If the members of none of the resulting partnerships owned an interest of more than 50 percent in the capital and profits of the divided partnership, the divided partnership is terminated. ...

Example. Partnership ABCD is in the real estate and insurance business. A owns a 40-percent interest, and B, C, and D each owns a 20-percent interest, in the capital and profits of the partnership. The partnership and the partners report their income on a calendar year. They agree to separate the real estate and insurance business as of November 1, 1955, and to form two partnerships; partnership AB to take over the real estate business, and partnership CD to take over the insurance business. Since members of resulting partnership AB owned more than a 50-percent interest in the capital and profits of partnership ABCD (A, 40 percent, and B, 20 percent), partnership AB shall be considered a continuation of partnership ABCD. Partnership AB is required to file a return for the taxable year January 1 to December 31, 1955, indicating thereon that until November 1, 1955, it was partnership ABCD. In forming partnership CD, partners C and D may contribute the property distributed to them in liquidation of their entire interests in divided partnership ABCD. Partnership CD will be required to file a return for the taxable year ....

A partnership can accomplish a partnership division in one of two ways: (1) the assets-over form and (2) the assets-up form.

1. Assets-over form

Treasury Regulation 1.708-1. Continuation of partnership

...

(d) Division of partnership.—

...

(3) Form of a division.—

(i) Assets-over form. When a partnership divides into two or more partnerships under applicable jurisdictional law without undertaking a form for the division, or undertakes a form that is not described in paragraph (d)(3)(ii) of this section, the transaction will be characterized under the assets-over form for Federal income tax purposes.

(A) Assets-over form where at least one resulting partnership is a continuation of the prior partnership. In a division under the assets-over form where at least one resulting partnership is a continuation of the prior partnership, the divided partnership (as defined in paragraph (d)(4)(i) of this section) contributes certain assets and liabilities to a recipient partnership (as defined in paragraph (d)(4)(iii) of this section) or recipient partnerships in exchange for interests in such recipient partnership or partnerships; and, immediately thereafter, the divided partnership distributes the interests in such recipient partnership or partnerships to some or all of its partners in partial or complete liquidation of the partners' interests in the divided partnership.

(B) Assets-over form where none of the resulting partnerships is a continuation of the prior partnership. In a division under the assets-over form where none of the resulting partnerships is a continuation of the prior partnership, the prior partnership will be treated as contributing all of its assets and liabilities to new resulting partnerships in exchange for interests in the resulting partnerships; and, immediately thereafter, the prior partnership will be treated as liquidating by distributing the interests in the new resulting partnership to the prior partnership's partners.

. . .

2. Assets-up form

Treasury Regulation 1.708-1. Continuation of partnership

. . .

(d) Division of partnership.—

. . .

(3) Form of a division.—

(A) Assets- up form where the partnership distributing assets is a continuation of the prior partnership. Despite the partners' transitory ownership of some of the prior partnership's assets, the form of a partnership division will be respected for Federal income tax purposes if the divided partnership (which, pursuant to § 1.708-1(d)(4)(i), must be a continuing partnership) distributes certain assets (in a manner that causes the partners to be treated, under the laws of the applicable jurisdiction, as the owners of such assets) to some or all of its partners in partial or complete liquidation of the partners' interests in the divided partnership, and immediately thereafter, such partners contribute the distributed assets to a recipient partnership or partnerships in exchange for interests in such recipient partnership or partnerships. In order for such form to be respected for transfers to a particular recipient partnership, all assets held by the prior partnership that are transferred to the recipient partnership must be distributed to, and then contributed by, the partners of the recipient partnership.

(B) Assets-up form where none of the resulting partnerships are a continuation of the prior partnership. If none of the resulting partnerships are a continuation of the prior partnership, then despite the partners' transitory ownership of some or all of the prior partnership's assets, the form of a partnership division will be respected for Federal income tax purposes if the prior partnership distributes certain assets (in a manner that causes the partners to be treated, under the laws of the applicable jurisdiction, as the owners of such assets) to some or all of its partners in partial or complete liquidation of the partners' interests in the prior partnership, and immediately thereafter, such partners contribute the distributed assets to a resulting partnership or partnerships in exchange for interests in such resulting partnership or partnerships. In order for such form to be respected for transfers to a particular resulting partnership, all assets held by the prior partnership that are transferred to the resulting partnership must be distributed to, and then contributed by, the partners of the resulting partnership. If the prior partnership does not liquidate under the applicable jurisdictional law, then with respect to the assets and liabilities that, in form, are not transferred to a new resulting partnership, the prior partnership will be treated as transferring these assets and liabilities to a new resulting partnership under the assets-over form described in paragraph (d)(3)(i)(B) of this section.

...

A tax practitioner should always be aware of potential partnership technical terminations and also the potential impact a merger or division will have on the partnership and its partners.

CHAPTER 13 QUESTIONS FOR REVIEW

1. *Partnership termination.* Explain the two ways in which a partnership can terminate for federal income tax purposes.

2. *Fensel v. United States.* Summarize the facts of the *Fensel v. United States* case. Discuss the issue, analysis, and conclusion of the court.

3. *Technical termination.* What is not considered a "sale or exchange" when determining if a partnership has technically terminated?

4. *Technical termination.* What are the consequences of a partnership's technical termination?

5. *Partnership termination.* R owns 70% of the profits and capital of a partnership. J owns the other 30%. On January 12, R sells a 40% interest in the partnership to M (leaving R with 30%). On August 10, R sells a 20% interest in the partnership to W (now leaving R with a 10% interest in partnership capital and profits). Does the partnership technically terminate as a result of these transactions? If so, when?

6. *Partnership termination.* Assume the same facts as in Problem 5 except that instead of selling 20% to W, R *gave* W the 20% interest in the partnership as a gift. Does the partnership technically terminate? If so, when?

7. *Partnership merger.* Explain the two different ways a partnership merger can be accomplished according to the regulations.

8. *Partnership division.* Explain the two different ways a partnership division can be accomplished according to the regulations.

Peter T. Fensel v. United States

United States District Court, Western District of Pennsylvania
617 F.Supp. 22 (1985)

Opinion

Mencer, District Judge:

The plaintiff, Peter T. Fensel, brought suit seeking a refund of part of the federal income taxes paid by him for 1978 and 1979. This tax was paid on partnership income attributed to the plaintiff by a partnership doing business as "The Pub" in which he was allegedly a partner. The plaintiff contends that he received no income or anything of value from The Pub in those years because the partnership had been terminated by mutual agreement in 1977. The defendant, the United States of America, alleges, on the other hand, that the partnership was not terminated and that the plaintiff is, therefore, liable for taxes on his share of the partnership's income in 1978 and 1979. The plaintiff further contends, however, that he never received a share of the partnership's income, which leads him to ask this Court, in the alternative, to allow him theft losses for the amounts attributed to him if we find that the partnership was not terminated in 1977. The plaintiff also seeks attorneys fees.

Both sides have filed Motions for Summary Judgment. The plaintiff's Motion is supported by his affidavit and exhibits while the defendant's Motion relies primarily on the plaintiff's deposition.
A court, when considering a motion for summary judgment, should only grant the motion "if the pleadings, depositions, answers to interrogatories, and admissions on file, together with the affidavits, if any, show that there is no genuine issue as to any material fact and that the moving party is entitled to a judgment as a matter of law." Fed. R. Civ. P. 56(c). All inferences, doubts and issues of credibility are to be resolved against the moving party. *E. E. O. C. v. Westinghouse Electric Corp.,* 725 F. 2d 211, 216 (3d Cir. 1983).

Partnership Termination

The plaintiff, in his Motion for Summary Judgment, asks this Court to find that the partnership in question was terminated in 1977 and to grant him a tax refund. The defendant requests that we find that the partnership was not terminated until 1980 and that the plaintiff is not entitled to any refund.

This Court is of the view that summary judgment is appropriate with regard to the partnership termination issue as there are no material facts left to be resolved. A partnership, to be viewed as terminated, must comply with the requirements of 26 U. S. C. §708(b)(1), which states in the appropriate part that:

[A] partnership shall be considered as terminated only if--

(A) no part of any business, financial operation, or venture of the partnership continues to be carried on by any of its partners in a partnership, or

(B) within a 12-month period there is a sale or exchange of 50 percent or more of the total interest in partnership capital and profits.

If there is not compliance with either provision of subsection (b)(1), "an existing partnership shall be considered as continuing...." 26 U. S. C. §708(a).

The plaintiff has attempted to convince this Court that the partnership in question here terminated in the fall of 1977 when he ceased his activities with The Pub, which left only his partner, Michael T. McGuire, involved with the business. This view is not in accord with those expressed by several courts. The court in *Ginsburg v. United States* [citation omitted] indicated that the apparent intention of Congress in adding §708 to subchapter K of the Internal Revenue Code of 1954 without a cross reference to the definition section (§761) was "that the issue of terminating an existing partnership [was] to be evaluated solely on the basis of Section 708 without regard to whether the 'organization' of individuals involved, if judged *ab initio,* would be considered a partnership under Section 761(a)." Based on this opinion, it would not matter that only one partner was left to continue carrying on the business of the partnership. As long as the business of the partnership is carried on by *any* partner, the partnership has not been terminated in accord with §708(b)(1)(A).

In a case very similar to this one, another court held that "even though the partnership dissolved ...when petitioner withdrew and ceased to be associated with the carrying on of the partnership business, there continued to be a valid partnership until such time as the partnership actually terminated." [Citation omitted.] The plaintiff here also withdrew and ceased to be associated with the running of The Pub, the partnership business, but the partnership continued to exist until he sold his interest in 1980.

Because the partnership did not terminate until 1980, the plaintiff is not entitled to a refund for the taxes paid for 1978 and 1979 on the share of the partnership's income attributed to him.

Theft Loss Deduction

This Court, having found that the plaintiff was a partner in a partnership in 1978 and 1979, must now consider whether he was entitled to take a theft loss deduction in those years for his allegedly unreceived share of the partnership's income.

Section 165 of the Internal Revenue Code states that "any loss arising from theft shall be treated as sustained during the taxable year in which the taxpayer discovers such loss." 26 U. S. C. §165(e). "The IRS has construed this as meaning that a theft loss deduction can be taken *only* in the year of discovery." [Citation omitted.] The plaintiff bears the burden of establishing when he discovered his theft loss. [Citation omitted.]

The plaintiff, in his affidavit, attempts to convince this Court that he learned of the theft losses when he received copies of Form 1065 and/or Schedule K during 1978 and 1979 at the times these documents were dated. The plaintiff further states that he has no recollection of looking at these documents or of their contents if he did look at them when they were received. These statements by the plaintiff are all that he offers to satisfy his burden of proving when he discovered the theft losses.

The plaintiff has failed to convince this Court that he discovered the thefts in 1978 and 1979, respectively, or that there is even a genuine issue of material fact as to his discovery of the thefts in those years. Therefore, he is not entitled to deduct the theft losses in 1978 or 1979. As to the theft losses which may be deductible in subsequent years, the plaintiff must resort to an amended return for the year in which such losses were discovered.

Attorneys Fees

The plaintiff also seeks attorneys fees under 26 U. S. C. §7430(a). In view of the disposition reached here, we deem that the plaintiff is not entitled to such fees.

An appropriate order will be issued.

ORDER

AND NOW, this 7th day of August, 1985,

IT IS ORDERED that the Motion for Summary Judgment filed by the plaintiff, Peter T. Fensel, is DENIED.

IT IS FURTHER ORDERED that the Motion for Summary Judgment filed by the defendant, the United States of America, is GRANTED for the reasons stated in the accompanying Opinion, and judgment is entered in favor of the defendant, the United States of America, and against the plaintiff, Peter T. Fensel.

Part V

Miscellaneous Partnership Tax Topics

Chapter 14

Miscellaneous Partnership Tax Topics

A. Carried Interests
B. Reportable Transactions and Material Advisors
C. Anti-abuse Rules

A. Carried Interests

Most individual taxpayers prefer long-term capital gains over ordinary income because of the preferential tax rate applied to long-term capital gains. This disparity in tax rates causes taxpayers to structure certain transactions in a manner so that they may benefit from the lower tax rate. Nevertheless, controversy sometimes arises on whether a partner's income from a partnership should really be classified as ordinary income instead. This controversy is very much alive in the "carried interests" area of partnership taxation.

Suppose that a limited partnership is organized and is able to attract millions of dollars in investment from limited partners. The partnership also has one general partner whose responsibility is to manage and invest the contributions of the limited partners. A typical arrangement has the partnership paying the general partner a guaranteed payment (ordinary income to the general partner) equal to 2% of the value of the assets in the partnership to compensate the general partner for the management services. Additionally, the agreement likely provides that the general partner's distributive share of partnership profits is, say, 20% (i.e., the carried interest) of the partnership's profits. Suppose the partnership's profits consist of millions of dollars in long-term capital gains due to investments in real estate and corporate stock of successful companies. As a result of the partnership's pass-through nature, the long-term capital gains pass-through to the partners including the general partner. *The question arises as to whether the general partner should be entitled to recognize the pass-through income as long-term capital gain because the general partner did not provide capital to the partnership; rather, the general partner provided services only.* Some politicians would like to pass legislation ensuring that the general partner recognizes ordinary income and not capital gain on the general partner's carried interest.

B. Reportable Transactions and Material Advisors

Most taxpayers do their best to comply with the tax laws and tax reporting requirements. Of course, there are always those who try to minimize or avoid paying taxes contrary to the letter and/or spirit of the laws. Tax advisors often spend a lot of time thinking about structuring transactions in a way that help clients generate tax deductions or avoid recognizing gains. Some of these transactions are of questionable legality, however. Consequently, the Code contains some specific provisions attempting to combat these abusive transactions that are often called "tax shelters." Partnerships may be required to disclose these transactions to the IRS.

1. Reportable Transactions and Related Penalties

Taxpayers entering into transactions identified as "reportable transactions" must disclose such transactions to the IRS.

Treas. Reg. § 1.6011-4. Requirement of statement disclosing participation in certain transactions by taxpayers

(a) In general. Every taxpayer that has participated, as described in paragraph (c)(3) of this section, in a reportable transaction within the meaning of paragraph (b) of this section and who is required to file a tax return must file within the time prescribed in paragraph (e) of this section a disclosure statement in the form prescribed by paragraph (d) of this section. The fact that a transaction is a reportable transaction shall not affect the legal determination of whether the taxpayer's treatment of the transaction is proper.

(b) Reportable transactions.—

(1) In general. A reportable transaction is a transaction described in any of the paragraphs (b)(2) through (7) of this section. The term transaction includes all of the factual elements relevant to the expected tax treatment of any investment, entity, plan, or arrangement, and includes any series of steps carried out as part of a plan.

(2) Listed transactions. A listed transaction is a transaction that is the same as or a substantially similar to one of the types of transactions that the Internal Revenue Service (IRS) has determined to be a tax avoidance transaction and identified by notice, regulation, or other form of published guidance as a listed transaction.

(3) Confidential transactions.—

(i) In general. A confidential transaction is a transaction that is offered to a taxpayer under conditions of confidentiality and for which the taxpayer has paid an advisor a minimum fee.

(ii) Conditions of confidentiality. A transaction is considered to be offered to a taxpayer under conditions of confidentiality if the advisor who is paid the minimum fee places a limitation on disclosure by the taxpayer of the tax treatment or tax structure of the transaction and the limitation on disclosure protects the confidentiality of that advisor's tax strategies. A transaction is treated as confidential even if the conditions of confidentiality are not legally binding on the taxpayer. A claim that a transaction is proprietary or exclusive is not treated as a limitation on disclosure if the advisor confirms to the taxpayer that there is no limitation on disclosure of the tax treatment or tax structure of the transaction.

(iii) Minimum fee. For purposes of this paragraph (b)(3), the minimum fee is—

(A) $250,000 for a transaction if the taxpayer is a corporation;

(B) $50,000 for all other transactions unless the taxpayer is a partnership or trust, all of the owners or beneficiaries of which are corporations (looking through any partners or beneficiaries that are themselves partnerships or trusts), in which case the minimum fee is $250,000.

...

(4) Transactions with contractual protection.

(i) In general. A transaction with contractual protection is a transaction for which the taxpayer or a related party (as described in Section 267(b) or 707(b)) has the right to a full or partial refund of fees (as described in paragraph (b)(4)(ii) of this section) if all or part of the intended tax consequences from the transaction are not sustained. A transaction with contractual protection also is a transaction for which fees (as described in paragraph (b)(4)(ii) of this section) are contingent on the taxpayer's realization of tax benefits from the transaction. All the facts and circumstances relating to the transaction will be considered when determining whether a fee is refundable or contingent, including the right to reimbursements of amounts that the parties to the transaction have not designated as fees or any agreement to provide services without reasonable compensation.

...

(5) Loss transactions.

(i) In general. A loss transaction is any transaction resulting in the taxpayer claiming a loss under Section 165 of at least—

(A) $10 million in any single taxable year or $20 million in any combination of taxable years for corporations;

(B) $10 million in any single taxable year or $20 million in any combination of taxable years for partnerships that have only corporations as partners (looking through any partners that are themselves partnerships), whether or not any losses flow through to one or more partners; or

(C) $2 million in any single taxable year or $4 million in any combination of taxable years for all other partnerships, whether or not any losses flow through to one or more partners;

(D) $2 million in any single taxable year or $4 million in any combination of taxable years for individuals, S corporations, or trusts, whether or not any losses flow through to one or more shareholders or beneficiaries; or

(E) $50,000 in any single taxable year for individuals or trusts whether or not the loss flows through from an S corporation or partnership, if the loss arises with respect to a Section 988 transaction... relating to foreign currency transactions.

...

(6) Transactions of interest. A transaction of interest is a transaction that is the same as or substantially similar to one of the types of transactions that the IRS has identified by notice, regulation, or other form of published guidance as a transaction of interest.

(7) [Reserved].

...

Penalties apply if a taxpayer fails to disclose reportable transactions.

Section 6707A. Penalty for failure to include reportable transaction information with return

(a) Imposition of penalty. Any person who fails to include on any return or statement any information with respect to a reportable transaction which is required under Section 6011 to be included with such return or statement shall pay a penalty in the amount determined under subsection (b).

(b) Amount of penalty.—

(1) In general. Except as otherwise provided in this subsection, the amount of the penalty under subsection (a) with respect to any reportable transaction shall be 75 percent of the decrease in tax shown on the return as a result of such transaction (or which would have resulted from such transaction if such transaction were respected for Federal tax purposes).

(2) Maximum penalty. The amount of the penalty under subsection (a) with respect to any reportable transaction shall not exceed—

(A) in the case of a listed transaction, $200,000 ($100,000 in the case of a natural person), or

(B) in the case of any other reportable transaction, $50,000 ($10,000 in the case of a natural person).

(3) Minimum penalty. The amount of the penalty under subsection (a) with respect to any transaction shall not be less than $10,000 ($5,000 in the case of a natural person).

(c) Definitions. For purposes of this section—

(1) Reportable transaction. The term "reportable transaction" means any transaction with respect to which information is required to be included with a return or statement because, as determined under regulations prescribed under Section 6011, such transaction is of a type which the Secretary determines as having a potential for tax avoidance or evasion.

(2) Listed transaction. The term "listed transaction" means a reportable transaction which is the same as, or substantially similar to, a transaction specifically identified by the Secretary as a tax avoidance transaction for purposes of Section 6011.

...

A taxpayer files IRS Form 8886 to disclose reportable transactions.

rzymuR /Shutterstock.com

For a court case analyzing a reportable transaction situation, see *United States v. Davison, 105 AFTR 2d 2010-2278*. Excerpts of the *Davison* case are included at the end of this chapter.

2. Disclosure by Material Advisors

The Code requires that tax advisors must disclose to the IRS reportable transactions that they advise taxpayers to enter into.

Section 6111. Disclosure of reportable transactions

(a) In general. Each material advisor with respect to any reportable transaction shall make a return (in such form as the Secretary may prescribe) setting forth—

(1) information identifying and describing the transaction,

(2) information describing any potential tax benefits expected to result from the transaction, and

(3) such other information as the Secretary may prescribe.

Such return shall be filed not later than the date specified by the Secretary.

(b) Definitions. For purposes of this section—

(1) Material advisor.—

(A) In general. The term "material advisor" means any person—

(i) who provides any material aid, assistance, or advice with respect to organizing, managing, promoting, selling, implementing, insuring, or carrying out any reportable transaction, and

(ii) who directly or indirectly derives gross income in excess of the threshold amount (or such other amount as may be prescribed by the Secretary) for such aid, assistance, or advice.

(B) Threshold amount. For purposes of subparagraph (A), the threshold amount is—

(i) $50,000 in the case of a reportable transaction substantially all of the tax benefits from which are provided to natural persons, and

(ii) $250,000 in any other case.

(2) Reportable transaction. The term "reportable transaction" has the meaning given to such term by Section 6707A(c).

. . .

Notice that the burden here is on the "material advisor" to make the report to the IRS regarding a "reportable transaction" entered into by a taxpayer with the advice, assistance, etc., of the material advisor.

Section 6707. Failure to furnish information regarding reportable transactions

(a) In general.—

If a person who is required to file a return under Section 6111(a) with respect to any reportable transaction—

(1) fails to file such return on or before the date prescribed therefor, or

(2) files false or incomplete information with the Secretary with respect to such transaction,

such person shall pay a penalty with respect to such return in the amount determined under subsection (b).

(b) Amount of penalty.—

(1) In general. Except as provided in paragraph (2), the penalty imposed under subsection (a) with respect to any failure shall be $50,000.

(2) Listed transactions. The penalty imposed under subsection (a) with respect to any listed transaction shall be an amount equal to the greater of—

(A) $200,000, or

(B) 50 percent of the gross income derived by such person with respect to aid, assistance, or advice which is provided with respect to the listed transaction before the date the return is filed under Section 6111.

...

A material advisor discloses these transactions by filing Form 8918.

Not only must material advisors disclose reportable transactions, they must keep a list of clients that they advised with respect to these transactions.

Section 6112. Material advisors of reportable transactions must keep lists of advisees, etc.

(a) In general. Each material advisor (as defined in Section 6111) with respect to any reportable transaction (as defined in Section 6707A)(c)) shall (whether or not required to file a return under Section 6111 with respect to such transaction) maintain (in such manner as the Secretary may by regulations prescribe) a list—

(1) identifying each person with respect to whom such advisor acted as a material advisor with respect to such transaction, and

(2) containing such other information as the Secretary may by regulations require.

(b) Special rules.—

(1) Availability for inspection; retention of information on list. Any person who is required to maintain a list under subsection (a) (or was required to maintain a list under subsection (a) as in effect before the enactment of the American Jobs Creation Act of 2004)—

(A) shall make such list available to the Secretary for inspection upon written request by the Secretary, and

(B) except as otherwise provided under regulations prescribed by the Secretary, shall retain any information which is required to be included on such list for 7 years.

. . .

C. Anti-abuse Rules

Taxpayers are very creative in finding ways to minimize their tax liabilities. In the partnership context, the Treasury Regulations contain what is commonly called the **anti-abuse rule**. In short, the Treasury Regulations state that partnerships should not be formed and utilized primarily for tax avoidance purposes that are inconsistent with the intent of Subchapter K. A few excerpts from those regulations are appropriate here.

Treasury Regulation § 1.701-2. Anti-abuse rule

(a) Intent of subchapter K. Subchapter K is intended to permit taxpayers to conduct joint businesses (including investment) activities through a flexible economic arrangement without incurring an entity-level tax. Implicit in the intent of subchapter K are the following requirements—

(1) The partnership must be bona fide and each partnership transaction or series of related transactions (individually or collectively, the transaction) must be entered into for a substantial business purpose.

(2) The form of each partnership transaction must be respected under substance over form principles.

(3) Except as otherwise provided in this paragraph 9a)(3), the tax consequences under subchapter K to each partner of partnership operations and of transactions between the partner and the partnership must accurately reflect the partners' economic agreement and clearly reflect the partner's income (collectively, *proper reflection of income*). However, certain provisions of subchapter K and the regulations thereunder were adopted to promote administrative convenience and other policy objectives, with the recognition that the application of those provisions to a transaction could, in some circumstances, produce tax results that do not properly reflect income. Thus, the proper reflection of income requirement of this paragraph (a)(3) is treated as satisfied with respect to a transaction that satisfies paragraphs (a)(1) and (2) of this section to the extent that the application of such a provision to the transaction and the ultimate tax results, taking into account all the relevant facts and circumstances, are clearly contemplated by that provision. ...

(b) Application of subchapter K rules. The provisions of subchapter K and the regulations thereunder must be applied in a manner that is consistent with the intent of subchapter K as set forth in paragraph (a) of this section (intent of subchapter K). Accordingly, if a partnership is formed or availed of in connection with a transaction a principal purpose of which is to reduce substantially the present value of the partners' aggregate federal tax liability in a manner that is inconsistent with the intent of subchapter K, the Commissioner can recast the transaction for federal tax purposes, as appropriate to achieve tax results that are consistent with the intent of subchapter K, in light of the applicable statutory and regulatory provisions and the pertinent facts and circumstances. Thus, even though the transaction may fall within the literal words of a particular statutory or regulatory provision, the Commissioner can determine, based on the particular facts and circumstances, that to achieve tax results that are consistent with the intent of subchapter K—

(1) The purported partnership should be disregarded in whole or in part, and the partnership's assets and activities should be considered, in whole or in part, to be owned and conducted, respectively, by one or more of its purported partners;

(2) One or more of the purported partners of the partnership should not be treated as a partner;

(3) The methods of accounting used by the partnership or a partner should be adjusted to reflect clearly the partnership's or the partner's income;

(4) The partnership's items of income, gain, loss, deduction, or credit should be reallocated; or

(5) The claimed tax treatment should otherwise be adjusted or modified.

...

CHAPTER 14 QUESTIONS FOR REVIEW

1. *Carried interests.* Explain what a "carried interest" Is. Why is the tax treatment so controversial?

2. *Reportable transactions.* What is a reportable transaction?

3. *Reportable transactions.* What is a "listed" transaction?

4. *Reportable transactions.* If a transaction is a reportable transaction, what must the partnership do?

5. *United States v. Davison.* Discuss the facts of the *United States v. Davison* case. What was/were the issue(s)? Discuss the court's analysis and conclusion.

6. *Material adviser.* With respect to a reportable transaction, who is a "material advisor"?

7. *Material adviser.* Explain what reporting requirements a material adviser must comply with.

8. *Anti-abuse rules.* What is the intent of Subchapter K?

9. *Anti-abuse rules.* What can the IRS do if it decides that a partnership transaction is contrary to the intent of Subchapter K?

United States v. Davison
105 AFTR 2d 2010-2278

OPINION

IN THE UNITED STATES DISTRICT COURT FOR THE WESTERN DISTRICT OF MISSOURI WESTERN DIVISION,

ORDER

Judge: Gary A. Fenner, Judge United States District Court

Defendant, Allen R. Davison, is a certified public accountant and an attorney, who is an active member of the Nebraska bar. Davison received his undergraduate degree and law degree with honors from the University of Nebraska. Since at least the mid-1990's, Davison has advised on tax-related matters and promoted tax-fraud schemes. He has had "hundreds of clients in thirty years of practice." He started his career at Coopers and Lybrand's Omaha office, moved to its Kansas City office, and then ultimately moved to Grant Thornton's Kansas City office, where he became a partner in the tax practice group. Davison left Grant Thornton in October of 2001, but continued to provide tax advice to clients. He became affiliated with Cheryl Womack's enterprises where he held an executive position and provided her with financial and tax advice until 2004, and then worked with Womack's enterprises as a contractor.

Davison has promoted several tax arrangements that involve sham companies and bogus deductions. Davison orchestrated these arrangements, including the creation of these companies. Davison knew at the time the companies were created and thereafter that the companies were shams created for the purpose of illegal tax avoidance. Davison did not intend for these companies to be operated in a legitimate fashion and knew that they were not intended by his clients to be operated in a legitimate fashion under the tax code. Nevertheless, Davison has deliberately promoted these arrangements and repeatedly advised his clients that each arrangement is a legal way to reduce tax liability.

Davison promoted a parallel C management company arrangement in which an operating company that elects sub-chapter S status (pass-through entity) makes purported management-fee payments pursuant to a recurring-item exception deduction under I.R.C. §461(h) to a management company with a staggered tax year. These "fees" were only sham journal entries, and the management company had no business purpose or economic substance. The management company claimed between $50,000 and $100,000 in income, in order to leverage the lower corporate tax rates. This arrangement results in a permanent deferral of income. Davison also promoted an ESOP-S arrangement, which functions similarly to the parallel C arrangement, except that the management company is an S corporation whose shares of stock are owned by an employee stock ownership plan. Here, too, the management company received no actual fees, but, because it is an S corporation, it does not report specific income on its return. Rather, the purported income passes through to its sole shareholder, the ESOP, where it accrues tax-free. Davison also promoted a Roth IRA-C arrangement, which follows the parallel C arrangement, except that the shares of the management company, which is also a C corporation, are owned by a Roth IRA, and the management company receives actual funds (as opposed to only journal entries), which then pass to the Roth IRA as purported dividends. Davison similarly promoted a sham 412(i) pension plan that also involves the formation of a sham entity that purports to sponsor a 412(i) pension plan that deliberately excludes an operating business' rank and file employees in contravention of well-established laws. Davison promoted a sham flock contract arrangement in which he advised clients to execute these contracts and then claim farmer-related deductions on their individual tax returns. His clients, however, are not farmers within the meaning of the Code, and not entitled to claim these deductions.

The IRS estimate that Davison's tax-fraud schemes have cost the United States at least $45 million in uncollected revenues is found to be a reasonable estimate. James Ley, the revenue agent who began the ...investigation nearly seven years ago, testified that "the IRS' resources that were being used to discover and combat these transactions was just staggering." Mr. Ley's testimony in this regard is credible. Davison's numerous and complex tax arrangements, coupled with his designs to disguise his true role in promoting these tax-fraud schemes, have all compounded the difficulty of deciphering these arrangements. Davison has flouted the law in a misguided and intentional attempt to assist his clients in illegal tax avoidance. The harm caused by Davison's actions is enormous.

Section 7402 of the Code provides a court with the authority to take action as necessary or appropriate to enforce the internal revenue laws. [Citations omitted.] The language of this statute is broad and manifests "a Congressional intention to provide the district courts with a full arsenal of powers to compel compliance with the internal revenue laws." [Citation omitted.] This includes issuance of an injunction "as may be necessary or appropriate for the enforcement of the internal revenue laws." [Citation omitted.]

The traditional factors for considering whether an injunction should issue are (1) the likelihood that a plaintiff will sustain irreparable injury in the absence of an injunction; (2) the balance between such harm and the injury that granting the injunction will inflict on other parties litigant; (3) whether the plaintiff has succeeded on the underlying merits of the case; and (4) the public interest. [Citation omitted.]

Here, all of these factors militate in favor of the Court issuing a comprehensive injunction under I.R.C. §7402. First, the government and the public fisc have suffered and will continue to suffer irreparable harm if Davison is not enjoined. Second, the balance between the harm to the government and the integrity of the tax laws balanced against the harm to Davison weighs in favor of the government. Third, the government has succeeded on the merits of its case, showing with overwhelming evidence that

Davison has long engaged in serious misconduct that interferes with enforcement of the internal revenue laws. Finally, the public interest is necessarily aligned with the government's interest. An injunction that bars Davison from providing tax advice in the manner that he has, is in the public interest, especially given the tax harm estimates stemming from Davison's promotion of his tax-fraud schemes, coupled with the substantial IRS resources needed to detect and respond to these tax-fraud schemes. Furthermore, Davison's record establishes that this cycle will continue unless he is barred from providing tax advice without significant restraint.

For nearly fifteen years, Davison has promoted a substantial number of unlawful tax arrangements that involve sham companies, bogus deductions, and fabricated documents. James Ley, the revenue agent who spearheaded this investigation, testified about its magnitude: "literally dozens of revenue agents were involved in conducting the income tax examinations," and the IRS was "dealing with literally hundreds of returns involving multiple tax years." To this end, IRS revenue agents also interviewed dozens of Davison's clients and logged hundreds of hours reviewing underlying paperwork that purported to justify sham transactions, all in an effort to unravel Davison's exceedingly complex tax arrangements. And for each and every examination, as revenue agent Lindsay Carlson has explained, the IRS must conduct a time versus benefit analysis to ensure the best use of its limited resources. An injunction is necessary and will "avoid the drain on the resources of the IRS required by auditing individual accounts, a multiplicity of suits on the same issue against individual taxpayers, and piecemeal litigation, all of which would only encourage violations in the doubtless accurate belief that the IRS would be unable to detect and pursue every taxpayer in violation." [Citation omitted.]

Davison has concocted numerous and complex tax-fraud schemes, including the parallel C; ESOP-S; Roth IRA-C; and a sham 412(i) pension plan, which all involved the creation of sham companies. Davison also advised clients to execute sham flock contracts in order to claim farmer-related deductions on their tax returns, notwithstanding the fact that none of these clients are actually small farmers within the meaning of the Code. For a couple of years, Davison advised his clients to claim a disabled access credit on grounds that they had made improvements to their businesses in accordance with the Americans with Disabilities Act, even though they made no such improvements and did nothing more than write his company, Handicapped Assistance Business Directory, an $11,000 check; his company purportedly provided telephone assistance for blind individuals. Davison also promoted a tax arrangement in which he advised a client, Mr. Lauerman, to inflate the basis in the shares of stock he held in his company at the time of sale, because of a purported contingent liability, even though there was neither legal nor factual support for this position. Davison also advised clients about a sham lease buyback program and about the bogus use of non-compete agreements as a way to reduce employee salaries and eliminate related employment taxes.

The IRS has spent countless hours unraveling Davison's tax-fraud schemes. For example, revenue agent Renato Quiason testified that he spent approximately 2,000 total hours unraveling the web of entities, payments and deductions set up by Davison for Kenny Thomas and Kelly Thomas, who are only two of Davison's hundreds of clients. Quiason testified about his examination of the Thomas' numerous tax arrangements, including an ESOP-S, Roth IRA-C, and sham 412(i) pension plan, that Davison had advised them to establish. During this examination process, Quiason reviewed the tax returns for the numerous management companies established to effect these arrangements, as well as the tax returns for their operating company, Olathe Toyota, and their individual tax returns. Quiason discovered a complicated web of payments for purported management services between the dealership and various management companies. Each purported management fee payment to one of the various management companies reduced the dealership's taxable income. There was no evidence that the management companies performed any sort of services for the dealership in order to justify the exorbitant fees paid to them, or the large corresponding deductions taken by the dealership. Kenny and Kelly Thomas reduced their total tax liability by hundreds of thousands of dollars during the 2002–2004 tax years.

Revenue agent Carlson audited Davison clients, Zaslavsky and Buterin, who maintained three separate unlawful tax arrangements: the parallel C arrangement, ESOP-S arrangement, and a sham 412(i) pension plan arrangement. In addition, Buterin also maintained a Roth IRA-C arrangement. In order to effect each tax-fraud scheme, Davison directed the formation of management companies. Carlson examined the tax returns for each of these management companies, Buterin and Zaslavsky's operating business, Country Hill Motors, and also each client's individual tax returns. Carlson also examined the books and records (or lack thereof) of the management companies, and the actual books and records of the operating business. Carlson's review concluded that not one of these management companies performed any services, conducted any business, adhered to any purported management agreement or otherwise had any business purpose. Here, Davison's tax-fraud schemes fraudulently reduced Buterin and Zaslavsky's reported tax liability by more than $2 million between the 2004–2006 tax years alone.

Michelle Paschke testified for a number of hours about another complex tax-fraud scheme. John Cimpl, one of Davison's clients, maintained a Roth IRA-C arrangement. Cimpl had a management company, BLHAT, that performed no management services. Paschke examined Cimpl's individual tax returns, BLHAT's corporate tax returns and its purported books, records and bank statements. During tax years, 1999–2002, Cimpl deducted management fees purportedly paid to BLHAT each year. In actuality, BLHAT received no management fees and performed no management services. In fact, the only funds reflected on BLHAT's general ledger were from an installment payment that Cimpl made on an outstanding promissory note owed to his father that concerned a transaction wholly unrelated to BLHAT's purported business purpose. At Davison's direction in 2001, Cimpl also funded a Roth IRA that was the sole shareholder of BLHAT, even though Cimpl's adjusted gross income exceeded the $160,000 statutory limit for each year that he maintained the Roth IRA.

Richard Troester testified about a number of tax-fraud schemes and his audits of several Davison clients, including 1) Tom Lauerman who had executed sham flock contracts and who also claimed an artificially inflated basis in shares of stock he owned in a company he sold in 2002; 2) David Lukens who executed sham flock contracts and claimed bogus small-farm related deductions on his tax returns; 3) Robert McGannon who maintained a Roth IRA-C arrangement; and 4) Philip Kneibert who maintained a series of sham management companies. At Davison's direction, Kneibert's salary of $490,000 for the 2001 and 2002 tax years from his mortgage lending business was re-characterized as purported management fees that had been paid to PhilBiz, one of Kneibert's sham management companies. PhilBiz claimed $490,000 as income for the tax year ending on November 30, 2002, and offset all but $75,000 of this purported income with purported expenses. A total of $415,000 was deducted in so-called expenses; $368,000 of these expenses were purported management fee payments purportedly paid to another Kneibert management company called BISOA25, which was an S corporation (pass-through entity). Although $368,000 in expenses were deducted and purportedly paid to BISOA25, none of these funds were ever transferred to BISOA25, which had no bank account or business purpose.

BISOA25, in turn purportedly paid a total of $200,000 in management fees, split equally among four purported management companies, so as to leverage the 15% corporate tax rate, which goes up for corporate income above $50,000. One of these four companies was purportedly owned by Kneibert, one company was purportedly owned by Kneibert's wife, and two management companies were purportedly owned by Kneibert's minor children. None of these companies had a business purpose or bank account either, and thus, never actually received any funds. In short, six different sham entities allowed Kneibert to report only $33,000 in income for the tax year ending November of 2002 when his total compensation for that tax year was actually $490,000.

Davison has worked hard to evade IRS detection. He has promoted deliberately complex tax-fraud schemes. He has expressed a willingness to change to new and different tax-fraud schemes when faced with heightened IRS scrutiny of older schemes. For example, James Adler explained what happened when he questioned Davison about the probable longevity of the Roth IRA-C arrangement: "I remember specifically saying to [Davison] what about when the IRS closes the loophole on this [the Roth IRA-C arrangement]? What's going to happen? And he said, we'll come up with another way to do this ... He said, we'll come up with something else." And Davison did precisely that when the ESOP-S arrangement came under heightened scrutiny and when single participant ESOPs (which benefit only one employee of a company with numerous employees) were challenged by the Internal Revenue Service. Davison encouraged his clients to unwind their sham ESOP-S arrangements and to instead establish sham 412(i) plans; he acknowledged this strategy to revenue agent Carlson when she interviewed him in his capacity as power of attorney for Yans Zaslavsky and Joshua Buterin during their audit. Zaslavsky and Buterin, in turn, confirmed that Davison recommended the sham 412(i) pension plan and advised them that it was a good and legal way to save for the future. Philip Beard, another Davison client who maintained an

ESOP-S arrangement, testified that Davison also recommended a replacement tax-fraud scheme to him; Beard, however, declined to follow Davison's advice.

In a further effort to obfuscate the facts of his tax arrangements and tax advice, Davison also fabricated records, prepared documents after the fact to address IRS concerns, and intentionally provided false information to the IRS during audits and examinations of his clients. For example, Brandy Wheeler, his former colleague at Womack's enterprises testified that at Davison's direction she helped him create documents after the fact and otherwise falsify documents, including management agreements, promissory notes, documents reflecting transactions between banks, and flight manifest logs. Davison also directed Wheeler to manufacture a sham promissory note and bogus flight manifest logs Davison directed the fabrication of other documents, as well, such as documents designed to give the appearance that funds had actually been moved between bank accounts and companies, in order to disguise paper transactions.

Davison deliberately disguised the nature of his work and his base of operations. Davison never advertises the fact of his tax advice or the specific tax arrangements he has long promoted. Rather, he has purported to provide business planning advice. At Grant Thornton, he was a self-described "rainmaker" who met with clients, learned about their particular businesses, "looked at their situation and gave them recommendations," usually concerning their participation in one or more tax arrangements. While he was at Grant Thornton as a partner in the tax group, Davison executed a partnership agreement that included a non-compete clause. Nevertheless, Davison designed his post-Grant Thornton life so as to enable him to continue providing tax advice to his clients, notwithstanding this agreement. After Grant Thornton, Davison went to work for Cheryl Womack's enterprises where he worked the equivalent of a four-day work week, in order to devote one work day to his clients from Grant Thornton. Davison also worked with Womack to found a bookkeeping operation, where he provided clients with tax advice.

Since leaving Grant Thornton, Davison also has provided tax advice by working through a loose network of four accounting firms, each of which was founded by a young accountant who had worked with Davison and his clients at Grant Thornton. In 2001, these accountants — Ruth Donovan, Charlie Hubbard, Tami Hughes and Heather Larsen — also left Grant Thornton and established their own firms. By virtue of their relatively junior status at Grant Thornton, none of these accountants had executed a non-compete agreement. In 2001, many of Davison's clients moved their business to one of these four firms, and Davison also referred his clients to these firms. Indeed, when Hubbard founded his firm, Alexander Key in 2001, nearly seventy percent of his clients were Davison clients, and when Larsen founded J. Larsen and Associates around the same time, nearly one hundred percent of her clients were Davison clients. Similarly, between 2001 and the present, nearly all of the tax returns that Donovan has prepared through her firm, Ellen Financial Services, were for Davison's clients. When Tami Hughes founded her bookkeeping firm, B.I. Services of America, Davison owned a 50% interest in the firm; he currently retains a 1% interest in the firm.

Davison has billed clients for his tax advice through each of these firms. Moreover, since 2001, Davison has even received 10% of the proceeds that his clients generate for Larsen's firm. Davison still provides Hughes with a time sheet that reflects the time he has spent providing tax advice to clients through B.I. Services of America, where Davison is considered a "tax guru." Hughes pays him up to $250 an hour for the tax advice he provides to clients. He maintains a desk at B.I. Services and uses that firm's offices for his client meetings. He has used this bookkeeping-services firm as a perch from which to provide tax advice and promote tax-fraud schemes. For example, he even wrote a so-called white paper that purported to lend support to the inflated basis in shares of stock that Tom Lauerman claimed on his 2002 tax return. Davison introduced Buterin and Zaslavsky to the sham 412(i) pension plan through the auspices of B.I. Services. Buterin testified that he met Davison at B.I. Services, but understood that Davison was the person who was "overseeing what was going on," with this tax arrangement. Kneibert similarly worked with Davison in this manner. Davison crafted Kneibert's multi-tiered sham management company arrangement, and B.I. Services prepared Kneibert's tax returns and helped incorporate his sham management companies.

Davison also has provided advice through Womack's bookkeeping-services company. For example, Daniel Bruning, a Davison client whose medical practice's books were managed by this bookkeeping company, explained that Davison was "apparently at the time [2003] ... used by VCW Accounting for consultation in tax matters and that's where we became acquainted." At Davison's direction, Bruning established a short-lived management company, which Bruning believed was intended to "alleviate tax liabilities." Similarly, Bruning's partner, Kimber Eubanks also ended up working with Davison under the same circumstances and Davison also advised Eubanks to establish a management company and also a Roth IRA-C arrangement, the latter of which Eubanks declined to do.

Davison avoids signing tax returns or executing engagement letters, and none of his clients maintain businesses that are publicly-traded companies. Essentially, there is little, if any, documentary proof of Davison's involvement in these tax arrangements. Thus, for this reason, too, it is especially difficult and time-consuming to ascertain the origins of his tax-fraud schemes. Davison's numerous, complex, ever-changing, tax-fraud schemes and his deliberate efforts to disguise his true involvement in the promotion of these tax-fraud schemes have required the IRS to expend a "staggering" amount of resources on discovering and combating these schemes. If this outlay of resources continues — and it almost certainly will continue in the absence of an injunction barring Davison from offering tax advice without significant restraint, then these resources will not be available to service honest tax paying Americans. Nor will these resources be available to investigate other promoters of tax-fraud schemes.
In considering the harm that Davison has caused to the government against the harm that will be suffered by Davison if he is enjoined in his ability to give tax advice, it is noted that Davison is a licensed attorney and has significant business interests separate and apart from his income derived by rendering tax advice.

In 2008, Davison's total income from the tax-related advice that he provided was approximately $100,000 that year. In 2009, he earned about the same amount from his tax-related advice. As he explained during his June 2009 deposition and confirmed at trial, as of the date of that deposition, he had earned approximately $50,000 in fees relating to his tax advice, and he was on target to earn approximately $100,000 for the 2009 year.

In contrast, Davison testified that he receives approximately $280,000 in annual income from non-tax-related work. Davison receives about $3,500 a month for his work on the administrative committee of Freemont Farms, a large Iowa-based, egg-producing farm, and between $22,500 to $40,000 each quarter for his partnership distribution from Freemont Farms. Davison also owns rental properties in Las Vegas, Kansas City and Louisiana and farm land in Nebraska. He receives a steady monthly income from his ownership interest in these properties. Finally, Davison co-owns with Tami Hughes, an Internet payday loan business from which he receives approximately $3,000 each month. None of these endeavors appears to relate to the provision of tax advice. Any harm that Davison would suffer from an injunction restricting his ability to offer tax advice is clearly outweighed by the potential for overwhelming continued harm to the government and the public interest in the absence of an injunction.

Davison contends that his associates or his clients are responsible for the sham entities used to effect his tax-fraud schemes. Davison testified that he has advised clients about numerous tax arrangements, sold them these arrangements and then passed clients to one of his associates, who was then charged with establishing the management companies necessary to effect these arrangements. Davison contends that he has never attended to the so-called corporate "details," which are indicia of a legitimate company, such as ensuring that each alleged entity maintained separate sets of books, employees, and office space. He does not believe that this was ever his responsibility, and he says he assumed his associates or clients handled these details. Davison even acknowledges that when a company neglects such details, the company starts to look like a sham entity. Numerous Davison clients testified about their lack of accounting expertise, including Yans Zaslavsky and Josh Buterin, who co-own a used car dealership; James Adler, who is an attorney; Philip Kneibert, who owns a home mortgage lending business; Daniel Bruning and Kimber Eubanks, who co-own a medical practice; Kelly Thomas, who co-owns an automobile dealership; and Philip Beard, who owned a healthcare consulting firm. Yet, Davison advised every single one of these clients to create at least one management company, and contends that he never confirmed, even once, that any of these companies performed actual services because he claimed it was not his responsibility to ensure that any of his client's companies conformed to even the most basic corporate formalities.

The record, however, shows that Davison was very much involved in and responsible for such details. Davison advised his clients to incorporate their management companies in Nevada, where there is no state income tax. NMN, a company in which Davison owns a 30% interest, incorporated these companies in that state. In an email to his-then employer, Cheryl Womack, Davison, in a candid acknowledgment of what was going on, described NMN as an company that was "responsible for window dress[ing] the companies in Nevada." Ruth Donovan, who also co-owned NMN along with Charlie Hubbard and his wife, testified at trial, via deposition, that she was primarily responsible for completing the paperwork associated with the incorporation of these management companies. She completed this paperwork at Davison's direction. Although Donovan was usually the management company's only officer and director, she often had no idea what the purported business of these companies was; Davison, she testified, made these decisions. Donovan similarly never confirmed whether any of these companies actually performed any services. Indeed, Donovan testified that she assumed that clients "had been told to set up a management company," and that "they had been talked to about what needed to be done" by Davison. She had attended meetings with Davison and clients during which time he had explained to clients the mechanics of forming a management company. Davison, in turn, has acknowledged that he drafted many of his clients' purported management agreements (supposedly in force between that company and the operating business). Donovan, who was the only designated officer and director for most of these management companies, signed and completed purported corporate minutes for Davison's clients by filling out a blank template form, at Davison's direction. Indeed, Donovan acknowledged the sham nature of this endeavor, as she noted that she could have held these so-called corporate meetings "in [her] head."

Davison's other associates also acted at his direction. For example, Heather Larsen helped set up Kenny and Kelly Thomas' sham 412(i) plan. Larsen, however, could not actually explain any of the plan details, including why an entirely new company was formed to sponsor the 412(i) plan. At trial, she conceded that she did not even understand the 412(i) arrangement and that "to the extent she was involved at all with the 412(i) plan that the Thomases [sic] implemented, that was really through Mr. Davison." Kenny Thomas confirmed that Davison had been the person who introduced him to this arrangement and advised him to establish a management company for the 412(i) plan and for other tax arrangements. Indeed, Larsen later sent the IRS a letter asking to "formally distance [her]self" from her prior role as power of attorney for Kelly and Kenny Thomas' audit relating to the sham 412(i) plan.

Tami Hughes also has worked with Davison's clients at his direction to help them establish numerous tax arrangements, none of which she truly understood, as her trial testimony made clear. She explained that her nominal understanding stemmed only from Davison's research memoranda or verbal explanations. For example, when Hughes incorporated Kneibert's numerous management companies at Davison's direction, it was Davison who determined and controlled those details. Davison acknowledged as much at trial when he testified about the specific details of Kneibert's sham management companies. Indeed, Davison clearly knew about and controlled the so-called details.

Davison deliberately advised his clients to break the law, and helped them go about doing so. For example, Davison has repeatedly insisted that the Roth IRA-C arrangement, which he actually introduced to his associates and clients while still employed at Grant Thornton, is a legal arrangement. He did so even though, by Davison's own admission, the arrangement's structure violates Code provisions that regulate Roth IRAs. For example, Roth IRA contributions are made with after-tax dollars, meaning these contributions are not tax deductible. [Citation omitted.] Davison acknowledges this aspect of the law. Roth IRA contributions are also subject to an excise tax of 6% if the owner of the Roth IRA's adjusted gross income exceeds the statutory limit in any given year. [Citation omitted.] Davison also acknowledges this. Yet, his Roth IRAC arrangement follows neither of these rules. Roth IRA contributions are disguised through the purported payment of management fees; by design the owner of the Roth IRA deducts these contributions. Davison's clients, such as John Cimpl and Robert McGannon, maintained Roth IRAs and contributed to these accounts, even when their adjusted gross incomes exceeded the statutory limit, and his clients paid no excise taxes.

Davison's tax arrangements flout other provisions of the Code, as well. For example, the 412(i) sham pension plan arrangement contradicts what Davison has described as the Internal Revenue Code's "aggregation rules," which govern whether a qualified plan properly covers the employees of a particular company. Davison testified that control group and affiliated service group rules, as defined in the Internal Revenue Code, apply to qualified plans, including ESOPs and 412(i) plans. Indeed, Davison even wrote at least one memorandum on this subject. Davison's memorandum explains that the pertinent aggregation rules consider employees of operating companies and management companies to belong to the same group of companies for purposes of assessing whether a qualified plan provides adequate coverage and comports with the Code's provisions. His memorandum explains that the "management company group affiliations is meant to combat situations where "a management company is set up which retains control of the operating company, and yet provides different benefits for the owners or highly paid employees. Congress wanted to preclude individuals from forming separate companies with no ownership synergies but who still maintain management control over the operating company." His memorandum also analyzes how qualified plans must cover both rank-and-file employees and highly-compensated employees. Nevertheless, Davison promoted the sham 412(i) plan arrangement and flouted these very Code provisions. He emailed one client, Daniel Bruning and told him that although Bruning's financial advisor was "concerned that [Bruning's C corporation] may provide management services and be included as an affiliated company with" Bruning's medical practice, this was not a concern to Davison. Davison advised Bruning that if his C corporation was treated as a management company, then "this would mean all Pain Care employees would be included in the 412(i) plan (not the desired result)." Instead Davison advanced an "opinion [that] the C corp provides administrative services and not management services and is not part of an affiliated group." Davison, however, also testified that Bruning's C corporation was previously referred to as a management company in an email sent by Ruth Donovan, who, at Davison's direction, had incorporated that same company for Bruning.

Nevertheless, Davison advised Bruning to simply describe his company in a different manner; Bruning declined to follow Davison's advice.

Section 6707(a) of the Code makes it clear that a person who is a material advisor as to a listed transaction must disclose to the IRS his or her role in promoting that arrangement. "[I]f a person who is required to file a return under Section 6111(a) with respect to a listed transaction" fails to make this disclosure, that individual is assessed with a penalty. I.R.C. § 6707(a). Section 6111(a) defines "material advisor," as being a person who provides "material aid, assistance, or advice" with respect to the organizing, establishing or selling of a listed transaction, and has earned at least $50,000 from these efforts. At the very least, the record shows that Davison was required to disclose his role in promoting the sham 412(i) arrangement. Davison made no such filing.

Davison has acknowledged that this tax arrangement is a listed transaction pursuant to Revenue Ruling 2004-20. Nevertheless, Davison contends that he did not know that he was required to disclose his role as a material advisor, because he was informed that the 412(i) plan that he promoted was not a listed transaction, by Economic Concepts, Inc. (ECI), the plan administrator.

The record tells a different story. Davison actually received an email from ECI announcing that on February 22, 2005 (shortly after the release of Revenue Ruling 2004-20), the company was holding a series of teleconferences on the question of whether the 412(i) plan that it administered and that Davison promoted was a listed transaction. Davison acknowledges that he received notice of this teleconference and that he chose not to participate in the event. He acknowledges that this teleconference that ECI convened was its effort to address Revenue Ruling 2004-20 and the consequences of that ruling. The email announcing this teleconference also included attachments, including a half-completed 8886 Form which is the disclosure form that material advisors of reportable transactions, including listed transactions, must file with the IRS.

Davison also sought and received advice from the IRS on this question. He conferred with Teresa Calvert, an IRS revenue agent who is a specialist in employee plans (including 412(i) plans). Calvert audited the 412(i) plan that Kenny and Kelly Thomas maintained, and for whom Davison was power of attorney. In her examination of the Thomas' 412(i) plan, Calvert actually noted that their particular arrangement was a listed transaction, for precisely those reasons listed in Revenue Ruling 2004-20, namely that the Thomas' 412(i) plan was funded with life insurance contracts that provided benefits in excess of what the 412(i) plan document stated. Davison has even admitted that Calvert's analysis of the Thomas' 412(i) plan identified the same issues identified in Revenue Ruling 2004-20. To this end, Davison asked Calvert whether the 412(i) plan that he was promoting was considered a listed transaction under Revenue Ruling 2004-20, and in a separate follow-up letter and phone call, she confirmed that the plan was a listed transaction. Thus, Davison received input from the plan administrator, ECI, and from the IRS, that his 412(i) arrangement was considered a listed transaction, and yet, he still never filed any disclosure form with the IRS.

Davison also knew that he was a material advisor within the meaning of I.R.C. § 6111. Hartford Life Insurance, which did file a disclosure form with the IRS, noted on its disclosure that it had paid Davison substantial commissions for his sales of life insurance policies used to fund the sham 412(i) plan. Indeed, Hartford paid Davison more than $100,000 for his sales of insurance policies, and as Davison testified, the largest portion of commissions he received from his efforts at selling insurance (he has a Kansas insurance license) came from his sales of life insurance policies used to fund the sham 412(i) plans. The threshold payment is $50,000 for listed transactions. [Citation omitted.] Furthermore, two of Davison's clients, Joseph and Salvatore Paris, filed disclosure forms as well, informing the IRS that they each had maintained a 412(i) arrangement and that Davison was their material advisor as to this arrangement.

Davison drafts purported flock contracts for his clients. He argues that by executing these agreements, his clients become farmers, who are eligible to claim deductions for the cost of purchasing a flock of layer hens during the tax year in which that cost is incurred, pursuant to Revenue Ruling 60-191. That revenue ruling provides "that farmers employing the cash method of accounting may deduct the cost of baby chicks and egg-laying hens in the year of payment therefor, provided such method is consistently followed and clearly reflects income." But the revenue ruling applies only to farmers within the meaning of the Code.

As common sense suggests and the Treasury Regulations make clear, merely executing a flock contract of the sort at issue here does not make a person a farmer. Treasury Regulations define who is a farmer: "A taxpayer is engaged in the business of farming if he cultivates, operates, or manages a farm for gain or profit, either as owner or tenant. For the purpose of Section 175, a taxpayer who receives a rental (either in cash or in kind) which is based upon farm production is engaged in the business of farming. However, a taxpayer who receives a fixed rental (without reference to production) is engaged in the business of farming only if he participates to a material extent in the operation or management of the farm." Treas. Reg. §1.175-3. Notwithstanding the Treasury Regulations, Davison maintains that when his clients execute a flock contract with fixed payments, they purchase flocks of layer hens and thus incur the risks inherent in owning these birds and are thus farmers within the meaning of the Code. Neither of these contentions is true or legally relevant.

When Davison's clients execute these flock contracts, they are not actually purchasing a flock of layer hens. For example, revenue agents Ley and Troester reviewed numerous audit files of Davison clients who executed flock agreements, and despite asking for them, neither revenue agent ever saw even one invoice or other form of documentation showing that a client had actually purchased a flock of layer hens.

Furthermore, even if executing the flock contract did confer ownership rights, this fact alone would not transform Davison's clients into farmers. Rather, his clients would simply be renting these flocks of layer hens for a fixed rate of return, and Treasury Regulations make it clear that taxpayers who receive fixed rates of return on farming-related endeavors, "without reference to production," must be engaged to "a material extent in the operation or management of the farm" in order to be called a farmer. [Citation omitted.] Davison's clients are not involved in the management of any farm, simply because they execute flock contracts. Davison's clients never have any control over or involvement in the farming process, as David Lukens testified at trial. Davison drafted flock contracts for Lukens, who is a self-employed insurance salesman. Lukens, however, never even saw the layer hens, did not purchase their feed, did not purchase their shelter, and did not know whether he was paying a fair price for the hens. None of Davison's flock contracts mention specific growing conditions of the birds. In contrast, in *Maple Leaf Farms, Inc. v. Commissioner*, [citation omitted], the court found that the petitioner, who actually owned a flock of ducks and had executed a duck-growing agreement, was a farmer, because the "petitioner selected and purchased the ducklings and determined all necessary feed and medication required by the growers, who served petitioner exclusively. It retained title to all ducks, feed, and medication while in the growers' possession. It exercised substantial supervision and control over the growing process." One condition of the duck-growing agreement was that the petitioner maintain control over this growth process. Davison's flock contracts contain no such condition.

Indeed, Davison's purported flock contracts are in substance loan agreements between Davison's client and the farming facility. The client loans the farming facility money in exchange for a promise that he will receive the loaned amount back, plus interest. Calling such a lender a farmer is like a bank calling itself a farmer because it makes loans to farming operations. The flock contracts provide a rate of return on investment, regardless of market conditions. In fact, in many instances the client who executes the contract receives all of his money back, plus interest, even before the layer hens have finished laying their eggs. Indeed, from Davison's clients' perspective, these flock contracts have all of the benefits of loans and additional benefits, as well. Unlike with loans, here, Davison's clients deduct the full amount of their loans because Davison falsely advises them that they can call their loans flock purchases and call themselves farmers.

Courts have rejected similar attempts by taxpayers to claim farming-related deductions. For example, in *Ward AG Products v. Commissioner*, [citation omitted], the court held that the petitioner, which sold fertilizer and seeds to farmers, was not a farming business and not entitled to use the cash basis method of accounting. The court held that in order to be designated a farmer, a taxpayer "must have participated to a significant degree in the growing process and borne a substantial risk of loss from that process," and specifically found that the petitioner had not borne this risk. Unlike farmers, who have no recourse if their crops fail or market conditions are harmful, the petitioner had liens, security interests and other means of protection against loss, just as Davison's flock contracts guarantee a return on investment, regardless of market conditions.

Davison promotes these flock agreements, notwithstanding the law. Davison has a monetary interest in having these contracts executed. For example, Davison drafted a flock agreement for his client, Tom Lauerman, in which Lauerman purportedly purchased a flock of layer hens to be raised at Freemont Farms, an entity that Davison helps manage and from which he receives approximately $140,000 a year in payments. Davison also signed (and possibly drafted) a document in which Lauerman agreed to assign his purported interest in these layer hens to Davison's entity, Cedar Valley Bird Company, which also serves as a third party broker that receives a 3% commission on the funds exchanged in connection with the flock contracts that Davison also drafts. Davison actually knows that his flock contracts do not reflect the real risks involved in raising layer hens and that his clients do not actually purchase layer hens when they execute these agreements. He also knows that even if they did purchase layer hens, that fact alone, would not entitle his clients to claim a farming-related deduction. Davison candidly testified that his flock contracts are like "renting a piece of real estate," as opposed to owning the property. Yet, he contends that his clients purchase layer hens, that the risk of ownership is inherent in his flock contracts, and that this enables his clients to call themselves farmers.

Davison's numerous, exceedingly complex tax fraud-schemes have caused great harm to the government and to the public fisc. He has promoted these arrangements with a reckless disregard for the law and refused to accept responsibility for his conduct. He routinely falsely and fraudulently advised clients that his tax arrangements were legal.

The Government requests the Court permanently enjoin Mr. Davison "from providing any tax advice" to any person in the future pursuant to I.R.C. § 7402 and argues that such a broad injunction is constitutionally permissible. Mr. Davison argues such a "broad preemptive injunction certainly violates [his] First Amendment right to free commercial speech." Unfortunately, neither parties' assertions regarding the constitutionality of such an injunction is completely accurate.

As previously referenced, in relevant part, I.R.C. § 7402(a) states, "[t]he district courts of the United States ... shall have such jurisdiction to make and issue in civil actions, writs and orders of injunction... necessary or appropriate for the enforcement of the internal revenue laws." This remedy does provide district courts broad discretion to prohibit a wide range of conduct that impedes enforcement of the internal revenue laws, but I.R.C. § 7402 may not be used by a court in a manner that would infringe upon rights guaranteed under the Constitution. See *Marbury v. Madison*, 1 Cranch 137, 176 (U.S. 1803) ("The powers of the legislature are defined, and limited; and that those limits may not be mistaken, or forgotten, the constitution is written ... It is a proposition too plain to be contested, that the constitution controls any legislative act repugnant to it; or, that the legislature may alter the constitution by an ordinary act."). In this case, the issuance of an injunction permanently barring Mr. Davison from offering tax advice, regardless of whether such advice comports truthfully and honestly with internal revenue laws, would affect Mr. Davison's right to freely speak, a right generally protected under the First Amendment. Thus, the question becomes whether such an injunction would violate Mr. Davison's First Amendment rights.

Generally, the First Amendment "prevents government from proscribing speech, ... or even expressive conduct, ... because of disapproval of the ideas expressed." [Citation omitted.] "Restrictions on speech based on its content are "presumptively invalid" and subject to strict scrutiny," which requires the government to demonstrate that the regulation protects or promotes a substantial state interest and the restriction represents the least restrictive means of protecting or promoting the state interest. [Citations omitted.] However, not all speech is entitled to protection under the First Amendment, and the Supreme Court has taken a limited categorical approach to exclusion. See e.g. *Gertz v. Robert Welch, Inc.*, 418 U.S. 323, 340 (1974) ("[T]here is no constitutional value in false statements of fact. Neither the intentional lie nor the careless error materially advances society's interest in "uninhibited, robust, and wide-open" debate on public issues."); *Rother v. United States*, 354 U.S. 476 (1957) (obscenity); Beauharnais v. Illinois, 343 U.S. 250 (1952) (defamation); *Chaplinsky v. New Hampshire*, 315 U.S. 568 (1942) ("fighting words").

Prior to 1975, one other category of speech was excluded from the protection of the First Amendment: commercial speech. See *Bolger v. Youngs Drug Prods. Corp.*, 463 U.S. 60, 64 (1983). Beginning with *Bigelow v. Virginia*, 421 U.S. 809 (1975), the Supreme Court has extended some protections of the First Amendment to commercial speech. [Citation omitted.] However, the Court has stated that "the Constitution accords less protection to commercial speech than to other constitutionally safeguarded forms of expression." [Citation omitted.] For example, the First Amendment "does not protect commercial speech about unlawful activities." [Citation omitted.] Further, due to the "greater potential for deception or confusion[,] ... content-based restrictions on commercial speech may be permissible." [Citation omitted.] Content-based restrictions on commercial speech are reviewed under intermediate scrutiny, and if the communication being restricted is neither misleading nor related to unlawful activity, (1) the state actor imposing the restriction must "assert a substantial interest to be achieved" by the restriction; (2) the restriction must directly advance that interest; and (3) the restriction must not be more extensive than is necessary to protect the substantial interest. [Citation omitted.]

In this case, because the "degree of protection afforded by the First Amendment depends on whether the activity sought to be regulated constitutes commercial or non-commercial speech," it must be determined whether a permanent injunction completely barring Mr. Davison's ability to offer tax advice or services would constitute a restriction of commercial speech, non-commercial speech, or a mixture of each. [Citation omitted.] The line separating commercial speech from non-commercial speech has not yet been clearly drawn. At its core, commercial speech consists of "speech proposing a commercial transaction." [Citation omitted.] Almost all cases reviewed by the Supreme Court have involved commercial expressions in the form of commercial advertisements for the sale of goods or services. [Citations omitted.] However, in *Bolger*, the Supreme Court indicated that commercial speech is not limited to pure commercial advertising that does no more than propose a commercial transaction. [Citation omitted.] In *Bolger*, there was a question of whether certain mailings consisting of "informational pamphlets discussing the desirability and availability of prophylactics in general or [a specific corporation's] products in particular," fell within the category of commercial speech. The pamphlets did more than merely propose commercial transactions, although they were designed to be advertisements and were conceded by the parties to the action to be advertisements. The Court viewed the pamphlets in their totality to arrive at a conclusion that a combination of three factors - advertising format, product references, and commercial motivation - provided "strong support" for classifying the pamphlets as commercial speech. The Court made clear, however, that it was the combination of all three of the factors that led to the classification and that pamphlets may have been classified differently had one or more of the three factors not been present.

In this case, a permanent injunction completely barring Mr. Davison from ever again offering any tax advice or service would constitute such a broad restriction that both Mr. Davison's non-commercial free speech and commercial free speech rights would be implicated. Such an injunction would effectively prohibit Mr. Davison from advertising or otherwise promulgating forms of expression intended primarily to merely propose commercial transactions involving the tax laws, thus implicating commercial free speech rights. The injunction would also prohibit Mr. Davison from offering tax advice or expressing his opinions of tax related matters that have no relation to advertising in the common sense and, under *Bolger's* three part test, would likely fall into the category of non-commercial free speech.

An injunction that would deprive Mr. Davison of his right to express non-commercial, truthful, non-misleading thoughts, ideas, and opinions regarding the internal revenue laws would be per se unconstitutional. [Citation omitted.] Strict scrutiny review of the injunction would be questionable since speech related to the tax laws does not fit within any of the limited categorical exceptions to First Amendment protection and a complete ban on such speech may not be the least restrictive means of protecting the internal revenue tax laws. Thus, contrary to the Government's claims, I.R.C. § 7402 cannot confer power upon this Court to enjoin Mr. Davison from offering any advice or service relating to the internal revenue laws because to do so would impermissibly violate Mr. Davison's right to engage in non-commercial free speech in contravention of the First Amendment.

The conclusion that a permanent injunction completely barring Mr. Davison from offering any advice or service relating to the internal revenue laws would be improper does not negate the Court's ability to fashion a more limited and more appropriate remedy in this case.

WHEREFORE, for all of these foregoing reasons, Davison is hereby enjoined from organizing, establishing, promoting, selling, offering for sale or helping to organize, establish, promote, sell or offer for sale any tax plan, as addressed herein, involving sham parallel C management companies, sham 412(i) plans, sham flock contracts or any other illegal tax scheme, plan, or device, even if not specifically addressed herein. Additionally, Davison shall not organize, establish, promote, sell, offer for sale or assist in any financial or tax related arrangement without submitting in writing to an IRS designee, a detailed plan explaining the financial or tax arrangement and all steps necessary for the arrangement to be legal under the tax code. The plan submitted to the IRS for approval shall set forth the provisions of the tax code relied upon and the requirements necessary to be undertaken by the client for the plan to function in accordance with all legal requirements. The plan submitted to the IRS for approval shall be signed by Davison. The plan submitted shall also include the signature of the client, individual, or entity wishing to implement such plan, or for whom the plan is proposed, acknowledging the client's understanding of all requirements, conditions and terms of the plan. No such plan shall be implemented by or with the assistance of Davison within thirty (30) days of submission to the IRS unless IRS approval is granted. If the IRS does not respond within thirty (30) days, Davison and his client may proceed subject to later review by the IRS. The IRS has no affirmative duty to respond to any plan submitted and does not waive the right to challenge any matter submitted by not responding. The IRS shall file with the court the name, address, and contact information for its initial designee within thirty (30) days of this Order. Any subsequent change of designee shall be provided to Davison in writing at the last address given by Davison. It is Davison's responsibility to keep the IRS informed of his address through its designee.

Furthermore, Davison is required to inform the United States within sixty (60) days hereof, through its attorney herein, Allyson Baker, of every client, together with contact information for each client, for whom he has provided any type of tax-related advice or consultation directly or indirectly within the last five years. Davison is also required to provide each such client with a copy of this Order within sixty (60) days. Subsequent hereto, on May 1 of each year hereafter, Davison is required to provide the IRS, through the IRS designee referenced above, a list of all clients, groups, entities or individuals, with whom he has consulted or provided any type of tax advice, assistance, or tax-related guidance within the preceding twelve (12) months, unless and until Davison notifies the IRS designee and provides proof that he has surrendered his license to practice as a CPA and has ceased giving and will not in the future give any financial or tax-related advice, assistance, or guidance in any capacity.

Gary A. Fenner, Judge

United States District Court

DATED: May 11, 2010

Appendix

Internal Revenue Code

Subchapter K

Internal Revenue Code

Subtitle A, Chapter 1, Subchapter K

Section 701. Partners, not partnership, subject to tax

A partnership as such shall not be subject to the income tax imposed by this chapter. Persons carrying on business as partners shall be liable for income tax only in their separate or individual capacities.

Section 702. Income and credits of partner

(a) General rule. In determining his income tax, each partner shall take into account separately his distributive share of the partnership's—

(1) gains and losses from sales or exchanges of capital assets held for not more than 1 year,

(2) gains and losses from sales or exchanges of capital assets held for more than 1 year,

(3) gains and losses from sales or exchanges of property described in Section 1231 (relating to certain property used in a trade or business and involuntary conversions),

(4) charitable contributions (as defined in Section 170(c)),

(5) dividends with respect to which Section 1(h)(11) or part VIII of subchapter B applies,

(6) taxes, described in Section 901, paid or accrued to foreign countries and to possessions of the United States,

(7) other items of income, gain, loss, deduction, or credit, to the extent provided by regulations prescribed by the Secretary, and

(8) taxable income or loss, exclusive of items requiring separate computation under other paragraphs of this subsection.

(b) Character of items constituting distributive share. The character of any item of income, gain, loss, deduction, or credit included in a partner's distributive share under paragraphs (1) through (7) of subsection (a) shall be determined as if such item were realized directly from the source from which realized by the partnership, or incurred in the same manner as incurred by the partnership.

(c) Gross income of a partner. In any case where it is necessary to determine the gross income of a partner for purposes of this title, such amount shall include his distributive share of the gross income of the partnership.

(d) Cross reference. For rules relating to procedures for determining the tax treatment of partnership items see subchapter C of chapter 63 (Section 6221 and following).

Section 703. Partnership computations

(a) Income and deductions. The taxable income of a partnership shall be computed in the same manner as in the case of an individual except that—

(1) the items described in Section 702(a) shall be separately stated, and
(2) the following deductions shall not be allowed to the partnership:
(A) the deductions for personal exemptions provided in Section 151,
(B) the deduction for taxes provided in Section 164(a) with respect to taxes, described in Section 901, paid or accrued to foreign countries and to possessions of the United States,
(C) the deduction for charitable contributions provided in Section 170,
(D) the net operating loss deduction provided in Section 172,
(E) the additional itemized deductions for individuals provided in part VII of subchapter B (sec. 211 and following), and
(F) the deduction for depletion under Section 611 with respect to oil and gas wells.

(b) Elections of the partnership. Any election affecting the computation of taxable income derived from a partnership shall be made by the partnership, except that any election under—
(1) subsection (b)(5) or (c)(3) of Section 108 (relating to income from discharge of indebtedness),
(2) Section 617 (relating to deduction and recapture of certain mining exploration expenditures), or
(3) Section 901 (relating to taxes of foreign countries and possessions of the United States),

shall be made by each partner separately.

Section 704. Partner's distributive share

(a) Effect of partnership agreement. A partner's distributive share of income, gain, loss, deduction, or credit shall, except as otherwise provided in this chapter, be determined by the partnership agreement.

(b) Determination of distributive share. A partner's distributive share of income, gain, loss, deduction, or credit (or item thereof) shall be determined in accordance with the partner's interest in the partnership (determined by taking into account all facts and circumstances), if—
(1) the partnership agreement does not provide as to the partner's distributive share of income, gain, loss, deduction, or credit (or item thereof), or
(2) the allocation to a partner under the agreement of income, gain, loss, deduction, or credit (or item thereof) does not have substantial economic effect.

(c) Contributed property.
(1) In general. Under regulations prescribed by the Secretary—
(A) income, gain, loss, and deduction with respect to property contributed to the partnership by a partner shall be shared among the partners so as to take account of the variation between the basis of the property to the partnership and its fair market value at the time of contribution,
(B) if any property so contributed is distributed (directly or indirectly) by the partnership (other than to the contributing partner) within 7 years of being contributed—
(i) the contributing partner shall be treated as recognizing gain or loss (as the case may be) from the sale of such property in an amount equal to the gain or loss which would have been allocated to such partner under subparagraph (A) by reason of the variation described in subparagraph (A) if the property had been sold at its fair market value at the time of the distribution,
(ii) the character of such gain or loss shall be determined by reference to the character of the gain or loss which would have resulted if such property had been sold by the partnership to the distributee, and

(iii) appropriate adjustments shall be made to the adjusted basis of the contributing partner's interest in the partnership and to the adjusted basis of the property distributed to reflect any gain or loss recognized under this subparagraph, and

(C) if any property so contributed has a built-in loss—

(i) such built-in loss shall be taken into account only in determining the amount of items allocated to the contributing partner, and

(ii) except as provided in regulations, in determining the amount of items allocated to other partners, the basis of the contributed property in the hands of the partnership shall be treated as being equal to its fair market value at the time of contribution.

For purposes of subparagraph (C), the term "built-in loss" means the excess of the adjusted basis of the property (determined without regard to subparagraph (C)(ii)) over its fair market value at the time of contribution.

(2) Special rule for distributions where gain or loss would not be recognized outside partnerships. Under regulations prescribed by the Secretary, if—

(A) property contributed by a partner (hereinafter referred to as the "contributing partner") is distributed by the partnership to another partner, and

(B) other property of a like kind (within the meaning of Section 1031) is distributed by the partnership to the contributing partner not later than the earlier of—

(i) the 180th day after the date of the distribution described in subparagraph (A), or

(ii) the due date (determined with regard to extensions) for the contributing partner's return of the tax imposed by this chapter for the taxable year in which the distribution described in subparagraph (A) occurs,

then to the extent of the value of the property described in subparagraph (B), paragraph (1)(B) shall be applied as if the contributing partner had contributed to the partnership the property described in subparagraph (B).

(3) Other rules. Under regulations prescribed by the Secretary, rules similar to the rules of paragraph (1) shall apply to contributions by a partner (using the cash receipts and disbursements method of accounting) of accounts payable and other accrued but unpaid items. Any reference in paragraph (1) or (2) to the contributing partner shall be treated as including a reference to any successor of such partner.

(d) Limitation on allowance of losses. A partner's distributive share of partnership loss (including capital loss) shall be allowed only to the extent of the adjusted basis of such partner's interest in the partnership at the end of the partnership year in which such loss occurred. Any excess of such loss over such basis shall be allowed as a deduction at the end of the partnership year in which such excess is repaid to the partnership.

(e) Partnership interest created by gift.

(1) Distributive share of donee includible in gross income. In the case of any partnership interest created by gift, the distributive share of the donee under the partnership agreement shall be includible in his gross income, except to the extent that such share is determined without allowance of reasonable compensation for services rendered to the partnership by the donor, and except to the extent that the portion of such share attributable to donated capital is proportionately greater than the share of the donor attributable to the donor's capital. The distributive share of a partner in the earnings of the partnership shall not be diminished because of absence due to military service.

(2) Purchase of interest by member of family. For purposes of this subsection, an interest purchased by one member of a family from another shall be considered to be created by gift from the seller and the fair market value of the purchased interest shall be considered to be donated capital. The "family" of any individual shall include only his spouse, ancestors, and lineal descendants, and any trusts for the primary benefit of such persons.

(f) Cross reference. For rules in the case of the sale, exchange, liquidation, or reduction of a partner's interest, see Section 706(c)(2).

Section 705. Determination of basis of partner's interest

(a) General rule. The adjusted basis of a partner's interest in a partnership shall, except as provided in subsection (b), be the basis of such interest determined under Section 722 (relating to contributions to a partnership) or Section 742 (relating to transfers of partnership interests)—

(1) increased by the sum of his distributive share for the taxable year and prior taxable years of—

(A) taxable income of the partnership as determined under Section 703(a),

(B) income of the partnership exempt from tax under this title, and

(C) the excess of the deductions for depletion over the basis of the property subject to depletion;

(2) decreased (but not below zero) by distributions by the partnership as provided in Section 733 and by the sum of his distributive share for the taxable year and prior taxable years of—

(A) losses of the partnership, and

(B) expenditures of the partnership not deductible in computing its taxable income and not properly chargeable to capital account; and

(3) decreased (but not below zero) by the amount of the partner's deduction for depletion for any partnership oil and gas property to the extent such deduction does not exceed the proportionate share of the adjusted basis of such property allocated to such partner under Section 613A(c)(7)(D).

(b) Alternative rule. The Secretary shall prescribe by regulations the circumstances under which the adjusted basis of a partner's interest in a partnership may be determined by reference to his proportionate share of the adjusted basis of partnership property upon a termination of the partnership.

Section 706. Taxable years of partner and partnership

(a) Year in which partnership income is includible. In computing the taxable income of a partner for a taxable year, the inclusions required by Section 702 and Section 707(c) with respect to a partnership shall be based on the income, gain, loss, deduction, or credit of the partnership for any taxable year of the partnership ending within or with the taxable year of the partner.

(b) Taxable year.

(1) Partnership's taxable year.

(A) Partnership treated as taxpayer. The taxable year of a partnership shall be determined as though the partnership were a taxpayer.

(B) Taxable year determined by reference to partners. Except as provided in subparagraph (C), a partnership shall not have a taxable year other than—

(i) the majority interest taxable year (as defined in paragraph (4)),

(ii) if there is no taxable year described in clause (i), the taxable year of all the principal partners of the partnership, or

(iii) if there is no taxable year described in clause (i) or (ii), the calendar year unless the Secretary by regulations prescribes another period.

(C) Business purpose. A partnership may have a taxable year not described in subparagraph (B) if it establishes, to the satisfaction of the Secretary, a business purpose therefor. For purposes of this subparagraph, any deferral of income to partners shall not be treated as a business purpose.

(2) Partner's taxable year. A partner may not change to a taxable year other than that of a partnership in which he is a principal partner unless he establishes, to the satisfaction of the Secretary, a business purpose therefor.

(3) Principal partner. For the purpose of this subsection, a principal partner is a partner having an interest of 5 percent or more in partnership profits or capital.

(4) Majority interest taxable year; limitation on required changes.

(A) Majority interest taxable year defined. For purposes of paragraph (1)(B)(i)—

(i) In general. The term "majority interest taxable year" means the taxable year (if any) which, on each testing day, constituted the taxable year of 1 or more partners having (on such day) an aggregate interest in partnership profits and capital of more than 50 percent.

(ii) Testing days. The testing days shall be—

(I) the 1st day of the partnership taxable year (determined without regard to clause (i)), or

(II) the days during such representative period as the Secretary may prescribe.

(B) Further change not required for 3 years. Except as provided in regulations necessary to prevent the avoidance of this section, if, by reason of paragraph (1)(B)(i), the taxable year of a partnership is changed, such partnership shall not be required to change to another taxable year for either of the 2 taxable years following the year of change.

(5) Application with other sections. Except as provided in regulations, for purposes of determining the taxable year to which a partnership is required to change by reason of this subsection, changes in taxable years of other persons required by this subsection, Section 441(i), Section 584(h), Section 644, or Section 1378(a) shall be taken into account.

(c) Closing of partnership year.

(1) General rule. Except in the case of a termination of a partnership and except as provided in paragraph (2) of this subsection, the taxable year of a partnership shall not close as the result of the death of a partner, the entry of a new partner, the liquidation of a partner's interest in the partnership, or the sale or exchange of a partner's interest in the partnership.

(2) Treatment of dispositions.

(A) Disposition of entire interest. The taxable year of a partnership shall close with respect to a partner whose entire interest in the partnership terminates (whether by reason of death, liquidation, or otherwise).

(B) Disposition of less than entire interest. The taxable year of a partnership shall not close (other than at the end of a partnership's taxable year as determined under subsection (b)(1)) with respect to a partner who sells or exchanges less than his entire interest in the partnership or with respect to a partner whose interest is reduced (whether by entry of a new partner, partial liquidation of a partner's interest, gift, or otherwise).

(d) Determination of distributive share when partner's interest changes.

(1) In general. Except as provided in paragraphs (2) and (3), if during any taxable year of the partnership there is a change in any partner's interest in the partnership, each partner's distributive share of any item of income, gain, loss, deduction, or credit of the partnership for such taxable year shall be determined by the use of any method prescribed by the Secretary by regulations which takes into account the varying interests of the partners in the partnership during such taxable year.

(2) Certain cash basis items prorated over period to which attributable.

(A) In general. If during any taxable year of the partnership there is a change in any partner's interest in the partnership, the (except to the extent provided in regulations) each partner's distributive share of any allocable cash basis item shall be determined—

(i) by assigning the appropriate portion of such item to each day in the period to which it is attributable, and

(ii) by allocating the portion assigned to any such day among the partners in proportion to their interests in the partnership at the close of such day.

(B) Allocable cash basis item. For purposes of this paragraph, the term "allocable cash basis item" means any of the following items with respect to which the partnership uses the cash receipts and disbursements method of accounting:

(i) Interest.

(ii) Taxes.

(iii) Payments for services or for the use of property.

(iv) Any other item of a kind specified in regulations prescribed by the Secretary as being an item with respect to which the application of this paragraph is appropriate to avoid significant misstatements of the income of the partners.

(C) Items attributable to periods not within taxable year. If any portion of any allocable cash basis item is attributable to—

(i) any period before the beginning of the taxable year, such portion shall be assigned under subparagraph (A)(i) to the first day of the taxable year, or

(ii) any period after the close of the taxable year, such portion shall be assigned under subparagraph (A)(i) to the last day of the taxable year.

(D) Treatment of deductible items attributable to prior periods. If any portion of a deductible cash item is assigned under subparagraph (c)(i) to the first day of any taxable year—

(i) such portion shall be allocated among persons who are partners in the partnership during the period to which such portion is attributable in accordance with their varying interests in the partnership during such period, and

(ii) any amount allocated under clause (i) to a person who is not a partner in the partnership on such first day shall be capitalized by the partnership and treated in the manner provided for in Section 755.

(3) Items attributable to interest in lower tier partnership prorated over entire taxable year. If—

(A) during any taxable year of the partnership there is a change in any partner's interest in the partnership (hereinafter in this paragraph referred to as the "upper tier partnership"), and

(B) such partnership is a partner in another partnership (hereinafter in this paragraph referred to as the "lower tier partnership"),

then (except to the extent provided in regulations) each partner's distributive share of any item of the upper tier partnership attributable to the lower tier partnership shall be determined by assigning the appropriate portion (determined by applying principles similar to the principles of subparagraphs (C) and (D) of paragraph (2)) of each such item to the appropriate days during which the upper tier partnership is a partner in the lower tier partnership and by allocating the portion assigned to any such day among the partners in proportion to their interests in the upper tier partnership at the close of such day.

(4) Taxable year determined without regard to subsection (c)(2)(A). For purposes of this subsection, the taxable year of a partnership shall be determined without regard to subsection (c)(2)(A).

Section 707. Transactions between partner and partnership

(a) Partner not acting in capacity as partner.

(1) In general. If a partner engages in a transaction with a partnership other than in his capacity as a member of such partnership, the transaction shall, except as otherwise provided in this section, be considered as occurring between the partnership and one who is not a partner.

(2) Treatment of payments to partners for property or services. Under regulations prescribed by the Secretary—

(A) Treatment of certain services and transfers of property. If—

(i) a partner performs services for a partnership or transfers property to a partnership,

(ii) there is a related direct or indirect allocation and distribution to such partner, and

(iii) the performance of such services (or such transfer) and the allocation and distribution, when viewed together, are properly characterized as a transaction occurring between the partnership and a partner acting other than in his capacity as a member of the partnership,

such allocation and distribution shall be treated as a transaction described in paragraph (1).

(B) Treatment of certain property transfers. If—

(i) there is a direct or indirect transfer of money or other property by a partner to a partnership,

(ii) there is a related direct or indirect transfer of money or other property by the partnership to such partner (or another partner), and

(iii) the transfers described in clauses (i) and (ii), when viewed together, are properly characterized as a sale or exchange of property,

such transfers shall be treated either as a transaction described in paragraph (1) or as a transaction between 2 or more partners acting other than in their capacity as members of the partnership.

(b) Certain sales or exchanges of property with respect to controlled partnerships.

(1) Losses disallowed. No deduction shall be allowed in respect of losses from sales or exchanges of property (other than an interest in the partnership), directly or indirectly, between—

(A) a partnership and a person owning, directly or indirectly, more than 50 percent of the capital interest, or the profits interest, in such partnership, or

(B) two partnerships in which the same persons own, directly or indirectly, more than 50 percent of the capital interests or profits interests.

In the case of a subsequent sale or exchange by a transferee described in this paragraph, Section 267(d) shall be applicable as if the loss were disallowed under Section 267(a)(1). For purposes of Section 267(a)(2), partnerships described in subparagraph (B) of this paragraph shall be treated as persons specified in Section 267(b).

(2) Gains treated as ordinary income. In the case of a sale or exchange, directly or indirectly, of property, which in the hands of the transferee, is property other than a capital asset as defined in Section 1221—

(A) between a partnership and a person owning, directly or indirectly, more than 50 percent of the capital interest, or profits interest, in such partnership, or

(B) between two partnership in which the same persons own, directly or indirectly, more than 50 percent of the capital interest or profits interests, any gain recognized shall be considered as ordinary income.

(3) Ownership of a capital or profits interest. For purposes of paragraphs (1) and (2) of this subsection, the ownership of a capital or profits interest in a partnership shall be determined in accordance with the

rules for constructive ownership of stock provided in Section 267(c) other than paragraph (3) of such section.

(c) Guaranteed payments. To the extent determined without regard to the income of the partnership, payments to a partner for services or the use of capital shall be considered as made to one who is not a member of the partnership, but only for the purposes of Section 61(a) (relating to gross income) and, subject to Section 263, for purposes of Section 162(a) (relating to trade or business expenses).

Section 708. Continuation of partnership

(a) General rule. For purposes of this subchapter, an existing partnership shall be considered as continuing if it is not terminated.

(b) Termination.
(1) General rule. For purposes of subsection (a), a partnership shall be considered as terminated only if—
(A) no part of any business, financial operation, or venture of the partnership continues to be carried on by any of its partners in a partnership, or
(B) within a 12-month period there is a sale or exchange of 50 percent or more of the total interest in partnership capital and profits.
(2) Special rules.
(A) Merger or consolidation. In the case of the merger or consolidation of two or more partnerships, the resulting partnership shall, for purposes of this section, be considered the continuation of any merging or consolidating partnership whose members own an interest of more than 50 percent in the capital and profits of the resulting partnership.
(B) Division of a partnership. In the case of a division of a partnership into two or more partnerships, the resulting partnerships (other than any resulting partnership the members of which had an interest of 50 percent or less in the capital and profits of the prior partnership) shall, for purposes of this section, be considered a continuation of the prior partnership.

Section 709. Treatment of organization and syndication fees

(a) General rule. Except as provided in subsection (b), no deduction shall be allowed under this chapter to the partnership or to any partner for any amounts paid or incurred to organize a partnership or to promote the sale of (or to sell) an interest in such partnership.

(b) Deduction of organization fees.
(1) Allowance of deduction. If a partnership elects the application of this subsection (in accordance with regulations prescribed by the Secretary) with respect to any organizational expenses—
(A) the partnership shall be allowed a deduction for the taxable year in which the partnership begins business in an amount equal to the lesser of—
(i) the amount of organizational expenses with respect to the partnership, or

(ii) $5,000, reduced (but not below zero) by the amount by which such organizational expenses exceed $50,000, and

(B) the remainder of such organizational expenses shall be allowed as a deduction ratably over the 180-month period beginning with the month in which the partnership begins business.

(2) Dispositions before close of amortization period. In any case in which a partnership is liquidated before the end of the period to which paragraph (1)(B) applies, any deferred expenses attributable to the partnership which were not allowed as a deduction by reason of this section may be deducted to the extent allowable under Section 165.

(3) Organizational expenses defined. The organizational expenses to which paragraph (1) applies, are expenditures which—

(A) are incident to the creation of the partnership;

(B) are chargeable to capital account; and

(C) are of a character which, if expended incident to the creation of a partnership having an ascertainable life, would be amortized over such life.

Section 721. Nonrecognition of gain or loss on contribution

(a) General rule. No gain or loss shall be recognized to a partnership or to any of its partners in the case of a contribution of property to the partnership in exchange for an interest in the partnership.

(b) Special rule. Subsection (a) shall not apply to gain realized on a transfer of property to a partnership which would be treated as an investment company (within the meaning of Section 351) if the partnership were incorporated.

(c) Regulations relating to certain transfers to partnerships. The Secretary may provide by regulations that subsection (a) shall not apOply to gain realized on the transfer of property to a partnership if such gain, when recognized, will be includible in the gross income of a person other than a United States person.

(d) Transfers of intangibles. For regulatory authority to treat intangibles transferred to a partnership as sold, see Section 367(d)(3).

Section 722. Basis of contributing partner's interest

The basis of an interest in a partnership acquired by a contribution of property, including money, to the partnership shall be the amount of such money and the adjusted basis of such property to the contributing partner at the time of the contribution increased by the amount (if any) of gain recognized under Section 721(b) to the contributing partner at such time.

Section 723. Basis of property contributed to partnership

The basis of property contributed to a partnership by a partner shall be the adjusted basis of such property to the contributing partner at the time of the contribution increased by the amount (if any) of gain recognized under Section 721(b) to the contributing partner at such time.

Section 724. Character of gain or loss on contributed unrealized receivables, inventory items, and capital loss property

(a) Contributions of unrealized receivables. In the case of any property which—
(1) was contributed to the partnership by a partner, and
(2) was an unrealized receivable in the hands of such partner immediately before such contribution,

Any gain or loss recognized by the partnership on the disposition of such property shall be treated as ordinary income or ordinary loss, as the case may be.

(b) Contributions of inventory items. In the case of any property which—
(1) was contributed to the partnership by a partner, and
(2) was an inventory item in the hands of such partner immediately before such contribution,

any gain or loss recognized by the partnership on the disposition of such property during the 5-year period beginning on the date of such contribution shall be treated as ordinary income or ordinary loss, as the case may be.

(c) Contributions of capital loss property. In the case of any property which—
(1) was contributed by a partner to the partnership, and
(2) was a capital asset in the hands of such partner immediately before such contribution,

any loss recognized by the partnership on the disposition of such property during the 5-year period beginning on the date of such contribution shall be treated as a loss from the sale of a capital asset to the extent that, immediately before such contribution, the adjusted basis of such property in the hands of the partner exceeded the fair market value of such property.

(d) Definitions. For purposes of this section—
(1) Unrealized receivable. The term "unrealized receivable" has the meaning given such term by Section 751(c) (determined by treating any reference to the partnership as referring to the partner).
(2) Inventory item. The term "inventory item" has the meaning given such term by Section 751(d) (determined by treating any reference to the partnership as referring to the partner and by applying Section 1231 without regard to any holding period therein provided).
(3) Substituted basis property.
(A) In general. If any property described in subsection (a), (b) or (c) is disposed of in a nonrecognition transaction, the tax treatment which applies to such property under such subsection shall also apply to any substituted basis property resulting from such transaction. A similar rule shall also apply in the case of a series of non-recognition transactions.
(B) Exception for stock in C corporation. Subparagraph (A) shall not apply to any stock in a C corporation received in an exchange described in Section 351.

Section 731. Extent of recognition of gain or loss on distribution

(a) Partners. In the case of a distribution by a partnership to a partner—

(1) gain shall not be recognized to such partner, except to the extent that any money distributed exceeds the adjusted basis of such partner's interest in the partnership immediately before the distribution, and

(2) loss shall not be recognized to such partner, except that upon a distribution in liquidation of a partner's interest in a partnership where no property other than that described in subparagraph (A) or (B) is distributed to such partner, loss shall be recognized to the extent of the excess of the adjusted basis of such partner's interest in the partnership over the sum of—

(A) any money distributed, and

(B) the basis to the distributee, as determined under Section 732, of any unrealized receivables (as defined in Section 751(c)) and inventory (as defined in Section 751(d)).

Any gain or loss recognized under this subsection shall be considered as gain or loss from the sale or exchange of the partnership interest of the distributee partner.

(b) Partnerships. No gain or loss shall be recognized to a partnership on a distribution to a partner of property, including money.

(c) Treatment of marketable securities.

(1) In general. For purposes of subsection (a)(1) and Section 737—

(A) the term "money" includes marketable securities, and

(B) such securities shall be taken into account at their fair market value as of the date of the distribution.

(2) Marketable securities. For purposes of this subsection:

(A) In general. The term "marketable securities" means financial instruments and foreign currencies which are, as of the date of the distribution, actively traded (within the meaning of Section 1092(d)(1)).

(B) Other property. Such term includes—

(i) any interest in—

(I) a common trust fund, or

(II) a regulated investment company which is offering for sale or has outstanding any redeemable security (as defined in Section 2(a)(32) of the Investment Company Act of 1940) of which it is the issuer,

(ii) any financial instrument which, pursuant to its terms or any other arrangement, is readily convertible into, or exchangeable for, money or marketable securities,

(iii) any financial instrument the value of which is determined substantially by reference to marketable securities,

(iv) except to the extent provided in regulations prescribed by the Secretary, any interest in a precious metal which, as of the date of the distribution, is actively traded (within the meaning of Section 1092(d)(1)) unless such metal was produced, used, or held in the active conduct of a trade or business by the partnership,

(v) except as otherwise provided in regulations prescribed by the Secretary, interests in any entity if substantially all of the assets of such entity consist (directly or indirectly) of marketable securities, money, or both, and

(vi) to the extent provided in regulations prescribed by the Secretary, any interest in an entity not described in clause (v) but only to the extent of the value of such interest which is attributable to marketable securities, money, or both.

(C) Financial instrument. The term “financial instrument” includes stocks and other equity interests, evidences of indebtedness, options, forward or futures contracts, notional principal contracts, and derivatives.

(3) Exceptions.

(A) In general. Paragraph (1) shall not apply to the distribution from a partnership of a marketable security to a partner if—

(i) the security was contributed to the partnership by such partner, except to the extent that the value of the distributed security is attributable to marketable securities or money contributed (directly or indirectly) to the entity to which the distributed security relates,

(ii) to the extent provided in regulation prescribed by the Secretary, the property was not a marketable security when acquired by such partnership, or

(iii) such partnership is an investment partnership and such partner is an eligible partner thereof.

(B) Limitation on gain recognized. In the case of a distribution of marketable securities to a partner, the amount taken into account under paragraph (1) shall be reduced (but not below zero) by the excess (if any) of—

(i) such partner’s distributive share of the net gain which would be recognized if all of the marketable securities of the same class and issuer as the distributed securities held by the partnership were sold (immediately before the transaction to which the distribution relates) by the partnership for fair market value, over

(ii) such partner’s distributive share of the net gain which is attributable to the marketable securities of the same class and issuer as the distributed securities held by the partnership immediately after the transaction, determined by using the same fair market value as used under clause (i).

Under regulation prescribed by the Secretary, all marketable securities held by the partnership may be treated as marketable securities of the same class and issuer as the distributed securities.

(C) Definitions relating to investment partnerships. For purposes of subparagraph (A)(iii):

(i) Investment partnership. The term “investment partnership” means any partnership which has never been engaged in a trade or business and substantially all of the assets (by value) of which have always consisted of—

(I) money,

(II) stock in a corporation,

(III) notes, bonds, debentures, or other evidences of indebtedness,

(IV) interest rate, currency, or equity notional principal contracts,

(V) foreign currencies,

(VI) interests in or derivative financial instruments (including options, forward or futures contracts, short positions, and similar financial instruments) in any asset described in any other subclause of this clause or in any commodity traded on or subject to the rules of a board of trade or commodity exchange,

(VII) other assets specified in regulations prescribed by the Secretary, or

(VIII) any combination of the foregoing.

(ii) Exception for certain activities. A partnership shall not be treated as engaged in a trade or business by reason of—

(I) any activity undertaken as an investor, trader, or dealer in any asset described in clause (i), or

(II) any other activity specified in regulations prescribed by the Secretary.

(iii) Eligible partner.

(I) In general. The term “eligible partner” means any partner who, before the date of the distribution, did not contribute to the partnership any property other than assets described in clause (i).

(II) Exception for certain nonrecognition transactions. The term “eligible partner” shall not include the transferor or transferee in a nonrecognition transaction involving a transfer of any portion of an interest in a partnership with respect to which the transferor was not an eligible partner.

(iv) Look-thru of partnership tiers. Except as otherwise provided in regulations prescribed by the Secretary—

(I) a partnership shall be treated as engaged in any trade or business engaged in by, and as holding (instead of a partnership interest) a proportionate share of the assets of, any other partnership in which the partnership holds a partnership interest, and

(II) a partner who contributes to a partnership an interest in another partnership shall be treated as contributing a proportionate share of the assets of the other partnership.

If the preceding sentence does not apply under such regulations with respect to any interest held by a partnership in another partnership, the interest in such other partnership shall be treated as if it were specified in a subclause of clause (i).

(4) Basis of securities distributed.

(A) In general. The basis of marketable securities with respect to which gain is recognized by reason of this subsection shall be—

(i) their basis determined under Section 732, increased by

(ii) the amount of such gain.

(B) Allocation of basis increase. Any increase in basis attributable to the gain described in subparagraph (A)(ii) shall be allocated to marketable securities in proportion to their respective amounts of unrealized appreciation before such increase.

(5) Subsection disregarded in determining basis of partner's interest in partnership and of basis of partnership property. Sections 733 and 734 shall be applied as if no gain were recognized, and no adjustment were made to the basis of property, under this subsection.

(6) Character of gain recognized. In the case of a distribution of a marketable security which is an unrealized receivable (as defined in Section 751(c)) or an inventory item (as defined in Section 751(d)), any gain recognized under this subsection shall be treated as ordinary income to the extent of any increase in the basis of such security attributable to the gain described in paragraph (4)(A)(ii).

(7) Regulations. The Secretary shall prescribe such regulations as may be necessary or appropriate to carry out the purposes of this subsection, including regulations to prevent the avoidance of such purposes.

(d) Exceptions. This section shall not apply to the extent otherwise provided by Section 736 (relating to payments to a retiring partner or a deceased partner's successor in interest), Section 751 (relating to unrealized receivables and inventory items), and Section 737 (relating to recognition of precontribution gain in case of certain distributions).

Section 732. Basis of distributed property other than money

(a) Distributions other than in liquidation of a partner's interest.

(1) General rule. The basis of property (other than money) distributed by a partnership to a partner other than in liquidation of the partner's interest shall, except as provided in paragraph (2), be its adjusted basis to the partnership immediately before such distribution.

(2) Limitation. The basis to the distributee partner of property to which paragraph (1) is applicable shall not exceed the adjusted basis of such partner's interest in the partnership reduced by any money distributed in the same transaction.

(b) Distributions in liquidation. The basis of property (other than money) distributed by a partnership to a partner in liquidation of the partner's interest shall be an amount equal to the adjusted basis of such partner's interest in the partnership reduced by any money distributed in the same transaction.

(c) Allocation of basis.

(1) In general. The basis of distributed properties to which subsection (a)(2) or (b) is applicable shall be allocated—

(A)

(i) first to any unrealized receivables (as defined in Section 751(c)) and inventory items (as defined in Section 751(d)) in an amount equal to the adjusted basis of each such property to the partnership, and

(ii) if the basis to be allocated is less than the sum of the adjusted bases of such properties to the partnership, then, to the extent any decrease is required in order to have the adjusted bases of such properties equal the basis to be allocated, in the manner provided in paragraph (3), and

(B) to the extent of any basis remaining after the allocation under subparagraph (A), to other distributed properties—

(i) first by assigning to each such other property such other property's adjusted basis to the partnership, and

(ii) then, to the extent any increase or decrease in basis is required in order to have the adjusted bases of such other distributed properties equal such remaining basis, in the manner provided in paragraph (2) or (3), whichever is appropriate.

(2) Method of allocating increase. Any increase required under paragraph (1)(B) shall be allocated among the properties—

(A) first to properties with unrealized appreciation in proportion to their respective amounts of unrealized appreciation before such increase (but only to the extent of each property's unrealized appreciation), and

(B) then, to the extent such increase is not allocated under subparagraph (A), in proportion to their respective fair market values.

(3) Method of allocating decrease. Any decrease required under paragraph (1)(A) or (1)(B) shall be allocated—

(A) first to properties with unrealized depreciation in proportion to their respective amounts of unrealized depreciation before such decrease (but only to the extent of each property's unrealized depreciation), and

(B) then, to the extent such decrease is not allocated under subparagraph (A), in proportion to their respective adjusted bases (as adjusted under subparagraph (A)).

(d) Special partnership basis to transferee. For purposes of subsections (a), (b), and (c), a partner who acquired all or a part of his interest by a transfer with respect to which the election provided in Section 754 is not in effect, and to whom a distribution of property (other than money) is made with respect to the transferred interest within 2 years after such transfer, may elect, under regulations prescribed by the Secretary, to treat as the adjusted partnership basis of such property the adjusted basis such property would have if the adjustment provided in Section 743(b) were in effect with respect to the partnership property. The Secretary may be regulations require the application of this subsection in the case of a distribution to a transferee partner, whether or not made within 2 years after the transfer, if at the time of the transfer the fair market value of the partnership property (other than money) exceeded 110 percent of its adjusted basis to the partnership.

(e) Exception. This section shall not apply to the extent that a distribution is treated as a sale or exchange of property under Section 751(b) (relating to unrealized receivables and inventory items).

(f) Corresponding adjustment to basis of assets of a distributed corporation controlled by a corporate partner.

(1) In general. If—

(A) a corporation (hereafter in this subsection referred to as the "corporate partner") receives a distribution from a partnership of stock in another corporation (hereafter in this subsection referred to as the "distributed corporation"),

(B) the corporate partner has control of the distributed corporation immediately after the distribution or at any time thereafter, and

(C) the partnership's adjusted basis in such stock immediately before the distribution exceeded the corporate partner's adjusted basis in such stock immediately after the distribution,

then an amount equal to such excess shall be applied to reduce (in accordance with subsection (c)) the basis of property held by the distributed corporation at such time (or, if the corporate partner does not control the distributed corporation at such time, at the time the corporate partner first has such control).

(2) Exception for certain distributions before control acquired. Paragraph (1) shall not apply to any distribution of stock in the distributed corporation if—

(A) the corporate partner does not have control of such corporation immediately after such distribution, and

(B) the corporate partner establishes to the satisfaction of the Secretary that such distribution was not part of a plan or arrangement to acquire control of the distributed corporation.

(3) Limitations on basis reduction.

(A) In general. The amount of the reduction under paragraph (1) shall not exceed the amount by which the sum of the aggregate adjusted bases of the property and the amount of money of the distributed corporation exceeds the corporate partner's adjusted basis in the stock of the distributed corporation.

(B) Reduction not to exceed adjusted basis of property. No reduction under paragraph (1) in the basis of any property shall exceed the adjusted basis of such property (determined without regard to such reduction).

(4) Gain recognition where reduction limited. If the amount of any reduction under paragraph (1) (determined after the application of paragraph (3)(A)) exceeds the aggregate adjusted bases of the property of the distributed corporation—

(A) such excess shall be recognized by the corporate partner as long-term capital gain, and

(B) the corporate partner's adjusted basis in the stock of the distributed corporation shall be increased by such excess.

(5) Control. For purposes of this subsection, the term "control" means ownership of stock meeting the requirements of Section 1504(a)(2).

(6) Indirect distributions. For purposes of paragraph (1), if a corporation acquires (other than in a distribution from a partnership) stock the basis of which is determined (by reason of being distributed from a partnership) in whole or in part by reference to subsection (a)(2) or (b), the corporation shall be treated as receiving a distribution of such stock from a partnership.

(7) Special rule for stock in controlled corporation. If the property held by a distributed corporation is stock in a corporation which the distributed corporation controls, this subsection shall be applied to reduce the basis of the property of such controlled corporation. This subsection shall be reapplied to any property of any controlled corporation which is stock in a corporation which it controls.

(8) Regulations. The Secretary shall prescribe such regulations as may be necessary to carry out the purposes of this subsection, including regulations to avoid double counting and to prevent the abuse of such purposes.

Section 733. Basis of distributee partner's interest

In the case of a distribution by a partnership to a partner other than in liquidation of a partner's interest, the adjusted basis to such partner of his interest in the partnership shall be reduced (but not below zero) by—

(1) the amount of any money distributed to such partner, and

(2) the amount of the basis to such partner of distributed property other than money, as determined under Section 732.

Section 734. Adjustment to basis of undistributed partnership property where Section 754 election or substantial basis reduction

(a) General rule. The basis of partnership property shall not be adjusted as the result of a distribution of property to a partner unless the election, provided in Section 754 (relating to optional adjustment to basis of partnership property), is in effect with respect to such partnership or unless there is a substantial basis reduction with respect to such distribution.

(b) Method of adjustment. In the case of a distribution of property to a partner by a partnership with respect to which the election provided in Section 754 is in effect or with respect to which there is a substantial basis reduction, the partnership shall—

(1) increase the adjusted basis of partnership property by—

(A) the amount of any gain recognized to the distributee partner with respect to such distribution under Section 731(a)(1), and

(B) in the case of distributed property to which Section 732(a)(2) or (b) applies, the excess of the adjusted basis of the distributed property to the partnership immediately before the distribution (as adjusted by Section 732(d)) over the basis of the distributed property to the distributee, as determined under Section 732, or

(2) decrease the adjusted basis of partnership property by—

(A) the amount of any loss recognized to the distributee partner with respect to such distribution under Section 731(a)(2), and

(B) in the case of distributed property to which 732(b) applies, the excess of the basis of the distributed property to the distributee, as determined under Section 732, over the adjusted basis of the distributed property to the partnership immediately before such distribution (as adjusted by Section 732(d)).

Paragraph (1)(B) shall not apply to any distributed property which is an interest in another partnership with respect to which the election provided in Section 754 is not in effect.

(c) Allocation of basis. The allocation of basis among partnership properties where subsection (b) is applicable shall be made in accordance with the rules provided in Section 755.

(d) Substantial basis reduction.

(1) In general. For purposes of this section, there is a substantial basis reduction with respect to a distribution if the sum of the amounts described in subparagraphs (A) and (B) of subsection (b)(2) exceeds $250,000.

(2) Regulations. For regulations to carry out this subsection, see Section 743(d)(2).

(e) Exception for securitization partnerships. For purposes of this section, a securitization partnership (as defined in Section 743(f)) shall not be treated as having a substantial basis reduction with respect to any distribution of property to a partner.

Section 735. Character of gain or loss on disposition of distributed property

(a) Sale or exchange of certain distributed property.

(1) Unrealized receivables. Gain or loss on the disposition by a distributee partner of unrealized receivables (as defined in Section 751(c)) distributed by a partnership, shall be considered as ordinary income or as ordinary loss, as the case may be.

(2) Inventory items. Gain or loss on the sale or exchange b y a distributee partner of inventory items (as defined in Section 751(d)) distributed by a partnership shall, if sold or exchanged within 5 years from the date of the distribution, be considered as ordinary income or as ordinary loss, as the case may be.

(b) Holding period for distributed property. In determining the period for which a partner has held property received in a distribution from a partnership (other than for purposes of subsection (a)(2)), there shall be included the holding period of the partnership, as determined under Section 1223, with respect to such property.

(c) Special rules.

(1) Waiver of holding periods contained in Section 1231. For purposes of this section, Section 751(d) (defining inventory item) shall be applied without regard to any holding period in Section 1231(b).

(2) Substituted basis property.

(A) In general. If any property described in subsection (a) is disposed of in a nonrecognition transaction, the tax treatment which applies to such property under such subsection shall also apply to any substituted basis property resulting from such transaction. A similar rule shall also apply in the case of a series of nonrecognition transactions.

(B) Exception for stock in C corporation. Subparagraph (A) shall not apply to any stock in a C corporation received in an exchange described in Section 351.

Section 736. Payments to a retiring partner or a deceased partner's successor in interest

(a) Payments considered as distributive share or guaranteed payment. Payments made in liquidation of the interest of a retiring partner shall, except as provided in subsection (b), be considered—

(1) as a distributive share to the recipient of partnership income if the amount thereof is determined with regard to the income of the partnership, or

(2) as a guaranteed payment described in Section 707(c) if the amount thereof is determined without regard to the income of the partnership.

(b) Payments for interest in partnership.

(1) General rule. Payments made in liquidation of the interest of a retiring partner or a deceased partner shall, to the extent such payments (other than payments described in paragraph (2)) are determined, under regulations prescribed by the Secretary, to be made in exchange for the interest of such partner in partnership property, be considered as a distribution by the partnership and not as a distributive share or guaranteed payment under subsection (a).

(2) Special rules. For purposes of this subsection, payments in exchange for an interest in partnership property shall not include amounts paid for—

(A) unrealized receivables of the partnership (as defined in Section 751(c)), or

(B) good will of the partnership, except to the extent that the partnership agreement provides for a payment with respect to good will.

(3) Limitation on application of paragraph (2). Paragraph (2) shall apply only if—

(A) capital is not a material income-producing factor for the partnership, and

(B) the retiring or deceased partner was a general partner in the partnership.

Section 737. Recognition of precontribution gain in case of certain distributions to contributing partner

(a) General rule. In the case of any distribution by a partnership to a partner, such partner shall be treated as recognizing gain in an amount equal to the lesser of—

(1) the excess (if any) of (A) the fair market value of property (other than money) received in the distribution over (B) the adjusted basis of such partner's interest in the partnership immediately before the distribution reduced (but not below zero) by the amount of money received in the distribution, or

(2) the net precontribution gain of the partner.

Gain recognized under the preceding sentence shall be in addition to any gain recognized under Section 731. The character of such gain shall be determined by reference to the proportionate character of the net precontribution gain.

(b) Net precontribution gain. For purposes of this section, the term "net precontribution gain" means the net gain (if any) which would have been recognized by the distributee partner under Section 704(c)(1)(B) if all property which—

(1) had been contributed to the partnership by the distributee partner within 7 years of the distribution, and

(2) is held by such partnership immediately before the distribution,

Had been distributed by such partnership to another partner.

(c) Basis rules.

(1) Partner's interest. The adjusted basis of a partner's interest in a partnership shall be increased by the amount of any gain recognized by such partner under subsection (a). For purposes of determining the basis of the distributed property (other than money), such increase shall be treated as occurring immediately before the distribution.

(2) Partnership's basis in contributed property. Appropriate adjustments shall be made to the adjusted basis of the partnership in the contributed property referred to in subsection (b) to reflect gain recognized under subsection (a).

(d) Exceptions.

(1) Distributions of previously contributed property. If any portion of the property distributed consists of property which had been contributed by a distributee partner to the partnership, such property shall not be taken into account under subsection (a)(1) and shall not be taken into account in determining the amount of the net precontribution gain. If the property distributed consists of an interest in an entity, the preceding

sentence shall not apply to the extent that the value of such interest is attributable to property contributed to such entity after such interest had been contributed to the partnership.

(2) Coordination with Section 751. This section shall not apply to the extent Section 751(b) applies to such distribution.

(e) Marketable securities treated as money. For treatment of marketable securities as money for purposes of this section, see Section 731(c).

Section 741. Recognition and character of gain or loss on sale or exchange

In the case of a sale or exchange of an interest in a partnership, gain or loss shall be recognized to the transferor partner. Such gain or loss shall be considered as gain or loss from the sale or exchange of a capital asset, except as otherwise provided in Section 751 (relating to unrealized receivables and inventory items).

Section 742. Basis of transferee partner's interest

The basis of an interest in a partnership acquired other than by contribution shall be determined under part II of subchapter O (sec. 1011 and following).

Section 743. Special rules where Section 754 election or substantial built-in loss

(a) General rule. The basis of partnership property shall not be adjusted as the result of a transfer of an interest in a partnership by sale or exchange or on the death of a partner unless the election provided by Section 754 (relating to optional adjustment to basis of partnership property) is in effect with respect to such partnership or unless the partnership has a substantial built-in loss immediately after such transfer.

(b) Adjustment to basis of partnership property. In the case of a transfer of an interest in a partnership by sale or exchange or upon the death of a partner, a partnership with respect to which the election provided in Section 754 is in effect or which has a substantial built-in loss immediately after such transfer shall—

(1) increase the adjusted basis of the partnership property by the excess of the basis to the transferee partner of his interest in the partnership over his proportionate share of the adjusted basis of the partnership property, or

(2) decrease the adjusted basis of the partnership property by the excess of the transferee partner's proportionate share of the adjusted basis of the partnership property over the basis of his interest in the partnership.

Under regulations prescribed by the Secretary, such increase or decrease shall constitute an adjustment to the basis of partnership property with respect to the transferee partner only. A partner's proportionate share of the adjusted basis of partnership property shall be determined in accordance with his interest in partnership capital and, in the case of property contributed to the partnership by a partner, Section 704(c)(relating to contributed property) shall apply in determining such share. In the case of an adjustment under this subsection to the basis of partnership property subject to depletion, any depletion allowable shall be determined separately for the transferee partner with respect to his interest in such property.

(c) Allocation of basis. The allocation of basis among partnership properties where subsection (b) is applicable shall be made in accordance with the rules provided in Section 755.

(d) Substantial built-in loss.

(1) In general. For purposes of this section, a partnership has a substantial built-in loss with respect to a transfer of an interest in a partnership if the partnership's adjusted basis in the partnership property exceeds by more than $250,000 the fair market value of such property.

(2) Regulations. The Secretary shall prescribe such regulations as may be appropriate to carry out the purposes of paragraph (1) and Section 734(d), including regulations aggregating related partnerships and disregarding property acquired by the partnership in an attempt to avoid such purposes.

(e) Alternative rules for electing investment partnerships.

(1) No adjustment of partnership basis. For purposes of this section, an electing investment partnership shall not be treated as having a substantial built-in loss with respect to any transfer occurring while the election under paragraph (6)(A) is in effect.

(2) Loss deferral for transferee partner. In the case of a transfer of an interest in an electing investment partnership, the transferee partner's distributive share of losses (without regard to gains) from the sale or exchange of partnership property shall not be allowed except to the extent that it is established that such losses exceed the loss (if any) recognized by the transferor (or any prior transferor to the extent not fully offset by a prior disallowance under this paragraph) on the transfer of the partnership interest.

(3) No reduction in partnership basis. Losses disallowed under paragraph (2) shall not decrease the transferee partner's basis in the partnership interest.

(4) Effect of termination of partnership. This subsection shall be applied without regard to any termination of a partnership under Section 708(b)(1)(B).

(5) Certain basis reductions treated as losses. In the case of a transferee partner whose basis in property distributed by the partnership is reduced under Section 732(a)(2), the amount of the loss recognized by the transferor on the transfer of the partnership interest which is taken into account under paragraph (2) shall be reduced by the amount of such basis reduction.

(6) Electing investment partnership. For purposes of this subsection, the term "electing investment partnership" means any partnership if—

(A) the partnership makes an election to have this subsection apply,

(B) the partnership would be an investment company under Section 3(a)(1)(A) of the Investment Company Act of 1940 but for an exemption under paragraph (1) or (7) of Section 3(c) of such Act,

(C) such partnership has never been engaged in a trade or business,

(D) substantially all of the assets of such partnership are held for investment,

(E) at least 95 percent of the assets contributed to such partnership consist of money,

(F) no assets contributed to such partnership had an adjusted basis in excess of fair market value at the time of contribution,

(G) all partnership interest of such partnership are issued by such partnership pursuant to a private offering before the date which is 24 months after the date of the first capital contribution to such partnership,

(H) the partnership agreement of such partnership has substantive restrictions on each partner's ability to cause a redemption of the partner's interest, and

(I) the partnership agreement of such partnership provides for a term that is not in excess of 15 years.

The election described in subparagraph (A), once made, shall be irrevocable except with the consent of the Secretary.

(7) Regulations. The Secretary shall prescribe such regulations as may be appropriate to carry out the purposes of this subsection, including regulations for applying this subsection to tiered partnerships.

(f) Exception for securitization partnerships.

(1) No adjustment of partnership basis. For purposes of this section, a securitization partnership shall not be treated as having a substantial built-in loss with respect to any transfer.

(2) Securitization partnership. For purposes of paragraph (1), the term "securitization partnership" means any partnership the sole business activity of which is to issue securities which provide for a fixed principal (or similar) amount and which are primarily serviced by the cash flows of a discrete pool (either fixed or revolving) of receivables or other financial assets that by their terms convert into cash in a finite period, but only if the sponsor of the pool reasonably believes that the receivables and other financial assets comprising the pools are not acquired so as to be disposed of.

Section 751. Unrealized receivables and inventory items

(a) Sale or exchange of interest in partnership. The amount of any money, or the fair market value of any property, received by a transferor partner in exchange for all or a part of his interest in the partnership attributable to—

(1) unrealized receivables of the partnership, or

(2) inventory items of the partnership,

shall be considered as an amount realized from the sale or exchange of property other than a capital asset.

(b) Certain distributions treated as sales or exchanges.

(1) General rule. To the extent a partner receives in a distribution—

(A) partnership property which is—

(i) unrealized receivables, or

(ii) inventory items which have appreciated substantially in value,

in exchange for all or a part of his interest in other partnership property (including money), or

(B) partnership property (including money) other than property described in subparagraph (A)(i) or (ii) in exchange for all or a part of his interest in partnership property described in subparagraph (A)(i) or (ii),

such transactions shall, under regulations prescribed by the Secretary, be considered as a sale or exchange of such property between the distributee and the partnership (as constituted after the distribution).

(2) Exceptions. Paragraph (1) shall not apply to—

(A) a distribution of property which the distributee contributed to the partnership, or

(B) payments, described in Section 736(a), to a retiring partner or successor in interest of a deceased partner.

(3) Substantial appreciation. For purposes of paragraph (1)—

(A) In general. Inventory items of the partnership shall be considered to have appreciated substantially in value if their fair market value exceeds 120 percent of the adjusted basis to the partnership of such property.

(B) Certain property excluded. For purposes of subparagraph (A), there shall be excluded any inventory property if a principal purpose for acquiring such property was to avoid the provisions of this subsection relating to inventory items.

(c) Unrealized receivables. For purposes of this subchapter, the term "unrealized receivables" includes, to the extent not previously includible in income under the method of accounting used by the partnership, any rights (contractual or otherwise) to payment for—

(1) goods delivered, or to be delivered, to the extent the proceeds therefrom would be treated as amounts received from the sale or exchange of property other than a capital asset, or

(2) services rendered, or to be rendered.

For purposes of this section and, sections 731, 732, and 741 (but not for purposes of Section 736), such term also includes mining property (as defined in Section 617(f)(2)), stock in a DISC (as described in Section 992(a)), Section 1245 property (as defined in Section 1245(a)(3)), stock in certain foreign corporations (as described in Section 1248), Section 1250 property (as defined in Section 1250(c)), farm land (as defined in Section 1252(a)), franchises, trademarks, or trade names (referred to in Section 1253(a)), and an oil, gas, or geothermal property (described in Section 1254) but only to the extent of the amount which would be treated as gain to which Section 617(d)(1), 995(c), 1245(a), 1248(a), 1250(a), 1252(a), 1253(a) or 1254(a) would apply if (at the time of the transaction described in this section or Section 731, 732, or 741, as the case may be) such property had been sold by the partnership at its fair market value. For purposes of this section and, sections 731, 732, and 741 (but not for purposes of Section 736), such term also includes any market discount bond (as defined in Section 1278) and any short-term obligation (as defined in Section 1283) but only to the extent of the amount which would be treated as ordinary income if (at the time of the transaction described in this section or Section 731, 732, or 741, as the case may be) such property had been sold by the partnership.

(d) Inventory items. For purposes of this subchapter, the term "inventory items" means—

(1) property of the partnership of the kind described in Section 1221(a)(1),

(2) any other property of the partnership which, on sale or exchange by the partnership, would be considered property other than a capital asset and other than property described in Section 1231, and

(3) any other property held by the partnership which, if held by the selling or distributee partner, would be considered property of the type described in paragraph (1) or (2).

(e) Limitation on tax attributable to deemed sales of Section 1248 stock. For purposes of applying this section and sections 731 and 741 to any amount resulting from the reference to Section 1248(a) in the second sentence of subsection (c), in the case of an individual, the tax attributable to such amount shall be limited in the manner provided by subsection (b) of Section 1248 (relating to gain from certain sales or exchanges of stock in certain foreign corporation).

(f) Special rules in the case of tiered partnerships, etc. In determining whether property of a partnership is—

(1) an unrealized receivable, or

(2) an inventory item,

such partnership shall be treated as owning its proportionate share of the property of any other partnership in which it is a partner. Under regulations, rules similar to the rules of the preceding sentence shall also apply in the case of interests in trusts.

Section 752. Treatment of certain liabilities

(a) Increase in partner's liabilities. Any increase in a partner's share of the liabilities of a partnership, or any increase in a partner's individual liabilities by reason of the assumption by such partner of partnership liabilities, shall be considered as a contribution of money by such partner to the partnership.

(b) Decrease in partner's liabilities. Any decrease in a partner's share of the liabilities of a partnership, or any decrease in a partner's individual liabilities by reason of the assumption by the partnership of such individual liabilities, shall be considered as a distribution of money to the partner by the partnership.

(c) Liability to which property is subject. For purposes of this section, a liability to which property is subject shall, to the extent of the fair market value of such property, be considered as a liability of the owner of the property.

(d) Sale or exchange of an interest. In the case of a sale or exchange of an interest in a partnership, liabilities shall be treated in the same manner as liabilities in connection with the sale or exchange of property not associated with partnerships.

Section 753. Partner receiving income in respect of decedent

The amount includible in the gross income of a successor in interest of a deceased partner under Section 736(a) shall be considered income in respect of a decedent under Section 691.

Section 754. Manner of electing optional adjustment to basis of partnership property

If a partnership files an election, in accordance with regulations prescribed by the Secretary, the basis of partnership property shall be adjusted, in the case of a distribution of property, in the manner provided in Section 734 and, in the case of a transfer of a partnership interest, in the manner provided in Section 743. Such an election shall apply with respect to all distributions of property by the partnership and to all transfers of interests in the partnership during the taxable year with respect to which such election was filed and all subsequent taxable years. Such election may be revoked by the partnership, subject to such limitations as may be provided by regulations prescribed by the Secretary.

Section 755. Rules for allocation of basis

(a) General rule. Any increase or decrease in the adjusted basis of partnership property under Section 734(b) (relating to the optional adjustment to the basis of undistributed partnership property) or Section 743(b) (relating to the optional adjustment to the basis of partnership property in the case of a transfer of an interest in a partnership) shall, except as provided in subsection (b), be allocated—

(1) in a manner which has the effect of reducing the difference between the fair market value and the adjusted basis of partnership properties, or

(2) in any other manner permitted by regulations prescribed by the Secretary.

(b) Special rule. In applying the allocation rules provided in subsection (a), increases or decreases in the adjusted basis of partnership property arising from a distribution of, or a transfer of an interest attributable to, property consisting of—

(1) capital assets and property described in Section 1231(b), or

(2) any other property of the partnership,

shall be allocated to partnership property of a like character except that the basis of any such partnership property shall not be reduced below zero. If, in the case of a distribution the adjustment to basis of property described in paragraph (1) or (2) is prevented by the absence of such property or by insufficient adjusted basis for such property, such adjustment shall be applied to subsequently acquired property of a like character in accordance with regulations prescribed by the Secretary.

(c) No allocation of basis decrease to stock of corporate partner. In making an allocation under subsection (a) of any decrease in the adjusted basis of partnership property under Section 734(b)—

(1) no allocation may be made to stock in a corporation (or any person related (within the meaning of sections 267(b) and 707(b)(1)) to such corporation) which is a partner in the partnership, and

(2) any amount not allocable to stock by reason of paragraph (1) shall be allocated under subsection (a) to other partnership property.

Gain shall be recognized to the partnership to the extent that the amount required to be allocated under paragraph (2) to other partnership property exceeds the aggregate adjusted basis of such other property immediately before the allocation required by paragraph (2).

Section 761. Terms defined

(a) Partnership. For purposes of this subtitle, the term "partnership" includes a syndicate, group, pool, joint venture, or other unincorporated organization through or by means of which any business, financial operation, or venture is carried on, and which is not, within the meaning of this title, a corporation or a trust or estate. Under regulations the Secretary may, at the election of all the members of an unincorporated organization, exclude such organization from the application of all or part of this subchapter, if it is availed of—

(1) for investment purposes only and not for the active conduct of a business,

(2) for the joint production, extraction, or use of property, but not for the purpose of selling services or property produced or extracted, or

(3) by dealers in securities for a short period for the purpose of underwriting, selling, or distributing a particular issue of securities,

if the income of the members of the organization may be adequately determined without the computation of partnership taxable income.

(b) Partner. For purposes of this subtitle, the term "partner" means a member of a partnership. In the case of a capital interest in a partnership in which capital is a material income-producing factor, whether a person is a partner with respect to such interest shall be determined without regard to whether such interest was derived by gift from any other person.

(c) Partnership agreement. For purposes of this subchapter, a partnership agreement includes any modifications of the partnership agreement made prior to, or at, the time prescribed by law for the filing of the partnership return for the taxable year (not including extensions) which are agreed to by all the partners, or which are adopted in such other manner as may be provided by the partnership agreement.

(d) Liquidation of a partner's interest. For purposes of this subchapter, the term "liquidation f a partner's interest" means the termination of a partner's entire interest in a partnership by means of a distribution, or a series of distributions, to the partner by the partnership.

(e) Distributions of partnership interests treated as exchanges. Except as otherwise provided in regulations, for purposes of—

(1) Section 708 (relating to continuation of partnership),
(2) Section 743 (relating to optional adjustment to basis of partnership property), and
(3) any other provision of this subchapter specified in regulations prescribed by the Secretary,

any distribution of an interest in a partnership (not otherwise treated as an exchange) shall be treated as an exchange.

(f) Qualified joint venture.

(1) In general. In the case of a qualified joint venture conducted by a husband and wife who file a joint return for the taxable year, for purposes of this title—

(A) such joint venture shall not be treated as a partnership,

(B) all items of income, gain, loss, deduction, and credit shall be divided between the spouses in accordance with their respective interests in the venture, and

(C) each spouse shall take into account such spouse's respective share of such items as if they were attributable to a trade or business conducted by such spouse as a sole proprietor.

(2) Qualified joint venture. For purposes of paragraph 91), the term "qualified joint venture" means any joint venture involving the conduct of a trade or business if—

(A) the only members of such joint venture are a husband and wife,

(B) both spouses materially participate (within the meaning of Section 469(h) without regard to paragraph (5) thereof) in such trade or business, and

(C) both spouses elect the application of this subsection.

(g) Cross reference. For rules in the case of the sale, exchange, liquidation, or reduction of a partner's interest, see sections 704(b) and 706(c)(2).

CPSIA information can be obtained
at www.ICGtesting.com
Printed in the USA
LVOW04s0549100617
537614LV00001B/1/P

9 781524 934286